D1069275

The Making of the Third Party System

Voters and Parties in Illinois, 1850-1876

Studies in
American History and Culture, No. 14

Robert Berkhofer, Series Editor
Director of American Culture Programs
and Richard Hudson Research Professor of History
The University of Michigan

Other Titles in This Series

The Making of the Third Party System

Voters and Parties in Illinois, 1850-1876

by
Stephen L. Hansen

umi
RESEARCH PRESS

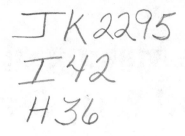

Produced and distributed by
UMI Research Press
an imprint of
University Microfilms International
Ann Arbor, Michigan 48106

Library of Congress Cataloging in Publication Data

Hansen, Stephen L
   The making of the third party system.

   (Studies in American history and culture ; no. 14)
   Bibliography: p.
   Includes index.
   1. Political parties—Illinois—History. 2. Elections—
Illinois—History. 3. Voting—Illinois—History.   I. Title.
II. Series.

JK2295.I42H36   324.2773'09   80-22447
ISBN 0-8357-1096-3

Contents

Tables

Acknowledgments

I was assisted in the writing and research of this book by a number of people and institutions. For financial assistance, I wish to thank the Illinois State Historical Society for awarding me their Fellowship in 1975 and the University of Illinois for granting me a fellowship in 1976. I also wish to acknowledge the free computer time provided to me by the Chicago Circle Computer Center. For helping me collect research material, I am particularly indebted to the staff of the Inter-Library Loan Office at the University of Illinois Chicago Circle. I also wish to extend my appreciation to the Regenstein Library at the University of Chicago for allowing me to examine and quote from the Stephen A. Douglas Papers.

My greatest debt of gratitude is to those people who labored with me over the writing of the manuscript. In particular, I wish to thank Professor Robert V. Remini, and Professors Richard Jensen, Michael Perman, Paul Kleppner, Daniel Scott Smith and Richard Fried for their helpful comments and criticisms. In the actual writing, I received invaluable help from my colleagues Arnold Hirsch, Deborah White, and Kurt Leichtle, and I greatly appreciate their assistance.

Finally, I am grateful to my wife, Julie, who provided me with financial, editorial, and emotional assistance, without which none of this would have been possible.

Introduction

For generations, historians have analyzed the political struggles that took place during the turbulent years of the Civil War era. Most of this literature has concentrated upon the causes of the sectional conflict and the motives of Reconstruction.[1] Despite the great amount of research undertaken and the valuable information gathered, a number of aspects of the political conflict remain confused. For example, there has never been a complete analysis of the fundamental changes in the party system from 1850 to 1876. The voter realignment in 1854, the war, and Reconstruction had a profound effect upon politics, yet the impact of these events upon the party system has been largely ignored. While most historians have recognized that the Second Party System was already in a state of decline in 1850 and that it was destroyed by the sectional conflict, they have failed to discuss what emerged to fill the political void. What replaced the Jacksonian parties was an entirely new party system. This Third Party System differed from the old order in terms of principles, structure, and behavior.

Traditionally, historians have ended their discussion of the American party system with Andrew Jackson. Much attention has been paid to the emergence and character of the First Party System during the early national period, but, according to most historians, it was the Age of Jackson that introduced the modern political party.[2] This Second Party System was characterized by mass-based parties, professional politicians, real party competition, and organized party structures.[3] Few historians would argue with Felice A. Bonadio, who concluded that the Jacksonians created "a modern party system, with all the forms and devices we today associate with it."[4]

While all historians have recognized that the Second Party System crumbled under the strain of sectionalism, there has been virtually no discussion of the political order that replaced the Jacksonian parties. The belief that the Jacksonians had created "modern political parties" is partially responsible for this myopia. The few historians who have written about the new political order have tended to acknowledge the Third Party System only with general references to the "corruption" of the Gilded Age.[5]

The refusal to recognize the profound changes in politics during the Civil War era is reflected in the discussion of the transition of politics during the 1850s. The literature devoted to politics prior to the Civil War ties the realignment of politics to the Jacksonian parties. The Republicans, for example, have been submerged into a continuum of Whiggery.[6] The result is that not only the parties, but also the voters, are seen as remaining aligned essentially as they had been since Jackson, albeit with new issues and party labels.

The difficulty in recognizing the changes in politics is due to the lack of a precise understanding of what constitutes a party system.[7] It is only recently that historians, in combination with political scientists, have addressed this problem. Through the efforts of William Chambers, Walter Dean Burnham, and James Sundquist, a definition of a party system has emerged.[8] According to Chambers, voter realignments cause fundamental changes in politics. The change is so distinct that a new party system is created. A realignment has a profound effect upon politics because the voters move into new combinations in reaction to a new set of issues, which destroys the basis for the old system. Around the new issues develop the principles which define the new voter coalitions and which provide the rationale for the political parties. With the composition and principles of the parties altered, Chambers concluded, a new party system is formed with its own distinct style.[9]

Expanding upon Chambers' contention that realignments create new party systems, James Sundquist identified the dynamics of a party system which shape politics.[10] According to Sundquist, the principles of a party system fade with time. The issues are resolved and the principles lose relevance. When a party system reaches this stage, the voter coalitions begin to weaken and the lines of distinction in the electorate become blurred. The reaction of the parties is to rely more heavily upon structure and voter loyalty in order to maintain unity.[11] Side issues begin to plague politics, a development that further weakens the system. Eventually, one of these new issues becomes powerful enough to cause another realignment, which creates a new party system. Each party system, then, has its own "life," character, composition, and style.

The works of Chambers and Sundquist have provided a means of recognizing changes in American politics. Instead of concentrating upon specific issues and men, it is possible to achieve a more complete view of the interaction between voters, politicians, and issues. In particular, through an analysis of party systems, a number of the confusing aspects of politics in the Civil War era become clear. For example, the disintegration of the Second Party System and the chaos in politics caused by the realignment in 1854 are best understood in terms of political systems rather than in the more conventional context of platforms and politicians. Furthermore, it is through the perspective of party systems that the dramatic changes in politics caused by the War and Reconstruction become apparent. Only by examining the principles, organization, and voter coalitions of the Second and Third Party Systems can the profound differences in politics be fully appreciated.

The analysis of party systems also provides a broader perspective for understanding voting patterns. Previously, historians have concentrated upon the motives of voter behavior and have ignored the composition of a political party's entire coalition.[12] This limited view of voting patterns has led to a number of erroneous assumptions. The "ethno-cultural" historians, for example, have concluded that because pietistic religious groups voted Whig, and then Republican, that the Republican party was a rebirth of Whiggery.[13] By examining voting patterns in terms of party systems, however, it becomes evident that this assumption is incorrect. Certainly many pietists did vote Whig, and later, Republican, but the voter coalitions of these two parties were strikingly different. Through the analysis of coalitions, instead of voter behavior alone, it is easier to recognize the importance of each group in the make-up of the political parties. Also, it is only in the context of the party system that any judgement can be made on the effect of the realignment in 1854 and on the stability of the voting pattern.

Illinois provides a good setting in which to analyze the impact of the Civil War and Reconstruction upon politics and the differences between the Second and Third Party Systems. In many ways, the State reflected the nation. Economically, Illinois developed industrially during the 1850s, as symbolized by the rapid growth of Chicago. Like the nation as a whole, however, agriculture still provided the main source of wealth. Illinois agriculture was quickly becoming commercialized, yet pockets of subsistence farming still existed.

The population of Illinois also resembled the nation's. The northern portion of the State was settled primarily by New Englanders, while the population in southern Illinois, called Egypt, came predominantly from the slave States. The presence of a large Southern-born population is one of the crucial reasons for examining Illinois. One of the major weaknesses of most voter studies is that by concentrating upon local areas or upon States dominated by Yankees, they have ignored Southern voting patterns.[14] The presence of Southerners and of Yankees makes Illinois important to examine not only because Southern voting patterns can be analyzed, but also because the State better reflected the reality of the nation.

Illinois also had a large immigrant population representing the major foreign-born groups in the United States. Over 130,000 Germans, close to 90,000 Irish, and 40,000 English had settled in the State. There was also a significant French, Scandinavian, and Canadian population. Before 1850, one-eighth of Illinois' population was foreign-born, but by 1860, the number of immigrants had trebled, representing 20 percent of the population.[15] The total population of Illinois doubled in the 1850s, making it the nation's fourth largest State.

The growth of Illinois made it one of the more significant States in national elections, and observers recognized the importance of Illinois in politics. The *Washington States*, for example, noted during the Senatorial battle between Lincoln and Douglas in 1858 that "the battle of the Union is to be fought in Illinois. In every respect, then, Illinois becomes, as it were, the Union for the time being."[16] Joshua Giddings also understood the political importance of Illinois. In explaining the nomination of Lincoln for President in 1860, he wrote that "Lincoln was selected on account of his *location*."[17]

Nothing reflects the importance of Illinois in national politics as much as the role played by the State's politicians in the Civil War era. Of the 5 presidents of the United States between 1850 and 1876, 2 were from Illinois. The terms of Lincoln and Grant spanned about half of the 26 year period. Stephen A. Douglas was a candidate for President within the Democratic party in 1852 and 1856 before finally winning the nomination in 1860. Besides these 3 giants who dominated the political scene, a number of other Illinois politicians played important roles in national politics. John A. McClernand and William A. Richardson, Democratic Congressmen from Illinois, were both candidates for Speaker of the House. Orville Hickman Browning was in Andrew Johnson's cabinet and in charge of the President's defense during the impeachment trial. David Davis, Supreme Court Justice, and Lyman Trumbull, author of the Freedmen's Bureau Bill, were leading candidates for the Liberal Republican nomination for President in 1872. The national recognition given to all of these men signified, at the very least, that the nation recognized the political importance of Illinois during the Civil War era.

By analyzing Illinois from 1850 to 1876 in terms of party systems, the profound changes in politics can be more easily understood. The realignment in 1854 destroyed the basis of the Second Party System. A new issue, slavery, superseded the principles of the Jacksonian parties and the old voter coalitions broke apart under the pressure. As the slavery issue expanded and the principles were clarified, new voter coalitions began to form. The principles and the voter patterns of the Third Party System dominated politics by 1860, but the political style of the new party system remained tied to the Jacksonian era. The Civil War and Reconstruction, however, forged a distinctive character for the Third Party System. The turbulent decade of the 1860s acted as a crucible fusing patriotism and party loyalty into one inseparable emotion. The voter in the Jacksonian era had no reason to remain loyal to the party after the inevitable fading of principles, but in the Third Party System, the identification of party loyalty with patriotism resulted in a more tightly disciplined and stable party system.

The profound differences between the Second and Third Party Systems are most evident when the two are compared after their respective principles had lost relevance. The Second Party System fragmented and began to disintegrate almost immediately. Endeavoring to preserve the party system as long as possible, the Whigs and the Democrats put a heavy reliance upon flamboyant personalities to keep the voter coalitions together. In the case of the Third Party System, however, the parties remained stable long after their principles lost relevance. Voter loyalty and a highly disciplined organization successfully sustained the Third Party System for two more decades.

The voter realignment, the war, and Reconstruction changed the shape of American politics. Not only were the rationale and the composition of the political parties fundamentally altered, but also the whole character of politics. The relationship between the voter, the politician, and the party was reshaped so that the political party became paramount. Instead of politicians linking the people to the party, the voter was directly engaged by the party organization. The War and Reconstruction turned the political parties into machines and the role of the politician was reduced to that of a mechanic. Whereas the generation before 1860 lived in the shadow of Jackson, Clay, Calhoun, and Webster, the generation after the Civil War was dominated by party machinery. The War and Reconstruction changed the principles, personalities, and politics of the nation from the institutionalization of the two party system to the establishment of political parties as institutions.

1

The Second Party System

In his analysis of party formation in the Jacksonian era, Richard McCormick argued that the Second Party System was firmly established in Illinois by 1840. Based upon broad principles rather than specialized interests, the Second Party System was characterized by an "intricate and elaborate exterior type of party apparatus."[1] Although McCormick acknowledged that the Whig party in Illinois remained peculiarly opposed to an efficient organization, he maintained that by 1840 personal factions had given way to professional party managers and that the Second Party System had become institutionalized.[2] While McCormick's analysis is essentially correct, he has exaggerated the strength and efficiency of the Second Party System in Illinois. The Democrats, and to a lesser extent, the Whigs, did develop "intricate and elaborate" organizations, but these structural devices failed to function in a coherent and regular fashion. The Second Party System in Illinois was not a model of efficiency, but instead, haphazard and ad hoc.

The weakness of the party organizations was evident in Illinois between 1850 and 1854. In that period the principles that had defined the parties since 1832 ceased to be relevant. In the absence of viable issues, a political party has only its organization to sustain it. The Whig and Democratic structures, however, proved to be too feeble to maintain party regularity. The voter coalitions began to dissolve as the parties split into factions. Side issues began to plague the parties, threatening to splinter the coalitions irrevocably. The Whigs and the Democrats desperately tried to forestall dissolution by emphasizing old party rhetoric. Ultimately, however, they were forced to rely upon the popularity of individual candidates to hold the system together.

The Democrats and the Whigs in Illinois clearly adopted all the party techniques that characterized the Second Party System. The caucus was replaced by the convention system for nominating party candidates. Committees were organized on the county level to coordinate activities and to be responsible for the local election. Deference gave way to mass politics as professional politicians appealed directly to the voter. All of the structural devices, however, did not result in an efficient party system. The party organizations lacked permanence and regularity. The agencies of the parties ceased to exist after elections and had to be created anew before each campaign. Once the party did organize for an election, it still had no formal lines of communication within the structure and no sense of a division of authority. Each county, and even each township within a county, adopted its own system of organization. Often all semblance of organization was simply ignored. In 1852, for example, the Democratic newspaper in Ottawa wrote that "should [Stephen] Douglass [*sic*] be the democratic candidate for the presidency, we will have an easy victory, and there will be little need for organization."[3]

For both parties the nominating process, in particular, lacked formalization. Some counties held conventions for nominating men for offices down to the ward level, while other areas might just have mass meetings to determine candidates. The Democrats of Greene County, for example, announced a meeting by declaring that "all of the democratic party are earnestly invited to attend and give free and full expression to their wishes." Those attending would have the opportunity to "express their preference for the candidate for Congress . . . for senator . . . and for representative."[4] Mass meetings like the one held in Greene County were not uncommon, nor were they confined to counties. Some Congressional districts also relied entirely upon such methods for nominating candidates.[5]

Other areas had no formal nominating process. A man would announce his candidacy for office by merely publishing a business card in the local newspaper. Often, candidates were so popular that nominations were unnecessary. In 1856, for example, the Springfield *Illinois State Journal* endorsed John Williams as the Congressional candidate with the "reservation that if the people expressed any dissatisfaction, we would leave his claims to be passed upon by a Convention." The *Journal* went on to say, however, that "we are gratified to observe that no such course is necessary."[6]

Even when counties and Congressional districts adhered to the convention system to select candidates for office, their procedures lacked consistency. Ideally, conventions were to bring unity to the party by giving all groups representation. The Democrats of Sangamon County, for example, began the nominating process by convening township mass meetings. Each of these meetings elected delegates to be sent to the county convention, with the number of delegates based upon the size of the Democratic vote in the preceding election. The county convention nominated local candidates and set up committees to formulate resolutions and platforms and to designate an executive committee to coordinate the campaign. The county convention then elected delegates to the Congressional convention.[7] Only in Sangamon County, however, were the Democrats so highly organized. If a county convention were held elsewhere, delegates were often self-appointed, or townships and precincts might send as many delegates as possible in order to pack the convention.[8]

Although conventions were designed to bring unity to the party, they often dissolved into brawls. If a convention did not proceed as intended by the local leaders, it might be adjourned and a new meeting convened. A group of dissatisfied Democrats in Springfield, for example, gained control of the city convention in 1852 and pushed through their own candidates in opposition to those of the party leaders. The *Illinois State Register*, the leading Democratic paper, did not approve of the action and refused to print the proceedings. Cooperating with the old leaders in the city, it declared the convention illegal and called for a new convention to nominate "proper men."[9]

It was not always so easy, however, to dismiss a convention that nominated the "wrong" man. In the Eighth Congressional district, which included Madison and St. Clair counties, the battles in the conventions had been so divisive that they had been suspended for six years until 1852. The convention system was revived because some Democrats felt that William H. Bissell had been in Congress long enough. A convention was called to meet in the town of Carlyle for the purpose of nominating a new candidate for Congress. In response to this call for a convention, the Bissell supporters held mass meetings to endorse his reelection and to repudiate the proposed Carlyle convention. The anti-Bissell group, nevertheless, held the convention. Only half of the counties were represented, but the convention proceeded with its work and nominated Phillip B. Fouke for Congress. The Bissell supporters were not allowed to address the convention and, at the point of violence, the lights were mysteriously extinguished, throwing everything into confusion.[10] The convention then adjourned with Fouke as the nominee, but the party was split for the election with both men claiming to be the legitimate candidate.

Candidates for State offices were usually nominated in a more orderly fashion. The State convention rarely erupted into brawls, and nominations were made in accord with established procedures. The selection of delegates to the State convention, however, was just as haphazard as it was for county conventions. If a county sent a delegation at all, it was often self-appointed and as large as the local party could organize. It was not until the 1850s that the Democratic party finally settled upon an apportionment so that one area could not dominate the entire State.[11] When the system ran smoothly, about 90 percent of the counties sent delegations to the State convention. Usually, however, only half of the counties were represented.

The nominating process took such varied forms because the parties lacked permanent governing councils. Typically, the parties lurched into a campaign in one of several indirect ways. Usually, a newspaper would suggest a need for a convention or mass meeting. For example, in 1857, the *Macoupin Spectator* proposed a grand mass meeting in Springfield of all the Democrats in Illinois to ratify Senator Douglas' course in Congress. The *Illinois State Register* agreed with the suggestion, but also decided that it was necessary to call a "state *convention* [to] be held *some time* . . ." for the purpose of nominating candidates for the state treasurer."[12] Sometimes a convention or mass meeting would be called for by a group of voters, who in one instance published an announcement in the local paper along with a list of over a hundred citizens who endorsed the proposal.[13] Another means by which the party apparatus began to move towards a campaign was to have leading politicians issue the call for a meeting.[14]

As in the case of the nominating process, the devices employed by the parties to conduct the campaign were haphazard. The model of the party structure called for an umbrella of committees to coordinate the campaign. Local conventions were to create committees to oversee different aspects of the party during the campaign, such as committees on resolutions, conventions, organization, and platforms. In charge of the entire State would be a provisional Central Committee appointed by the State convention for each election. The main duty of the Central Committee was to coordinate the counties and to select and appoint in each a county executive committee. The county committee would then select a prominent man in each town to be responsible for the campaign.[15] This plan was the ideal but it was rarely realized. The *Illinois State Register* complained that it has "often been found to be the case that many counties, when the proper time for assembling county conventions arrived, were not provided with . . . committees."[16] All through the summer of an election year the paper would urge the counties to organize properly. "Is the democracy of Illinois fully organized for the coming presidential and state campaign?" cried the *Register* in 1852. "Are executive, corresponding and vigilance committees appointed in every county? Are arrangements [made] for circulating political documents and democratic newspapers?"[17] The answer was usually no.

When the provisions of the organizing committees were not carried out, the State party, as well as individual candidates for office, was forced to rely upon local politicians for assistance. When Stephen Douglas ran for Congress in 1838, he found, in many counties, no organization to present his credentials as a candidate. In such cases, a candidate was forced to ask friends for assistance in conducting his campaign. Douglas wrote to Lewis W. Ross that "[I will] have to rely to a great extent upon you and other friends to present [my] pretensions."[18] State and national executive committees often found themselves in the same situation. When there was no local committee to take charge of the campaign, the committees at the higher levels sent circular letters to prominent men instructing them to lead the local party in the campaign. They requested local politicians to collect campaign funds and provide lists of names to the Central Committee for the purposes of sending campaign materials. A letter from the National Democratic Committee in 1852 was typical of these circulars:

> The Democratic National Committee has assessed one hundred dollars upon each Congressional District of the U.S. and it is the duty of the Democratic Resident Committee to see to the fulfillment of this suggestion. We have the honor to call upon you to aid in the collection of that sum.
>
> The Resident Committee will return for all money subscribed an abundance of documents for each district . . . and will have them directed whenever the names and places to which they are to go are sent to the Resident Committee.[19]

Without an efficient organization to do the work of a campaign the parties often resorted to private political clubs. These clubs were formed by local party leaders for presidential campaigns with the primary purpose of rallying the voters. Most towns had their own clubs and in the larger cities, each ward had its own group. Besides turning out the voters, the clubs were to organize meetings and rallies, distribute campaign literature, escort speakers to and from meetings, keep order at rallies, run errands for politicians, participate in parades, and engage in other campaign rituals, such as pole raisings.[20] Clubs adopted their own name and they usually had some kind of home made uniform. In the 1852 campaign, for example, the Democrats formed "Pierce and King" clubs while the Whigs organized the "Friends of Scott." Most of these groups were semi-military in nature, marching in precision with drill sergeants, flags, uniforms, and martial music. While the clubs were valuable in arousing the voters for a particular election, their effectiveness was limited by the fact that the clubs were not coordinated and by the practice of disbanding after each contest.

Despite the various attempts to compensate for the weakness of their political organizations, the parties found it difficult to insure party regularity. It was not uncommon in the Second Party System for voters and politicians to change parties frequently. One politician recalled that in 1847, "the county of Macoupin was democratic, but the people refused to be controlled by mere partisan considerations" when electing members to the Illinois Constitutional Convention.[21] Voters switched parties often enough that when Archibald Williams, a Whig politician, was asked to define an old Whig, he answered that "an old-line whig is a gentleman who takes his toddy regularly, and votes the Democratic ticket occasionally."[22]

If voters shifted allegiance quickly, politicians did so with even less hesitation. Joseph Gillespie, a local Whig politician who later helped organize the Republican party, described Usher F. Linder as a Jackson man.

> His admiration for the old hero was so strong that he rather ignored the principles which characterized the Adams and Jackson parties, and followed his inclinations. When Jackson was out of the way, and the contest was between Clay and somebody else, he consulted his judgement and was profoundly convinced of the correctness of the old Whig principles.[23]

In the 1850s, Linder returned to the Democratic party, but he died a Republican. Friendship was often another reason for ignoring the party. Linder and James Semple were in the Legislature together in 1836, and Linder noted that "he and I were both members . . . of the same political sentiments; but I did not vote for him for Speaker, but voted for my friend, Col. John Dement. . . ."[24]

At times it became difficult to determine to which party a man belonged. Often mistakes were made when it came to doling out patronage. In 1850, for example, a prominent Whig in Taylorsville wrote to David Davis about the need to remove the postmaster there because he was paying the profits of the office to the old postmaster — a Democrat![25] The election of the wrong man to office was also a frequent mistake. In 1837, William L. May, elected to congress as a Democrat, refused to support the party and repudiated President Martin Van Buren's financial policy. Douglas tried to have May read out of the party and, failing in that, he prevented May's renomination to Congress. Instead of receiving the gratitude of the national party leaders for his efforts to punish May, however, Douglas was reprimanded for tampering with the convention system by Van Buren's Secretary of the Treasury, Levi Woodbury.[26]

The Democrats and the Whigs had difficulty maintaining party discipline because many politicians themselves regarded party organization with suspicion. Most resisted party regularity on the grounds that such efforts were "corrupting and anti-republican."[27]   Other politicians felt about party discipline as did John Palmer who, during the Kansas-Nebraska controversy in 1854, wrote: "I was mainly anxious to preserve my personal independence and the right . . . to act according to the dictates of my own sense of personal duty."[28] The feeling that to submit to party regularity was somehow akin to sacrificing one's freedom of choice prevented party organizations from bringing order to the political scene. The Whigs were so averse to party structures that in 1848 they dispensed with a State convention altogether. Instead, Ned Baker addressed the Whig members of the Illinois Constitutional Convention, urging them to endorse Zachary Taylor's nomination for the Presidency. The group pledged their support to Taylor and sent a report of their action to the Whig newspapers in the State. That was the extent of the Whig State organization in 1848.[29]

Despite the fact that the devices of the Second Party System did not operate efficiently or with any regularity, the Democrats and the Whigs in Illinois remained fairly stable as long as party principles were strong. Once the principles began to lose relevance, however, the parties quickly fragmented.

The principles of the Jacksonian parties remained energetic only as long as relevant problems, i.e., issues, agitated the public mind. An issue is a temporary political problem, but it plays a vital role for the party in that it keeps the principles alive. The task of the party is to emphasize those issues that reinforce the principles, while sidestepping issues that do not. Once original issues are resolved and replaced by new ones with little relevance to the principles of the party, then the party itself begins to lose relevance.

Originally, the Whig party had been born out of the controversy over the Bank of the United States. Within a short time, the party expanded to adopt a range of programs including aid for internal improvements, higher tariffs, and controlled land distribution in the West. Collectively, the Whig position on these issues constituted the principles, or motivating force of the party. The Whig principles were based on a general concept that the federal government should take an active part in fostering national development. In contrast, the Democrats' position on banking, internal improvements, and the tariff reflected their principles of a more laissez faire notion of American growth and freedom.

Traditional positions, however, became confused with time. The Bank of the United States was a dead issue by the late 1840s and preemption seemed to solve the land question. In addition to the fading of these issues, frontier States like Illinois demanded cheap land, internal improvements, banking, and low tariffs, making it difficult to maintain a strict party line.

By 1850, the principles of the Second Party System had become irrelevant. Stephen Douglas supported many internal improvement schemes even though he was a Democrat. Douglas sponsored and helped pass a bill in Congress giving federal land to Illinois to subsidize the building of the Illinois Central Railroad.[30] The old principles also gave way on the issue of a national bank. There was no plan in the 1850s to reinstitute another Bank of the United States. Even in Illinois, where the Whigs and the Democrats battled over incorporation of banks, many Democrats sided with the Whigs to support a new State chartered bank. After a Banking Law passed by special referendum in 1851, Douglas wrote to his followers that "however obnoxious the Banking Law may be to us and much as we might desire to defeat its adoption by the people, we are decidedly of the opinion that it will carry as often as it may be submitted to the people." Douglas saw that a sizeable portion of Democrats favored the law, so "a combination can always be formed to carry the measure." Douglas advised the party to drop banking as an issue because "to carry the question into the next general election would enable the combination to carry not only that measure, but the Legislature & state Government."[31]

If the Democratic stand on traditional issues was no longer relevant, then the Whig policy was completely anachronistic. As early as 1848, one prominent Whig complained about the lack of viable Whig principles.

> I have struggled for some time past to prevail upon the Whig members [of the Legislature] to adopt some suitable system of State Policy – Whig State Measures. Whig State Platform of separate principles from the Dems – but have found it utterly unavailing – either a [Stephen T.] Logan, or a somebody for selfish wishes of local measures or advantages, or from some other cause always held off and nothing has been done. . . .[32]

Typical of Whig platforms, the 1852 Illinois Convention endorsed a protective tariff and nonintervention in the affairs of foreign governments.[33] Not only did these issues not excite voters, they also had a dulling effect upon the politicians. David Davis wrote, in 1852, that "I have thought less about politics this summer than I ever have during a Presidential canvass. In Illinois there is no political excitement at all. The Whigs have made [a] fight so often and been beaten so often that they have thought it the part of wisdom to ground their arms during this contest."[34] Even the Whig newspapers, which always exaggerated the enthusiasm and support for the party, were forced to recognize the general decline of Whiggery. Most of them tried to restore confidence in the party through scolding editorials. The *Quincy Whig*, for example, wrote:

> It is time that the whigs of this State prepared to engage in the coming contest. . . . The elections to be held the present year in this State are of sufficient importance to enlist the energies and active cooperation of every whig . . . and in view of this, it is a duty incumbent upon the whigs . . . to arouse themselves from the lethargy which has always diminished their vote, and . . . been the sole cause of their defeat. So long as apathy and despondency pervade the whig camp, there is no chance of success; an effective and thorough organization is only necessary to reduce greatly the majority claimed by our opponents. . . .[35]

Despite the chiding from the newspapers, the Whigs neither created an effective organization nor raised themselves out of their lethargy. The old Whig principles had never mobilized a majority in Illinois, and now, with their principles irrelevant, the party was bankrupt. There was no hope of overcoming the habitual majority of the Democracy.

With the party structures so weak and the principles irrelevant, the Whigs and the Democrats had difficulty in controlling new issues. By 1850, new political questions which had no relation to the founding principles of the Jacksonian parties constantly plagued the Whigs and the Democrats. The new issues threatened to shatter the voter coalitions of both parties by cutting across the electorate and forming new voter combinations.

One of the new questions which threatened the Second Party System was temperance. In 1851, there was growing support for a law prohibiting the sale of intoxicating liquor. The temperance crusade attracted wide support from both Whig and Democratic ranks and thus blurred the lines of distinction between the two coalitions. The Whigs were completely immobilized by the new issue. Although a large number of Whigs advocated temperance, officially the party remained silent. The Democrats, however, actively tried to blunt the temperance issue since they realized the new question could only hurt their majority coalition. In an attempt to placate both sides of the temperance issue, the Democrats called liquor a "monstrous evil" that should be eradicated. But the party also argued that an effective prohibition law could not be made. At any rate, the Democrats declared, prohibition would not solve the problem of intemperance.[36] Despite the efforts of the Democrats to quell the temperance question, it persisted as a prominent political issue. It became so important, in fact, that the Illinois Legislature was forced to draw up a prohibition law and submit it as a referendum to be voted on in 1855.

Another new issue which threatened to destroy the Jacksonian parties was slavery. The Mexican War had opened the festering slavery problem, and the question of the expansion of slavery into the newly conquered territories led to the formation of the Free Soil Party.[37] In order to contain the new question and to restore the old coalitions, the Whigs and the Democrats sought to disarm the slavery issue through compromise. In 1850, a number of proposals passed through Congress which the parties hoped would resolve the problem.[38] Although the Free Soilers lost much of their support after the Compromise of 1850, the party persisted in Illinois, fielding candidates in the 1850 and 1852 elections. The anti-slavery forces did not carry a large percentage of voters in these contests, but they did manage to keep the question in the public eye.

Just as it seemed that the Free Soil movement would dissolve, the slavery issue was revived in Illinois by a referendum on a law governing the status of Negroes. In 1853, the Illinois Legislature passed a series of laws to prohibit the freeing of slaves in the State and the immigration of free blacks and mulattoes. This Black Law, coming upon the heels of the controversy over the Compromise of 1850, stirred great excitement in the State.

Rather than carefully avoiding direct attacks upon the new issues, as the Whigs and the Democrats had done with temperance, both parties took a firm stand for the Black Law. They hoped to avoid new divisions in the parties by attacking those opposed to the law as abolitionists while maintaining that free blacks were a nuisance.[39] As the agitation over the Black Law continued, one exasperated Whig newspaper complained that "they [the opposition] must certainly know that their anti-Negro law conventions can effect nothing and may do harm. Why can they not 'let well enough, alone'?"[40]

The Black Law was carried by a vast majority in a special referendum in 1853, but that did not put an end to the slavery question and its related issues. Despite the efforts of both parties to contain the new issue, the Free Soil movement, the Compromise of 1850, and the Black Law kept the parties internally divided in Illinois. The Whigs in particular were badly split over slavery, and when Horace Greeley, the powerful New York editor, urged that the party be reorganized on the basis of abolitionism, it seemed impossible that the party could be restored.[41] The deep division in the Whig party led one Democratic paper to predict that Whigs would have to find a new political home. The "union Whigs" would join the Democracy, while the "higher law" Greeley men would join the abolitionists.[42]

Without relevant principles and effective organizations, the

Democratic and Whig coalitions began to dissolve. Nothing reveals the disorder in the Second Party System as much as the weakness of the voter coalitions. The fluctuations and inconsistencies of the voting patterns in the early 1850s are well illustrated through the use of a statistical routine called regression.[43]

The regression technique is an important tool for voter analysis. Unlike other descriptive statistical routines, it can sort out the complex relationships of a wide range of population characteristics to party preference. While regression is not a causal analysis of voting behavior, it can evaluate the importance of each population characteristic in explaining a voter coalition. Consequently, instead of being limited by just one or two characteristics defining a party's voters, the historian can determine a complete picture of the voter coalitions.

Regression is also important for voter analysis since it can provide an estimate of the percentage of any population group voting Whig or Democratic while avoiding the dangers of relying upon homogeneous voting units.[44] The percentage of each group's voting preference is calculated by testing the ability of selected independent variables, such as ethnicity, religion, and economic status, to predict the value of the dependent variable, percent Whig and Democratic. Statistically, regression determines the predicting value of an independent variable by drawing a straight line between it and the dependent variable. If the data fall close to the line, then there is a good "fit." One can then be reasonably certain that for every change in the independent variable, the dependent variable will change in a predicted manner. Since the effect of an independent variable upon the dependent variable can be measured, it is possible to calculate the percentage of any population group voting Whig or Democratic. It must be remembered, however, that regression is a statistical generalization and that the percentage, say, of Germans voting Democratic, should be understood as an estimate and not an absolute number.

The weakness of the Second Party System in Illinois becomes evident when the regression technique is used to analyze Whig and Democratic coalitions. By 1850, the voting patterns in Illinois varied wildly from election to election. Contrary to what some historians have identified as a fixed ethnocultural pattern, there was a great amount of instability in the voter coalitions.[45] Few of the religious and ethnic groups in Illinois were firmly tied to one political party. A close look at the elections of 1850 and 1852 dramatically illustrates not only the absence of a rigid voting pattern, but also the ineffectiveness of the Second Party System in maintaining political order.

In the 1850 election for State Treasurer, the Democrats captured a majority of almost every ethnic group in Illinois. Nearly every Yankee-, English-, Irish-, Scandinavian-, and Canadian-born voter supported the Democracy. Additionally, close to 85 percent of the Southern-born and 57 percent of the Germans voted Democratic. Finally, 93 percent of those born in parts of the United States other than the South and New England went for the party. Only the Illinois-born voters and the small French population were strongly Whig.[46] Clearly, then, there was no ethnic division in the electorate for the State Treasurer's contest; both immigrants and native-born voters supported the Democracy in overwhelming numbers.

The instability of the voter coalitions is illustrated by comparing the State Treasurer's contest to other elections in 1850. In the Congressional election that year, the Democratic coalition changed dramatically (see Table 1). While Yankees and English-born gave nearly unanimous support to the Democratic candidate for Treasurer, only 52 percent of the Yankees and 69 percent of the English supported the party's Congressional candidates. The Southern, Irish, and Scandinavian vote held constant over both contests, but the Illinois-born and French made a complete about-turn, voting Whig in one election and Democratic in the other. Instead of the 57 percent of the Germans who voted for the Democratic candidate for Treasurer, nearly all of this group supported the Democratic Congressional candidates. Finally, the Canadians moved completely into the Whig column as did all but 17 percent of the "other" U.S.-born.[47]

Table 1. Comparative Breakdown of Democratic Voting in 1850

Ethnic Group	Percent Voting for State Treasurer	Percent Voting for Congressional Candidates
Yankee	100	52
Southern	85	70
Illinois	0	100
"Other" U.S.	93	18
German	57	100
English	100	69
Irish	100	86
Scandinavian	100	100
Canadian	100	0
French	0	100

The 1850 elections were not an exception in the voting pattern; the 1852 contests also lacked a coherent voter configuration. The Democratic vote for Franklin Pierce for President had little in common with that for the rest of the party ticket. Pierce captured nearly all of the Irish, Scandinavian, Canadian, and French voters, but only 27 percent of the English, 2 percent of the Yankees, and 54 percent of the Southerners. He also carried about 90 percent of the Germans, 69 percent of the Illinois-born, and 30 percent of the "other" U.S.-born. This pattern was notably different from that in either of the 1850 elections.[48]

The configuration that supported Pierce, however, did not persist for the entire Democratic ticket, demonstrating the inability of the party to maintain a stable coalition (see Table 2). The Congressional contests showed an increase in Yankee support from 2 to 30 percent and in the Southern vote from 54 to 71 percent, and the Illinois-born voters went almost solidly Democratic. Meanwhile, the percentage of English, Scandinavians, and French voting Democratic fell off sharply. The English voted only 5 percent for Democratic Congressional candidates as opposed to 27 percent for Pierce. Scandinavian support fell 53 points to 47 percent and the French made another about-turn, going entirely Whig in the Congressional contest. Only the Irish, Canadians, Germans, and "other" U.S.-born remained fairly consistent in the two elections.[49]

Table 2. Comparative Democratic Vote: 1850 and 1852

Ethnic Group	1850 Percent for Treasurer	1850 Percent for Congress	1852 Percent for President	1852 Percent for Congress
Yankee	100	52	02	29
Southern	85	70	54	71
Illinois	0	100	69	100
"Other" U.S.	93	18	30	28
German	57	100	90	93
English	100	69	27	05
Irish	100	86	83	66
Scandinavian	100	100	100	47
Canadian	100	0	100	92
French	0	100	100	0

The Whig coalitions in 1850 and 1852 were just as unstable as the Democratic voters had been. In the 1850 Treasurer's contest, the Whigs carried all of the Illinois-born and French voters along with as much as 45 percent of the Germans and 13 percent of the Southerners.[50] The Congressional vote, however, showed a different pattern. The Whig Congressional candidates captured 37 percent of the Yankees, 30 percent of the Southerners, 31 percent of the English, and 83 percent of the "other" U.S.-born. Along with these major shifts, Whig candidates also carried all the Canadians, but lost all the French and the Illinois-born.[51]

In the 1852 elections, not only were the Whig voting patterns different from the 1850 configurations, but the combinations were also different for the Presidential, State, and Congressional contests. Winfield Scott, the Whig Presidential candidate, carried 18 percent of the Yankees, but Whig Congressional candidates captured 71 percent of that group. Some 51 percent of the Southerners voted for Scott, while only 29 percent voted Whig in the Congressional contests. All the French voted for Whig Congressional candidates, but almost none for Scott. Likewise, the Scandinavians gave Pierce their total support, but in the contest for Congress only 53 percent voted Whig. The English shifted from 25 percent for Scott to 95 percent Whig, while the Illinois-born dropped from 65 percent Scott to virtually none in the Congressional elections. Finally, the "other" U.S.-born increased their Whig vote from 51 percent in the Presidential election to 72 percent Whig in the Congressional contest. Only the Germans, Canadians, and Irish remained consistently anti-Whig.[52]

If there was a consistent pattern in the voter coalitions, it should become apparent from a comparison of any one of the elections with the special referendum in 1851 on banking. The proposed Banking Law authorized the State of Illinois to incorporate banks and stood as a clear example of a traditional issue between the Whigs and the Democrats. Whigs gave full support to the law, while the Democrats opposed the referendum. The election returns, however, provided a voting pattern completely different from any of the elections held in 1850 or 1852.

The vote against the Banking referendum came from 62 percent of the Southerners, 81 percent of the English, and nearly all of the Illinois-born, Germans, Irish, and Scandinavians. Nearly all the Yankees, "other" U.S.-born, Canadians, and French voted for the referendum.[53] None of the other elections displayed this ethnic pattern. In fact, neither the pro- nor the anti-Bank vote correlates higher than .65 with any of the Whig and Democratic contests. Incredibly, the Democratic State Treasurer's vote in 1850 correlates at an insignificant .02 with the anti-Bank vote.

The wide variance in the ethnic voting in the 1850 and 1852 elections affected the religious composition of the coalitions. Again, contrary to the ethno-cultural interpretation, religion did not have a consistent effect upon the voters in Illinois in 1850. Instead of the Whigs being predominantly pietistic, and the Democrats liturgical, the influence of religion varied (see Table 3). In fact, the 1850 Democratic Treasurer's vote correlated with pietism at .32 and was negatively associated with liturgicalism at -.14. The 1850 Congressional vote, however, showed the Whig vote negatively correlated with both pietism and liturgicalism. The lack of a consistent religious division in the electorate persisted in the

1852 elections. The Democratic vote for Franklin Pierce, for example, had a negative -.17 correlation to pietism with the Congressional vote showing a stronger -.26. Liturgicalism correlated at .33 with the Pierce vote, but the Democratic Congressional vote had an insignificant .02 correlation. Clearly, then, the Whig and Democratic coalitions varied as much in religious structure as they did in ethnic composition.

Table 3. Pearson Correlations: Religion by Election

	Whig		Democratic	
	Pietist	Liturgical	Pietist	Liturgical
1850 Treasurer	-.32	.14	.32	-.14
1850 Congress	-.16	-.29	.18	.22
1852 President	.29	-.46	-.17	.33
1852 Governor	.14	-.28	-.12	.31
1852 Congress	.30	-.27	-.26	.02
1852 Bank Law	.31	-.39	-.30	.39

The only consistency in any of these elections was the persistence of an economic division in the electorate (see Table 4). The Democratic vote came from areas with poor farmers. Regions with low farm value, acreage value, and farm size consistently were Democratic while the richer farming regions voted Whig. Even this economic trend, however, fluctuated with each election. The 1850 Treasurer's election varied most from this pattern, but the other elections still had a wide range of correlations.

Table 4. Pearson Correlations: Farm Value by Election

	High Farm Value		High Acreage Value		Large Farm Size	
	Whig	Democrat	Whig	Democrat	Whig	Democrat
1850 Treasurer	-.28	.27	.29	-.29	-.53	.52
1850 Congress	.38	-.38	.23	-.23	.07	-.06
1852 President	.52	-.52	.29	-.28	.19	-.18
1852 Governor	.53	-.53	.28	-.26	.20	-.19
1852 Congress	.78	-.54	.25	-.13	.47	-.36
1852 Bank Law	.67	-.67	.38	-.38	.17	-.17

The variance in the voter patterns is reflected in the correlations between party contests (see Table 5). The voter coalitions were so weak that some of the contests are even negatively correlated with later elections for the same party. The Democratic Congressional contest in 1852, for example, has a -.24 correlation to the Democratic vote for

Table 5. Pearson Correlations: Election to Election

| | 1851 | | 1850 | | | |
	Pro-Bank	Anti-Bank	Democrat Congress	Whig Congress	Democrat Treasurer	Whig Treasurer
1851						
Pro-Bank	1.0	-.99	-.61	.62	-.02	.01
Anti-Bank	-.99	1.00	.61	-.61	.02	-.01
1850						
Congress						
Democrat	-.61	.61	1.00	-.99	.17	-.15
Whig	.62	-.61	-.99	1.00	-.17	.15
Treasurer						
Democrat	-.02	.02	.17	-.17	1.00	-.99
Whig	.01	-.01	-.15	.15	-.99	1.00
1852						
President						
Democrat	-.63	.63	.52	-.52	.11	-.09
Whig	.64	-.64	-.59	.59	-.16	.14
Congress						
Democrat	-.21	.21	-.24	.24	-.45	.45
Whig	.54	-.54	-.21	.21	.41	-.43
Governor						
Democrat	-.63	.63	.54	-.54	.09	-.07
Whig	.65	-.65	-.61	.60	-.15	.13

| | 1852 | | | | | |
	Democrat President	Whig President	Democrat Congress	Whig Congress	Democrat Governor	Whig Governor
1851						
Pro-Bank	-.63	.64	-.21	.54	-.63	.65
Anti-Bank	.63	-.64	.21	-.54	.63	-.65
1850						
Congress						
Democrat	.52	-.59	-.24	-.21	.54	-.61
Whig	-.52	.59	.24	.21	-.54	.60
Treasurer						
Democrat	.11	-.16	-.45	.41	.09	-.15
Whig	-.09	.14	.45	-.43	-.07	.13
1852						
President						
Democrat	1.00	-.95	.33	-.58	.99	-.95
Whig	-.95	1.00	-.24	.52	-.94	.99
Congress						
Democrat	.33	-.24	1.00	-.80	.34	-.25
Whig	-.58	.52	-.80	1.00	-.59	.52
Governor						
Democrat	.99	-.94	.34	-.59	1.00	-.95
Whig	-.95	.99	-.25	.52	-.95	1.00

Congress in 1850, and a -.45 correlation to the Treasurer's ticket. In fact, the Democratic Treasurer's vote in 1850 had a positive .41 correlation to the Whig Congressional vote in 1852!

The elections of 1850 and 1852 clearly demonstrate that the Whig and Democratic voter coalitions were dissolving. Realizing their predicament, both parties tried to forestall fragmentation by recalling the past glory of old principles. The hope was that emphasis on the original principles could divert attention from the new questions and restore party unity. The failure of this tactic forced the Whigs and the Democrats to rely entirely upon the popularity of individual candidates to keep the parties alive.

The Democratic platform in 1852 contained all the provisions included in every other party platform since Andrew Jackson. The National Convention at Baltimore declared that the powers of the Federal government were limited and that strict construction of the Constitution must be maintained. The platform also stated that Federal aid for internal improvements was unconstitutional and that there must be no national bank. Other traditional stands taken by the Baltimore convention included demands to extinguish the public debt, to preserve the rights of immigrants, and to protect the government from control by special interests. In order to put aside once and for all the divisions of 1848, the platform declared that the government could not interfere with the States' affairs and that the agitation of slavery was a threat to the Union. Therefore, the Compromise of 1850 was declared to be the final solution to the new issue of slavery. The Illinois Democratic platform simply restated the same provisions.[54]

In hopes of rallying the voters around the traditional issues, the Democrats emphasized the glory of the party. One newspaper wrote that Whigs and abolitionists might well despair because the Democratic "party in Illinois has stood firm for the true and old fashioned doctrines of republicanism." The paper declared that the reason for the success of the Democracy was its faithfulness "to the principles as laid down by Thomas Jefferson and Andrew Jackson. No combustible material has been allowed in our platform. No new-fangled notion has been endorsed as a portion of the party's creed."[55] By the summer of 1853, the *Register* was proclaiming a great future for the party.

> The storm which once raged has passed away, and the sky is clear and bright, and promising for the future. . . . We have a platform broad enough to hold all, and satisfy all. There are no freesoilers, no nullifiers . . . [and] there never was a time when our organization has been firmer, stronger and more likely to be enduring.[56]

Strict adherence to the old principles and the promise of a great future, however, did not stem the erosion of the party. The Democrats' only hope lay in emphasizing the popularity of their leaders. Always portraying the strength of the party, the Democratic newspapers talked incessantly about unity, Andrew Jackson, and Illinois' special champion, Stephen Douglas. "There is, at this moment," declared the *Register*, "a more complete unity of sentiment and agreement, touching opinions and measures, than have been exhibited since the days of Jackson."[57] When Illinois newspapers were not glorifying Jackson or Douglas, they printed articles from the rest of the nation's press which praised the "Little Giant." In 1852, for example, when Douglas was considered a candidate for President, the *Register* reprinted articles from across the country supporting Douglas in his bid for the nomination.[58]

Putting such a heavy emphasis upon personalities to preserve the party was a dangerous game. It paid off in immediate benefits for Illinois Democrats, as voters, excited over the prospects of one of their own running for President, forgot the troublesome issues of temperance and slavery. In the long run, however, reliance upon the popularity of candidates was no solution to the problem of new issues, and the policy proved to be a source of embarrassment. The Illinois press, beside itself with excitement over the idea of Douglas' candidacy in 1852, reported in great detail on the Baltimore convention, weighing Douglas' chances against those of all other possible candidates. When news arrived that Franklin Pierce had been chosen as the party's candidate, Illinois Democrats were at a loss as to how to react. They had not even heard Pierce mentioned as a possible candidate. Since they knew so little about him, and what they did learn indicated no outstanding personality characteristics, the party resorted to the rallying cry of "principles not men." "We vote not for the individual," stated the *Register*, "but for the great and glorious principles of the democracy, which ever remains the same."[59] The party in Illinois was greatly disappointed in Pierce's nomination and it showed in the lack of enthusiasm in the campaign. The Democrats concentrated upon personal attacks on Winfield Scott, the Whig nominee, rather than on either the greatness of Pierce or the "glorious principles of the democracy."[60]

The Whig party was even less capable than the Democrats of forestalling fragmentation. Adherence to the original Whig principles only meant continued defeat. Consequently, the Whigs had been willing to grasp at local issues in the hope of achieving some success. Now, however, that both parties were threatened by new issues, the Whigs could not return to the old rhetoric to find unity. The Democratic

Register correctly saw the Whig situation in 1852 and delighted in telling its readers about the elusive Whig principles.

> The Whig party of the Union uniformly coalesce with factions. Being in a minority, they are forced to depend upon pandering to every *ism* that makes its appearance. This is what makes them change from one track to another with such facility. This is what makes them free-soilers one day and compromisers the next; Native-Americans in one conjunction and ardent friends of the foreigner in another. They also seek constantly to draw within the circle of their influence the off shoots of all parties and every floating element, which defies all attempts at classification. To do this, they hesitate not to repudiate to-day what they advocated yesterday, and to welcome into their ranks as confreres those they had previously delighted to abuse and sought to destroy.[61]

The Whigs, like the Democrats, were forced to rely upon the popularity of individual candidates in an effort to preserve the party. In 1848, the Whigs had won the Presidency behind Zachary Taylor, the hero of the Mexican War. In 1852, they tried a similar strategy. They nominated Winfield Scott, another popular General in the war. Scott remained silent on all issues and since the party adopted no platform, local Whigs represented him in whatever way they thought best. The Democrats declared that Scott's motto was "no principle for the public eye."[62]

The Whig strategy was a disaster. Rumors circulated in Illinois that Daniel Webster had refused to endorse Scott and that the General was a tool of William H. Seward and the "Conscience Whigs." Other reports said that Scott was a nativist and had been against the Compromise of 1850 because he was a slave owner. Scott's image as a hero was tarnished by the rumors that he was indecisive and under the control of special interests. The Whigs in Illinois, nevertheless, bravely carried on the campaign emphasizing the General's exploits during the war. In hopes of attracting enough votes, the party, in many cases, dropped the Whig label and simply called themselves "Friends of Scott."[63]

The Whig party was so badly beaten in 1852 that the *Register* declared it "defunct, totally annihilated, beyond the hope of resurrection."[64] The paper correctly pointed to the Whigs' desperation in having nominated "Winfield Scott for president—a man in whose favor they could say nothing, save that he was 'available.'"[65] The mere popularity of a candidate was not enough to save a disintegrating party.

The Second Party System in Illinois was in a shambles by 1853. The principles of both parties were irrelevant. New issues divided the voter coalitions, and the party structures were too weak to prevent the dissolution of the parties. In this stage of disintegration, the Whigs and the Democrats reacted by relying more upon the appeal of individual politicians. The result was that the parties became dominated by personalities. They no longer had an existence separate from the fortunes of a few leaders.

Politics and Personalities

Once the principles of the Jacksonian parties had lost their vitality, personalities, not party structures, remained as the most important influence in politics. Without relevant principles and an effective party organization, voters transferred their loyalty to politicians.

The result was that Illinois was carved into political fiefdoms. Counties and even whole Congressional districts came under the control of a single politician. John A. McClernand, William A. Richardson, and John Wentworth created such personal bailiwicks. No man could be nominated for any office in these areas without their approval and patronage was given only to their loyal supporters. In short, they controlled all aspects of the party structure, which meant that the party no longer had a life separate from its politicians.

No man exemplified the role of personalities in politics better than Stephen A. Douglas. In his rise to power in Illinois, Douglas skillfully drew his own issues and manipulated the party to his advantage. He formed and broke many personal alliances, and eventually crushed all in the party who opposed him. By 1852, the "Little Giant" ruled the Illinois Democracy like a monarch. The party had become his personal property. According to one politician, "Douglas was absolutely supreme in the party in Illinois, and his supremacy was a despotism; his demand was to 'shoot the deserters,' and by deserters he meant all Democrats who were unwilling to follow him."[1]

Douglas launched his political career in 1834, at the age of 21, by being elected District Attorney for the First Judicial District in Illinois. While on the circuit, he was able to meet many local politicians and make other important contacts. During these years, Douglas sharpened his speaking skills and won for himself a reputation as a tough debater. Two years later, he was elected to the Illinois Assembly, but he resigned to accept a patronage job from the Van Buren administration as Registrar of the Land Office. Through this important post, Douglas laid the groundwork for future campaigns by widening his contacts with

Democratic politicians throughout the State and performing favors for many of them.

Having carefully cultivated the friendship of party leaders, Douglas had no trouble getting nominated to run for Congress in 1834 against the very popular Whig, John T. Stuart. But in his spectacular rise to prominence, he had offended a number of Democrats. One of those was Jim Turney, who had expected to be nominated for Congress instead of Douglas. According to Usher F. Linder, Douglas would have won the election if it had not been "for a rascally contrivance of old Jim Turney, who, pretending to be a friend of Douglas, got the Irish on the canal to vote for 'John A. Douglas,' 'James A. Douglas,' and every other Douglas you might imagine except the right one of Stephen A. Douglas." All of these votes were thrown out and Douglas was defeated. "Turney played this trick upon Douglas from the meanest and most envious of motives. He thought that he should have been run by the Democratic party instead of Douglas."[2] Douglas lost the election by only 36 votes out of 36,500 cast, proving his great appeal to the voters and demonstrating his ability as a tough campaigner.

In recognition of his popularity, Douglas was appointed Illinois Secretary of State in 1840. Controlling the patronage for that office, he now had an important base of power. Douglas felt secure enough to challenge Sidney Breese, Illinois' leading Democrat, for the Senate in 1842. Although he was defeated, the caucus vote was close enough to convince all Democrats that Douglas was a new power in the party.

To Douglas, however, the defeat demonstrated the need for a stronger base of support. He was quick to realize that the shortest route to political power was through a seat in the House. There he would have a voice in distribution of federal patronage and in policy decisions, and he could make further contacts with important men. Turning his attention to that goal, Douglas was elected to Congress in 1843, in 1844, and again in 1846. After his last election, he resigned his seat in order to prepare again to run for the Senate. He then helped William A. Richardson win his former Congressional seat in a special election, and thereby established a friendship and an alliance that would last until his death.

In his maneuverings to win the Senate seat in 1846, Douglas found that John A. McClernand, a powerful Southern Illinois Democrat, was his principal rival. In order to head off McClernand, Douglas made an alliance with Senator Breese, informing the Senator that his enemies were supporting McClernand in order to unseat him in the next election.[3] Breese rallied to Douglas' support and opened a vigorous correspondence with his friends, urging them all to support Douglas. McClernand was forced to back down under the pressure and Douglas was elected to his first term as a United States Senator.[4]

Douglas was now in a position of power, but he did not yet command the party. Breese and McClernand were still powerful, and the party was divided into contending factions. The opportunity for Douglas to seize complete control of the party came in 1849, when Breese's term in the Senate expired. Breese fully expected to be reelected with Douglas' help. Douglas, however, realized that Breese could never be made subservient to his wishes and that his own power could be greatly increased by helping a friend to the Senate. Douglas quietly threw his support behind his close friend, General James Shields, a hero of the Mexican War. Through the use of patronage and personal pressure, Douglas was able to take advantage of the private jealousies that many Democrats harbored against Senator Breese. Although McClernand again entered the contest, Shields carried the election in the caucus and replaced Breese as United States Senator from Illinois.[5] Douglas not only succeeded in elevating his friend Shields to the Senate; he also won the support of McClernand by making the Congressman believe that he had done all he could to help McClernand win the Senate seat![6]

Even though he had control of both Senate seats, Douglas still faced a challenge from Breese for control of the party. Breese, bitter over his defeat, hoped to damage Douglas in 1852 by claiming the credit for the federal land grant to Illinois subsidizing the Central Railroad. Breese had proposed similar legislation as early as 1836, and when he saw Douglas receiving all the recognition for passing virtually the same bill in 1851, the old Senator believed he had an opportunity to discredit the "Little Giant." Breese launched a personal attack upon Douglas in a letter in the *Illinois State Register.*[7] The scheme, however, backfired and Breese's own reputation was badly injured.

Later, when Breese attempted to rebuild his political career by running for Judge of the Illinois Supreme Court, Douglas advised his friends not to support the ex-Senator. He wanted no future challenges from Breese and he was determined to drive Breese from politics forever. Breese complained to William R. Morrison, an ally, that "Webb, an old whig of 30 years, and my special friend Josh. Allen and John Logan are determined to beat me. . . . I can't see why the Democrats of the state should prefer Webb to me. . . ."[8] Realizing his position was precarious, Breese declared in desperation that "it is for the interest of McClernand and his friends to elect me to the Bench. If I am elected, I quit politics forever. . . ."[9] After the election, Breese was never again an important force in Illinois politics. Douglas had effectively removed the old

Senator from the political scene and now nothing stood in his way of complete control of the party.

Douglas' spectacular rise to power in Illinois was aided by influence over party leaders, but the key to his success was his immense popularity with the voters. One man observed that Douglas "can carry [an election] for any man & on any platform."[10] Wherever Douglas went, a throng of people would gather and he would dazzle them with his oratory. One newspaper likened his speaking style to that of a prizefighter. "He has . . . pluck, quickness, and strength; adroitness in shifting his positions, avoiding his adversary's blows, and hitting him in unexpected places in return."[11] Douglas' speaking style won over many politicians directly, but in any case, his skill in appealing to the voters forced politicians to attach themselves to the "Little Giant."

Once in power, Douglas was able to keep most Democrats in line by the force of his personality. As early as 1841, the Chicago *American* noted that when Douglas "says 'stand aside', none of the party dare say otherwise. . . . The truth is the whole party are (*sic*) afraid of him; and they all obey his nod most implicitly."[12] Douglas was "aggressive, bold and defiant." He "always mapped out his own campaign, formed his own issues and supported them with unequaled power."[13] By 1854, he had grown so powerful that he could write to one of his lieutenants that he had no fear of a plan in the Illinois Assembly to instruct him against the Kansas-Nebraska Bill. "Of course I have no apprehension that the scheme can succeed," Douglas confidently wrote, "nor would it alter or change my course if the plan could be executed."[14]

The Illinois Democracy no longer had a life distinct from the career of the "Little Giant." While Douglas' rule gave the party a certain stability, his power rested upon a series of personal alliances, a system which allowed for numerous disruptions. McClernand and Richardson had become Douglas' chief lieutenants and their Congressional fiefdoms were pillars of stability for Douglas. The rest of the party, however, fought incessantly among themselves. Local quarrels over patronage and offices were frequent, and they often resulted in irreparable splits, as was the case with Phillip B. Fouke and William H. Bissell in 1852. When such a battle erupted, Douglas was forced to settle the dispute or form some new alliance in order to preserve harmony. The most celebrated of these incidents involved John Wentworth, the political boss of Chicago. Douglas' efforts to settle this dispute illustrate well the workings of the alliance system.

John Wentworth had been the Congressman from the Chicago district for a number of years and had effectively dominated the local party.[15] Wentworth had always been a thorn in Douglas' side, always arguing over patronage and policy. In 1848, Wentworth showed strong sympathies for the Free Soil movement, which provided the opportunity for some Chicago Democrats to challenge "Long John's" dominance. In 1852, Ebenezer Peck, leading the opposition to Wentworth, demanded that "Long John" be read out of the party. Douglas supported Peck and Democratic newspapers across the State opened attacks upon Wentworth. Once Douglas decided to work for the Democratic nomination for President, however, he encouraged reconciliation. The "Little Giant" needed a unified party in Illinois and Wentworth had many times in the past demonstrated his popularity with the voters. Rather than risk a divided delegation to the Baltimore convention, Douglas met with Wentworth to work out an agreement. Douglas agreed to support Wentworth for Congress, if "Long John" would cease his attacks upon the party and support whomever the convention nominated for president. If Douglas was not the nominee, then Wentworth must support him for re-election to the Senate.[16] Once this new alliance with Wentworth was completed, Douglas quickly abandoned the Peck revolt.

Both Wentworth and Douglas performed their parts of the agreement. After the election of 1852, President Pierce gave Douglas complete control of the patronage in Illinois. Douglas delegated to "Long John" control over all the offices in northern Illinois, except that of postmaster of Chicago.[17] Wentworth made a big show of supporting Douglas' re-election to the Senate, and the new alliance was established.

Personalities also came to dominate the Whig party in Illinois, but with far fewer alliances than existed in the Democracy. The Democratic party was a mass of entangling, and always shifting, personal combinations because the majority party had control of all the offices and patronage in Illinois. Since the Whigs had never carried Illinois, they had fewer opportunities to advance in politics and there was little reason for cooperation. Only in local enclaves where the Whigs were in a majority was there any chance of political advancement. In these areas the Whigs carried on personal struggles for control, and they did so to the exclusion of everything else.

The most famous example of Whig politics based on personalities was the Seventh Congressional District in Central Illinois, which included Sangamon County. In a number of the counties of the district, the Whigs had a majority, and they usually were able to elect a Congressman. Because this was the only Whig enclave in the State that could send a man to Washington, the most talented of the party resided in the district. Stephen T. Logan, John J. Hardin, John T. Stuart, Edward D. Baker, and Abraham Lincoln all battled for dominance in the district. All were young and ambitious, and craved political distinction.

The rivalry between these men almost destroyed the Whig majority in the Seventh District until they agreed to "take a turn apiece" as Congressman. The feud that brought this agreement into effect began in 1843, when Lincoln wrote an "Address to the People of Illinois" in which he explained Whig principles and sought to overcome the party's reluctance to organize.[18] Lincoln proposed that the party adopt the convention system. They must do so, he argued, or resign themselves to continued defeat and watch "the spoils chucklingly borne off by the common enemy...."[19]

The Whigs fell into line and began to elect delegates to a district convention. Lincoln had hopes of carrying the Sangamon County delegation for himself, but instead the county convention endorsed E.D. Baker, and named Lincoln as a delegate instructed for Baker. Having argued for the convention system and party harmony, Lincoln had no choice but to acquiesce. When the district convention met, however, it nominated John J. Hardin rather than Baker. In order to preserve harmony, Lincoln had the convention resolve that Baker would be the candidate two years hence. Lincoln's proposal was designed to establish a rotation of office whereby, after Baker succeeded Hardin, he would follow Baker.

Lincoln's plan worked to a point. Baker followed Hardin to Congress. In 1845, however, when it was Lincoln's turn, Hardin was unwilling to stand aside again. Lincoln tried to sidetrack Hardin by having him nominated for Governor, but Hardin declined the dubious honor, knowing that it was certain political death. As Lincoln had the convention nearly locked up, Hardin proposed that the convention be called off and that the Whig voters choose the candidate by a primary election. Lincoln declined this alternative, believing that Hardin would win. Lincoln wrote that "to yield to Hardin under the present circumstances seems to me as nothing else than yielding to one who [would] gladly sacrifice me altogether."[20]

Hardin found himself outmaneuvered and finally withdrew from the race, but not until the feud had become bitter. "It will be *just all we can do* to keep out of a quarrel," Lincoln wrote.[21] There was no sign that the feud would end, even after Lincoln's nomination, but an open split in the party was averted by the outbreak of the Mexican War. Hardin enlisted and was killed at the battle of Buena Vista, thus removing forever the only man who could have turned the Seventh Congressional District into his own fiefdom. Joseph Gillespie believed that Lincoln might not have become so famous if Hardin had lived. "Hardin had high aspirations, strong convictions, and resolute purposes, and, had he survived the Mexican War, he would have added to other elements of popularity great military renown."[22]

In accordance with the plan for taking turns, Lincoln stepped aside in 1848, and Stephen T. Logan was chosen as the Whig candidate for Congress. But that did not prevent Lincoln from pursuing his own quest for political power along other avenues. Lincoln hoped that through the patronage of President Taylor he would be put into a position controlling the Whigs of the Seventh District. However, he was ignored by the new Whig Administration. The battle to turn the district into a personal fiefdom ended in an uneasy stalemate, with Lincoln and Logan as the principal contestants.

There were few other areas in Illinois where Whig politicians were dominant. In the late 1840s and early 1850s, the only other Whig politicians of consequence were Cyrus Edwards of Edwardsville, J. L. D. Morrison of St. Clair County, Orville Hickman Browning of Quincy, and, to a lesser extent, David Davis of Bloomington. Each of these men, however, appeared less ambitious than the Whigs of Sangamon, probably because there was less opportunity for political gain. In many ways, the attitudes of each of these men were typified by O. H. Browning. In 1850, Browning received news that a Whig convention had nominated him for Congress. Unlike the Sangamon County Whigs, who battled to the end for such a nomination, Browning was disappointed. In his diary, he wrote: "I have not wanted to run — on the contrary have been averse to it — but in obedience to what seems to be the general wish of the whigs of the district I have yielded. . . ." Browning approached his nomination and impending campaign with such gloom because he had not much hope of success. There was a large Democratic majority in the district. As for the campaign, Browning declared that "my professional engagements are such as to forbid my canvassing the district to any tolerable extent."[23] Despite Browning's reluctance to run for Congress, the Whigs in the Fifth Congressional District continued to nominate him. Again, in 1852, he was a candidate and he wrote: "I am sorry I ever became a candidate, but am in for it now, and must go through with good heart, tho it is at great sacrifice."[24]

Browning's lack of enthusiasm was typical of Whigs in areas where the Democrats had a majority. In 1852, Browning had an opportunity to win the election but failed because it was a Presidential year and the national Whig ticket dragged him down to defeat. "It [the district] could not have been carried against [me] at any other time. Had no Presidential election pending [*sic*], I would have been elected easily. Genl Scott has beaten me."[25] Not only was there nothing to gain from cooperating with Whigs in other districts, it was a disadvantage. So local Whig leaders shunned attempts at unity and struggled on by themselves for political life.

Whenever there was an opportunity to gain some advantage, as in the case of patronage when Taylor was elected President, Illinois politicians turned to Sangamon County and made quick alliances with one of the Whig leaders there. In 1849, Baker and Lincoln each sought to control the federal patronage in Illinois, and Whigs throughout the State turned to these men for jobs. Cyrus Edwards enlisted the support of Lincoln for the post of Commissioner of the General Land Office, while Baker committed himself to J.L.D. Morrison for the same position. The contest was deadlocked when Justin Butterfield entered the fray. Desperate to control the patronage and enhance his own power, Lincoln offered himself as a candidate. Eventually, Butterfield received the post. The Sangamon Whigs were virtually left out of patronage and therefore lost any power they might otherwise have had to unify the State party through personal alliances.

Both political parties were divided into a series of political fiefdoms by the 1850s. Local politicians jealously guarded their bailiwicks and looked with distrust upon all other politicians. Consequently, men elected to State offices were generally compromise candidates. E. B. Webb, for example, was the perennial Whig candidate for Governor because he was unassuming and not very ambitious. Joel A. Matteson, the Democratic candidate for Governor in 1852, was a compromise between rival personalities who feared a strong candidate.[26]

The personal factions into which the parties were divided usually managed to cooperate only when there was something to be gained in opposition to some other personality. John Palmer, for example, remembered that after the death of William Henry Harrison in 1841, "[t]he discordant elements which had united to elect 'Tippecanoe and Tyler too' separated, never again to be reunited — their only bond of union was their opposition to Mr. Van Buren." Palmer concluded that "the political combination which placed Harrison and Tyler upon the same ticket had no common principles, and the accession of Tyler to the presidency destroyed it."[27]

Politics based on personalities had a profound effect upon the party system. Always ad hoc, the party organizations were susceptible to local pressures and individual ambition. Once personalities came to dominate the party, the agencies making up the State organization were changed, ignored, and turned into personal tools for advancement. Consequently, all aspects of the party became dependent upon the politician. The nominating process, the newspapers, patronage, and the campaigns were all manipulated by individual politicians.

Probably the most important tool used by personalities to control politics was the newspaper. As the most important link between the party and the voter, the newspaper was a crucial aspect of the political structure. A politician who owned his own paper had priceless opportunities to express his views, defend his actions, and attack his enemies without fear of having the "facts" proven wrong. John Reynolds, for example, an early Governor of Illinois, owned the *Belleville Advocate*, and through the paper he controlled the local party. Notice of all Democratic party activities had to be printed in the *Advocate* in order to be considered official. Reynolds would report on the proceedings of party meetings but, if a resolution did not meet his approval, the paper would simply ignore it. Joseph Gillespie remembered one mass meeting in which he and some other Whig friends got resolutions passed that Reynolds did not approve. The *Advocate*, however, reported the meeting as a great success and vindication of the Governor. Gillespie, upon meeting Reynolds, remarked "that the account of the meeting did not square very well with the actual proceedings." Reynolds replied, "'No; you damned fellows beat me in the meeting, but I can beat you in the papers.'"[28]

Few politicians had money enough to own their own presses but many were able to buy editorial support through judicious arrangements with publishers. Isaac R. Diller, for example, proposed to Douglas that a newspaper was needed in Chicago to present the Senator's case to the people. Diller asked for $5,000 from Douglas to help launch such a paper. In return Diller would support the Senator in the newspaper. Part of the deal stipulated that if Diller ever broke with Douglas, he would pay the money back.[29]

With individual politicians controlling the press, editors of newspapers carried on great debates with each other. These affairs usually resulted in clashes between personalities which always divided the party. The *Joliet Signal*, for example, observed in 1853 that:

> We regret to see that a large portion of the democratic papers of this State are engaged in a guerrilla warfare among themselves. While some are exhibiting a quarrelsome feeling of innuendoes, others . . . are openly opposing and denouncing prominent democrats. . . . This family warfare in our State, we regard as one founded more on variances and envious feelings between individuals, than upon reason or principle.[30]

The personal control of a newspaper was so important for the advancement of an individual politician that editors sometimes faced violence when they espoused the wrong man or cause. In 1860, John A. Logan, Democratic Congressman from Southern Illinois, led a mob at Benton to demand that the editors of the *Franklin Democrat*, who supported Lincoln, either sell the paper or suffer the consequences.

According to the editors, Logan first offered them money to return to the Douglas cause. They refused the bribe, so Logan offered to buy the paper, but for a price far below its value. Again the editors refused. At midnight, Logan returned to the newspaper office with about one hundred "friends" and demanded that the paper be sold. The crowd began to threaten the editors and warned them that they would "not come out of the office alive" if they persisted in refusing to sell. The editors sold the paper immediately at a ruinous price and left town.[31]

Another way politicians controlled politics was through the manipulation of the nominating process. Despite the existence of conventions, individual leaders easily managed the selection of candidates. Candidates for local offices were hand-picked by the more powerful leaders and, if a convention was held, it usually merely ratified what had already been decided. Local candidates found it necessary to receive the endorsement of an important politician before they could run for office. Joseph L. Hayes, for example, sought the support of John A. McClernand in order to run for Congress. Hayes pleaded with McClernand for his endorsement on the grounds "of seven years of friendship, in which I have never deceived you, of the labor I have undergone, the responsibility I have assumed, the eminity [sic] I have incurred, in your support, to come up to my help against your old antagonists and his allies."[32]

In some cases, the local party was so torn apart by personal rivalries that the political boss could not afford to openly endorse one man over another for fear of causing a rebellion. In such cases, the politician would either stand aside and allow the local candidates to battle it out in a convention or secretly help a favored man to the nomination. In 1854, after carefully checking all the aspirants for office, Lincoln wrote to Richard Yates that he would support him for Congress. Lincoln wrote: "I would like, by your leave, to get an additional paragraph into the *Journal* about as follows:

> 'To-day we place the name of Hon. Richard Yates at the head of our columns for reelection as the Whig candidate for this congressional district. We do this without consultation with him and subject to the decision of a whig convention, should the holding of one be deemed necessary; hoping, however, there may be unanimous acquiescence without a convention.'"[33]

Stephen Douglas had a more foolproof plan to help his friends win the nomination of the party. In his early political career when his own position was not so secure that he could risk political feuds, Douglas advised his friends to create their own party organization and thereby control all the political activity. In a letter to William S. Prentice, Douglas outlined the procedure.

> I am glad you have concluded to run for the Legislature. You ought to begin to make your arrangements immediately & take an early start, not publicly, but let your confidential friends understand it and act accordingly. Let the party in the county be thoroughly organized. The best way to do that, perhaps, would be to call a county meeting to appoint delegates to the State convention in December & then appoint a county corresponding committee. . . . Let the county committee appoint sub-committees in each precinct composed of three men each. In this way you can have the most perfect organization in the whole county & the Whigs need know nothing about it. . . . By producing a perfect organization this fall & becoming well acquainted with the committee men in each Precinct you can have any man you please nominated for the Legislature. . . . Any man who comes out against the regular nominee will be regarded as a Whig brought to divide the party.[34]

Once a politician followed this procedure, it was next to impossible for a rival candidate to get a nomination except by bolting the party. Many politicians did create their own party organization. John McClernand developed one in Southern Illinois. A supporter wrote, "Your friends I believe will again be able to nominate you for Congress. I have been out in Franklin, Williamson, & Saline Counties and find your old friends are all for you. . . ." The man concluded that to start the nominating process, he had "written to old Dr. Turney of Fairfield [to] get up a county meeting and appoint a delegate to the McLeansboro convention with instructions to go for you. . . ."[35]

Patronage was also an effective tool politicians used to control politics. Nominally, the Congressional delegation handled federal patronage to the State with each Congressman controlling the appointments to his own district. In the Democratic party, however, since Douglas was a figure of national importance, the "Little Giant" had the final word on all appointments. Douglas was careful enough not to run roughshod over the local politicians, and he used patronage with skill to keep everyone in line. After the Free Soil split in 1848, for example, Douglas kept John Wentworth of Chicago loyal to the party by allowing "Long John" to control the patronage in northern Illinois.[36]

The game of doling out patronage was dangerous. Douglas was under a constant barrage of letters from supporters appealing for jobs. If a mistake was made in appointing the wrong man to office or if some local politician was offended, the result could be disastrous. In 1853, John McClernand fired a letter to Douglas warning him about the consequences of not receiving a fair share of the offices. "I understand that several or the whole of the [Congressional] delegation . . . have declared it to be sufficient reason for denouncing a man's pretension to office who is known to be a friend of mine." If this is true, McClernand warned, "I will retaliate and we will see with what effect in the next session."[37] Usually, Douglas was able to avoid a blow-up over patronage among his supporters. Charles Lanphier, the editor of the *Illinois State Register*, asked Douglas to appoint a friend to the position of clerk of the U. S. District Court, but Douglas refused Lanphier's request on the grounds that the appointment belonged to the Judge, Samuel Treat.[38]

Patronage was more than just a reward system for loyalty. The offices themselves were important in furthering the career of a local politician. It was fully expected that the recipients of patronage would help pay for the next campaign. The political boss then was much like a landlord collecting the "rent" from the men who worked the patronage offices.

The patronage worker was also expected to use the office itself to further the ambition of his benefactor. Post office positions were regarded as the most important in this regard. One Chicago newspaper complained about Wentworth, who had control of all the post offices around Chicago.

> Mr. Wentworth has had the appointing of Postmasters here abouts for a great many years, and he has uniformly used the power so as to increase the circulation of his paper. No man could be Postmaster in his bailwick [*sic*] who could not perform the drudgery of an active agency for the *Chicago Democrat*, or who would use any exertion to secure subscribers for another Chicago paper.[39]

After Wentworth and Douglas split over the Kansas-Nebraska Act in 1854, the "Little Giant" was forced to start his own newspaper in Chicago, the *Times*. The Senator found, however, that the paper could not be distributed in the surrounding area until all of Wentworth's postmasters were removed from office.

> *Long John* claimed to name all the Postmasters in his district, except that of Chicago, which he conceded to Judge Douglas as a personal favor. . . . The main condition imposed by *Long John* on the appointee was that each Postmaster should circulate a given number of the *Chicago Democrat*. During the past summer an agent of the Douglas *organ* canvassed the county with the view of introducing the *Times* among the faithful, but it is said found the Postmasters along the river hostile to this movement. No one could be induced to touch the thing, and the Judge of course became indignant. Determined on bringing the *Long John* men to their sense, Judge Douglas applied privately to the Postmaster General and had the Postmasters at Elgin, Geneva, Batavia, Aurora, etc., removed, and Nebraska men appointed in their places.[40]

With all aspects of party politics controlled by personalities, the campaigns developed a special style. Electioneering was intense, spontaneous, and, at times, violent. Usually, a campaign began on the circuit, when the lawyers who were following the court from town to town would entertain the crowds with political speeches after the day's adjournment. John Palmer remembered that since all the lawyers were politicians, "the more ready and ambitious of them would on the first day of the term . . . make a speech either assailing the party opposed to him, or defending his own party, or both. Some orator would reply to him on the next day or evening, and thus the debate was kept up until the close of the term."[41] The debate was a favorite campaign technique of the time and it was held on any occasion for any reason. Sometimes, however, these exchanges included personal attacks that led to bloodshed.

Usher F. Linder was involved in such an incident. Linder had learned that "a low, dirty loco-foco . . . had been going around the county attacking . . . [his] personal character." Linder, in a speech, held the man up to the scorn and indignation of his audience. That night on his way home Linder was attacked by the man. According to Linder:

> [T]he cowardly wretch waylaid me . . . having hid himself behind a couple of good boxes, being armed with a large hickory cane, jumped out from his place of concealment just as I passed, and commenced striking me with his cane over my head, from behind. It is a wonder he did not kill me, for I had nothing with which to defend myself. . . .[42]

The man continued to beat Linder on the head until his cane broke, when Linder was able to grab his assailant by the hair and strike him until he broke loose. Linder went to a friend's house to get bandaged and to borrow a revolver and then he went looking for the man. According to Linder, "I was determined if I had met him in his own parlor to plaster its walls with his brains."[43]

Not all campaigns were so hazardous or bloody, but personal confrontations were more the rule than the exception. In 1860, Richard Yates was sent to Gallatin County, a strong Democratic area, to make a speech for the Republican party. The Democrats decided to kidnap Yates to prevent him from speaking. They guarded the road from the town of Carmi where Yates had spoken the day before and sat up all night to wait. Fortunately for Yates, the kidnappers fell asleep and he passed them by in the night unaware of their plans.[44]

With personalities in control of the parties, all electioneering was left to the individual candidates. After winning a Congressional term in 1852, Richard Yates revealed to a fellow Whig the technique necessary for success.

> There are in my estimates from 500 to 1000 votes to be materially effected
> in every District by the personal efforts of the candidates. His friends can
> do much. They can do every thing but their action will always be affected
> by the efforts of the candidate. . . . I knew I could be elected, if I could
> make them believe it. I wrote a letter & had 150 copies of it drawn off
> which I sent to as many whigs known & unknown to me—in ten days I
> went through each county in the District had a little night meeting in each
> . . . and at the end of that time I commenced speaking at the various
> county seats *on a run* and in twenty days the whole whig columns from
> center to circumference were moving in solid phalanx and shouting victory
> all along the line. . . .[45]

In addition to a candidate's own efforts, dignitaries and popular
politicians were always in great demand during a campaign. Much could
be gained by the appearance of an important man. During the 1858
campaign, Douglas canvassed the State covering every Legislative
District, hoping to influence enough voters with his personality to elect a
Democratic Assembly in Illinois. He spoke in 57 different counties and
delivered 59 speeches from 2 to 3 hours in length. In addition to those
efforts, he made 17 speeches from 20 to 45 minutes in response to
serenades and 37 speeches in reply to addresses of welcome. During the
campaign the "Little Giant" rode every railroad in the State except 3 and
travelled some 5000 miles throughout Illinois.[46] His efforts paid off as
the Assembly received a Democratic majority and Douglas was returned
to the Senate. In 1860, a nervous Republican worker wrote to Lyman
Trumbull requesting him to recall all of his appointments and to
campaign personally in the doubtful districts.

> I think you should refuse to go anywhere out of those districts. You had
> better travel from County to County going around among the people
> talking to them in their School Houses—counciling with, and encouraging
> the working man of the party. You will in this way double the good you
> would by attending large mass meetings. . . .[47]

By 1853, all aspects of political life in Illinois were dominated by
personalities. Individual politicians controlled the campaign style, the
newspapers, patronage, the nominating process, and the party structure
itself. The result was a fragile and easily disrupted party system.
Douglas was driven to the point of distraction after listening to the
constant bickering of his lieutenants and suffering the defections of a
number of Democrats. Exasperated, Douglas complained to James W.
Sheahan, the editor of the *Chicago Times*:

> [N]ever did a party throw away its favour & waste its strength so foolishly
> & uselessly by personal quarrels, resentments and desire for revenge. If this
> course is persisted in the consequences are obvious and inevitable. No

party, no matter how patriotic its men, and how fine its principles can survive such a suicidal course.[48]

Douglas was able to keep the Democrats together through his political genius and the force of his personality until his death in 1861. Then the whole party came tumbling down, making true Douglas' own prophecy. The Whig demise came much earlier but without the suddenness of the Democratic collapse. Whig politicians had no crowned head to follow and so were not so easily thrown into confusion by drastic changes. They had long been accustomed to fending for themselves due to the lack of patronage ties, and many Whigs proved their political agility by moving in new directions.

Politics based on personalities depended upon the voter. As long as the voter was unmotivated by principle and there was no effective party organization to sustain regularity, individual politicians ruled politics. With voter loyalty attached to personalities rather than the party structure, the Jacksonian parties were easily destroyed by the introduction of new principles.

3

The Realignment Begins

By 1853, the Democratic party throughout the nation was troubled by factionalism. Its political hegemony was further threatened by the weakness of President Franklin Pierce, whose attempts to unify the party only seemed to make matters worse. Even the traditional Democratic leaders could do little to help rally the party. Lewis Cass was too old and embittered by his defeat in 1848. Thomas Hart Benton had been discredited by the split in the party in his own State of Missouri, and James Buchanan was out of the country. Many Democrats began to look to Stephen Douglas as the savior of the party.[1] Aware of the opportunity that lay before him, Douglas understood that he needed an issue in order to unify the personal factions of the party. "Our first duty is the cause—the fate of individual politicians is of minor consequence," Douglas wrote. "The party is in a distracted condition & it requires all our wisdom, freedom & energy to consolidate its powers and perpetuate its principles."[2]

Douglas believed that westward expansion, an important corollary to the traditional Jacksonian program, could serve as the unifying principle for the Democrats.[3] In hopes of defining the expansion issue, Douglas worked hard for legislation to help build a transcontinental railroad and telegraph system, and he advocated free homesteads in the west to encourage the movement of settlers. Since expansion required organizing the newly opened lands, Douglas prepared a bill for the creation of the territories of Kansas and Nebraska.[4]

Early in 1854, Douglas presented his Kansas-Nebraska Bill to the Congress. Hoping to defuse Southern opposition to the Bill, Douglas included a provision for the question of slavery to be determined by popular sovereignty. Because it proposed to abrogate the Missouri Compromise line, the Kansas-Nebraska Bill became an explosive issue that polarized the electorate. Voters, aroused by the question of extending slavery, began a realignment that utterly destroyed the fragile Whig and Democratic coalitions. A new issue, and not the one Douglas had intended, had been interjected into the political scene, and it changed the shape of the voter pattern, destroying the Second Party System.

The historiography on the effects of the Kansas-Nebraska Act is divided between two general interpretations, but neither view accurately describes the process of the voter realignment. The older interpretation contends that the Nebraska Bill was the final step leading to the Civil War and that the eruption of the slavery issue created the Republican party which in effect replaced the destroyed Whig organization.[5] Stressing the revolutionary effect of the Kansas-Nebraska Act upon the nation, historians holding this position presented the formation of the Republican party as rapid and fairly simple. Although this view is correct in asserting the importance of the Kansas-Nebraska Act, it fails to take into account the complicated and uneven nature of the voter realignment. The Republican party was neither instantaneous nor a direct result of the Nebraska Act. Instead, the creation of the Republican coalition was a confused process of uniting numerous anti-Democratic factions.

The more recent interpretation accurately depicts the complex nature of politics in 1854, but sees the revolt against the Democratic party as rooted in local tensions and cultural conflicts.[6] The Kansas-Nebraska Act, in this view, did not cause the disruption of politics, but merely released long-festering hostilities. The problem with this interpretation is that while it corrects the overemphasis upon the suddenness of the realignment in 1854, it reduces the Kansas-Nebraska Act to a minor role and it misses the depth of the political changes by regarding politics as essentially a series of continuous ethno-cultural conflicts.

The one view, then, recognizes the importance of the Kansas-Nebraska Act upon politics but fails to understand the complexity of the changes, while the other interpretation, although acknowledging the uneven process of politics, declines to look beyond the influence of local tensions. Both interpretations miss the profound changes occurring within the Democratic party, and, consequently, neither can give a total picture of the voter realignment. Although the Kansas-Nebraska bill did not, in Illinois, produce a universal attack upon slavery nor the spontaneous creation of the Republican party, the measure was not of minor consequence. It did divert public attention from all other issues and begin to force the electorate into new voting patterns that would last until the end of the century. In Illinois, the key to understanding this new configuration was the presence of a large Southern-born population, and not, as ethno-cultural historians have maintained, a pietist-liturgical conflict.[7] Rather than being based on a fusion of native-born pietists with Protestant Germans and Scandinavians against the Catholic and liturgical groups, the realignment combined the various ethnic and cultural groups without regard to religion, in opposition to a Southern-based Democratic coalition.

The initial reaction in Illinois to the Kansas-Nebraska Act can best be described as confusion. A new issue had been introduced into politics and neither party was capable of responding in a coherent fashion. The Whigs were irrevocably destroyed as a party, but the Democracy was also dramatically altered. As the voters began to realign, the composition and character of the Democratic party changed, but the party managed to survive these changes because of the system of patronage and alliances controlled by Senator Douglas. The Whigs, however, could not respond to the voter movement, not only because they lacked the Democratic network of personal alliances, but also because the Whig coalition was more widely split by the realignment. The breaking up of the parties, however, was not an even affair. The result was that there was no coherent order to politics in Illinois in 1854.

Douglas was surprised by the force of the public opposition to the passage of the Kansas-Nebraska Act. At first, he was convinced that the protests were the result of agitation by a small group of abolitionists. Still confident that the measure would unify the Democratic party on the program of western expansion, Douglas defended his bill on the grounds that it rested upon "the great fundamental principle of self-government upon which our republican institutions are predicated." Eventually, however, he realized with dismay the depth of the opposition to the Nebraska Bill, though he found incomprehensible the cry that the act would introduce slavery into formerly free territories. Anxious to keep the slavery question out of the discussion and to make clear the purpose of the bill, Douglas declared that it was the "TRUE INTENT AND MEANING *of this act* NOT *to legislate slavery into any Territory or State,* NOR *to exclude it therefrom, but to leave the people thereof perfectly* FREE TO FORM AND REGULATE THEIR DOMESTIC INSTITUTIONS IN THEIR OWN WAY."[8]

Douglas' explanations, however, did not divert public attention from the question of slavery. Still hoping to unify the party on traditional Jacksonian questions, Douglas was forced to try to discredit those who claimed slavery was the issue. Party leaders in Illinois quickly rallied around the Senator, and following his lead, attacked the opposition leaders as demagogues. The Springfield *Register* tried to convince its readers that the anti-Nebraska movement was composed of soreheads in the bankrupted Whig party who hoped to capitalize upon the prejudices of the voters by agitating the slavery question.

> The fanatics declare truly that the Whig party as a party has no vitality and
> can never reorganize on any of the old issues. . . . [The] bank, tariff,
> internal improvements [are] all dead issues. The people have decided against
> the Whig issues of the last half century, and the national sentiment has
> now become so confirmed against them that the most devoted whigs
> themselves have ceased to advocate them.   All that they have left are
> merely personal affirmities and predilections.   It is natural that they should
> seek to elevate to office those with whom they have been associated
> politically. . . .[9]

While the *Register* attacked the anti-Nebraska leaders as being Whigs
who sought office by inflaming public passions because the old party had
no viable issue, other Democratic newspapers attacked the agitators on
the grounds that they were using the slavery question as a ruse to dupe
the voters and that the agitators really hoped to restore the old Whig
programs. One paper predicted that should these agitators "attain power
their anti-Nebraska zeal will all be forgotten in their schemes for the
restoration of a National Bank. . . ."[10]

The charges that the Whig party had fallen into the hands of
fanatics and demagogues did not stem the attacks upon Douglas and the
Nebraska Act. As the fear that slavery would spread into Kansas
continued to be the dominant theme of politics, the Democrats finally
turned to the argument that the natural limits of the territory would
prevent slavery from taking hold. "If Kansas were now a slave state,"
The *Register* reasoned, "there would be little or no influx of slaves there
for the reason that slave labor would be far less profitable there than in
the cotton and sugar districts of the south."[11] There would be no slaves
in Kansas, the *Register* argued, if the abolitionist agitators would stop
trying to bully the slave States out of their rights.

Despite all efforts, the Nebraska Act had clearly begun to polarize
the voters. Slavery had long been a festering problem under the surface
of the Whig and Democratic order of politics, but it had never had the
strength to cause a major realignment. The Kansas-Nebraska Act
changed everything. Now, for the first time, slavery could be introduced
into the northern territories. The implications of the law posed a threat
to the livelihood of the northern farmer, who feared competition if the
plantation system should be extended. Slavery became a question that
could no longer be ignored.

The realignment of the electorate, however, was disjointed and
confused. Some voters were reluctant to leave their old party even
though it no longer represented their views. Others simply sought to end
the agitation and restore the Missouri Compromise, while yet another
group directly embraced the new question and immediately adopted a
polar stand. The suddenness and complexity of the changes in the

electorate made it impossible for the parties to respond in a coherent manner. Old issues, principles, and in some cases, personalities lost their appeal. With the approach of the fall elections, politics in Illinois offered a spectacle of complete confusion of voters and parties. Silver-Grey Whigs, anti-Nebraska Whigs, Fusionists, Republicans, and anti-Nebraska Democrats all entered Congressional candidates in one district or another against the Douglas Democrats.

The process of the realignment in 1854 is best understood through the use of multiple regression.[12] The multiple regression routine can sort out the complicated movement of voters and construct a statistical picture of the composition of each of the factions in 1854. This identification of voters is important in understanding the realignment because it illustrates not only the fragmentation of the old coalitions, but also the impact of the Kansas-Nebraska Act upon the Jacksonian parties. Once the voter composition of the factions is known, the various political groups can be more easily characterized. Each of the factions represented a different constituency and ideological position against the Nebraska Act, and each stands as an example of the varying speed and direction in which the voters moved in the realignment over slavery.

The old Whig voters displayed the greatest variation in their reaction to the Nebraska Act. The State Whig organization split into at least three groups. One group favored the Bill and drifted into the Democratic party after some hesitation. Led by prominent men like James W. Singleton, these Whigs became important tools for Douglas against the anti-Nebraska forces. Singleton and others were pointed out as examples by the Democrats of true "Henry Clay Whigs," whose patriotism forced them to oppose the agitation of the slavery question. A larger group of Whigs sought to maintain the party on the old issues. Led by Stephen T. Logan and John T. Stuart, this Silver-Grey faction of the party fought both the Democrats and the anti-Nebraska factions. Eventually, most of these Whigs were forced out of politics by their own irrelevance. The bulk of the Whig party, however, adopted an anti-Nebraska position.

Only in a few cases, however, was there a distinct anti-Nebraska Whig organization. The Whigs opposed to the Nebraska Act were so widely divided by the question that cooperation was nearly impossible and the more radical anti-slavery Whigs found that they could not attract much outside support because of the lingering suspicions of and antagonisms to the Whig party. The anti-Nebraska Whigs who did maintain a distinct organization were the most conservative of the anti-slavery men in the old party. Essentially, their anti-slavery position was limited to advocating the restoration of the Missouri Compromise. The anti-Nebraska Whigs declared their purpose to be "to resist the tendency of the country to sectionalism; to endeavor to allay the strife of sectional feelings. . . ."[13]

The areas in which the anti-Nebraska Whigs thrived as a separate organization were the old strongholds in the central counties with a population composed mostly of Southerners and Baptists. (See Table 6.)[14] Other ethnic groups, such as the English and the Yankees, who had previously supported the party, turned to the more radical anti-Nebraska factions. The fact that the anti-Nebraska Whig faction had only limited support is demonstrated in the correlations of the 1854 election with previous Whig elections. The vote for Winfield Scott in 1852, for example, correlates at only .22 with the 1854 anti-Nebraska Whig voters.

Table 6. Regression: 1854 Congressional Anti-Nebraska Whig Vote

	Multiple R	R Square	RSQ Change	Simple R	B	Beta
Percent Southern	.372	.138	.138	.37	.320	.226
Average Farm Value	.520	.270	.132	.22	.006	.141
Pietist	.580	.336	.065	.14	17.67	.385
Average Acre Value	.614	.377	.040	-.15	-.041	-.056
Liturgical	.642	.413	.035	-.32	12.51	-.407
Percent Irish	.666	.443	.030	-.19	-.10	-.020
Percent Yankee	.684	.467	.024	-.17	-3.37	-.526
Baptist	.699	.488	.021	.21	2.86	.101
Percent Illinois	.717	.514	.025	-.19	-2.23	-.654
Percent Scandinavian	.723	.523	.009	-.004	10.16	.175
(constant)					-60.24	

The more radical anti-Nebraska Whigs generally joined what were called Fusion movements. These Fusion movements, involving a conglomeration of voters from all parties, sprang up in areas with large English, Yankee, French and Scandinavian populations (see Table 7). Significantly, the Fusion vote was dramatically reduced by the presence of Baptists and Southerners, which resulted in a strong -.54 correlation between the anti-Nebraska Whig and Fusion voters. The complete difference in the type of support received by these two anti-Nebraska factions reveals how fragmented the realignment was.

The Fusion movements succeeded instead of the anti-Nebraska Whig organization in the counties with large Yankee and English-born populations because these voters demanded stronger action against the Kansas-Nebraska Bill than many of the old Whigs were willing to concede. The Fusionists moved far beyond a mere call for the restoration of the Missouri Compromise, declaring that the extension of slavery was a threat to liberty and that the Kansas-Nebraska Act was "a disgrace to

Table 7. Regression: 1854 Congressional Fusion Vote

	Multiple R	R Square	RSQ Change	Simple R	B	Beta
Percent Other	.655	.429	.429	.65	.383	.211
Average Acre Value	.730	.533	.103	.37	.197	.220
Percent Canada	.791	.627	.093	.21	14.38	.259
Liturgical	.833	.694	.066	-.14	18.20	.493
Capital Investment	.839	.704	.010	.17	-.0002	-.844
Percent Yankee	.848	.720	.015	.29	-.388	-.050
Pietist	.857	.734	.013	.16	-7.11	-.129
Percent English	.861	.742	.008	.27	-1.83	-.247
Percent German	.867	.752	.009	-.13	-2.39	-.721
Percent French	.875	.765	.013	.29	12.38	.268
Percent Southern	.884	.782	.016	-.59	-1.58	-.928
Value Produced	.890	.792	.009	.20	.00005	.506
Average Farm Value	.891	.795	.002	.35	.004	.079
Baptist	.892	.796	.001	-.27	4.19	.124
Percent Illinois	.893	.797	.0006	-.38	-.306	-.074
Percent Scandinavian	.893	.797	.0001	.27	-1.59	-.022
(constant)					93.07	

the character of the age—a foul libel on every profession of Liberty and Equality of men." The result of the Nebraska Act, one Fusion newspaper stated, was that "Slavery is nationalized, and Freedom sectionalized. . . ." The paper declared that hereafter, the mission of the government "is to breed slaves and protect the interests of the inhuman whipper of women and children."[15]

Because of the success of the Fusionists, some radical anti-Nebraska Whigs tried to co-opt the Fusion movements and revitalize the old party on an anti-slavery platform. One Whig newspaper declared that the "death of the Whig Party is a favorite theme of . . . present. In the North the Whig Party was never stronger. *It is now taking its true position* and . . . it will give evidence of vitality never possessed by it before."[16] Scornful of the conservatism displayed by many Whigs, another Whig editor wrote:

> If there is a single 'National Whig' who . . . thinks the Whigs have really sold themselves out to the abolitionists and that our ship is really sinking through too much 'nigger' ballast, why, we hope he will immediately play the rat and leave the Whig party, espouse the cause of modern democracy and enlist at once under the black flag of Douglas.[17]

Generally, however, it was the radical anti-Nebraska whigs who were forced to abandon the old party. The party apparatus was controlled by conservative leaders who steadfastly refused to leave behind the old issues and move beyond the call for an end to the slavery agitation.

The persistence of the Whigs proved to be a major problem for the Fusionists. The leaders of the Fusion movements had to handle the Whigs with caution for fear of alienating the conservative wing of the party. Elihu Washburne, Whig Congressman from Rockford and Fusion leader, outlined in a letter to his supporters the strategy that was adopted by most Fusionists in dealing with the Whigs.

> The Whigs will call a convention and make a nomination. If our folks do not go with it then a Silver Grey Whig will be nominated. . . . Let the Whigs have their convention. . . . They will *probably* nominate me. . . . Let the free soilers have a convention at the same time and place. Let them resolve to maintain their organization if they please, but yet resolve to act as to make their power felt. If the candidate nominated by the Whig convention be satisfactory to them, they can resolve to support him, and they can ask the Whigs to support their men for Legislature, which they will readily do. This course will enable the two parties to come together.[18]

Following Washburne's advice, a Fusion and a Whig convention were held in Rockford on the same day. Resolutions, delegations, and conferences were exchanged between the two conventions. The Whig convention nominated Washburne for Congress and the Fusionists shortly did the same. Eventually, the two conventions agreed upon a whole slate of candidates and the coalition was formalized.

This pattern was repeated between Whigs and Fusionists in other northern Congressional districts. In one case, that of the Peoria district, the Fusionists adopted the name "Republicans," but their position was not materially different from any of the other Fusion groups. The only true Republican movement in Illinois in 1854 developed in the Chicago Congressional district.

Originally, the Fusion movement in Chicago was like that of Fusion movements elsewhere but through the summer, the tone of the campaign became more radical. These Fusionists moved beyond the resolutions and the rhetoric of other anti-Nebraska groups. Eventually, they came to define slavery as an aggressive institution and they attacked the South as the source of the problem. Southerners, they declared, have "determined and practiced upon a system of aggression, whereby they seek to extend that institution into all the territories of this Union, and by conquest or purchase . . . shall farther to extent [sic] its limits, until slavery shall acquire an undisputed and irresistible preponderance of power in the Councils of this nation."[19] These men, who began to call themselves "Republicans," saw the problem as far more than simply a question of the extension of slavery. They believed that the Constitution had been subverted and they doubted that freedom could continue to exist in the current state of affairs.

The Federal Government of this Union, has . . . widely departed from the objects of its founders in respect to slavery. The Constititution when adopted, found Slavery local and Freedom national: but a gradual misconstruction and perversion of the powers of that instrument has nearly reversed their positions, and hazarded the enjoyment and possession of those inalienable rights which it was the original object of this Government. . . .[20]

The radical posture of the Chicago district Republicans drove many of the Fusionists back into the Whig party, which nominated its own anti-Nebraska candidate for Congress. Anti-Nebraska Democrats also fielded a candidate in the district, which resulted in a four-man contest for Congress. Despite the fact that the anti-Nebraska forces were split into three factions, the Republican James R. Woodworth won the election.

A final faction of the anti-Nebraska movement was composed entirely of Democrats. The anti-Nebraska Democrats thrived as a separate organization only in traditionally strong Democratic communities with a large German-born population (see Table 8). Germans, liturgicals,

Table 8. Regression: 1854 Congressional Anti-Nebraska Democratic Vote

	Multiple R	R Square	RSQ Change	Simple R	B	Beta
Percent Other	.573	.329	.329	-.57	4.19	2.71
Percent Southern	.617	.381	.052	.10	4.70	3.23
Percent Irish	.651	.424	.043	.08	3.70	0.70
Value Produced	.689	.475	.050	.24	0.0001	2.11
Percent English	.722	.521	.046	.07	-1.98	-0.31
Capital Investment	.753	.567	.045	.19	-0.0002	-1.05
Percent Yankee	.774	.599	.032	.11	8.73	1.32
Percent Scandinavian	.805	.648	.048	-.14	-13.84	-0.23
Average Farm Value	.830	.688	.040	-.30	-0.01	-0.20
Liturgical	.837	.701	.012	.41	-7.54	-0.23
Baptist	.850	.723	.022	.01	-5.63	-0.19
Percent Canada	.859	.739	.015	.06	3.24	0.06
Percent Illinois	.862	.743	.004	.39	6.45	1.84
Percent German	.864	.748	.004	.35	5.55	1.96
Percent French	.868	.754	.006	.0007	7.99	0.20
Pietist	.869	.756	.001	-.01	4.16	0.08
(constant)					-380.38	

and Illinois-born voters, all Democrats of long standing, were dislodged from the Democracy by the slavery question, but their ties to the party remained so strong that they could not support a Whig or fuse with some other anti-Nebraska group. This anti-Nebraska Democratic faction was so different from the other anti-Nebraska movements that they correlated at -.41 with the Whigs and -.32 with the Fusion voters.

Some historians have portrayed anti-Nebraska Democrats as radical anti-slavery men.[21] In Illinois, however, this was not the case. Reacting to the introduction of a new issue, the extension of slavery, they sought to restore the Democratic party to a traditional Jacksonian program. The Nebraska Act, they felt, was a gross outrage committed upon the party. The anti-Nebraska Democratic Alton *Courier* declared in late 1854 that some of the party leaders "have proved recreant to the trust confided to them, and have endeavored to force the party into the support of measures repugnant to its moral sentiment in direct violation of its solemnly adopted platform, and calculated to distract and divide it." The Nebraska men were endeavoring "to foist their bastard upon the party" and the true Democrats stood against this new measure.[22] Douglas, of course, charged the anti-Nebraska men with being traitors and soreheads who had joined the abolitionists to gain the spoils of office. The anti-Nebraska Democrats consistently maintained, however, that their sole purpose was to restore the party.

> It is not true that we have joined the opponents of Democracy, and it is still more notoriously untrue that we have done anything to injure the Democratic party. We have joined the opponents of the Douglas-Nebraska party, and we have done what we could to induce the Democratic party to frown upon the fraud committed in the name of the party.[23]

The anti-Nebraska movement within the Democratic party developed slowly because of the desire to maintain old party lines. The first sign of dissatisfaction within the party did not come until the late spring, three months after the Nebraska Bill had passed Congress. The Alton *Courier* declared that the Bill "sanctions what we recognize as a great principle, but our objection is that in giving this sanction, it opens the door for a great outrage upon human rights, the introduction of slavery into territories now free."[24] As it became apparent, however, that the Nebraska Act was dividing the party, the *Courier* took a conciliatory position, attempting to convince the Democrats to avoid the issue and rally upon the traditional principles. "If no side issues are presented [i.e., the Nebraska question], any good Democrat can be elected, but if new tests are to be made and insisted upon, we are sure to be beat."[25] Douglas, however, insisted upon the Nebraska Act as the measure of a man's party loyalty. The anti-Nebraska press was finally forced to declare itself against the Douglas Bill, but it limited its opposition to statements opposing the agitation of slavery.

The anti-Nebraska Democrats made their strongest showing in the Congressional district that included Alton and Illinois counties across the river from St. Louis. Because the area was heavily German, the Whigs had never been a very strong party. Once the Nebraska Bill became the focus of politics, the Whigs passed out of existence and anti-Nebraska Democrats dominated the scene. The struggle in this Congressional district took the form of an intra-party battle.

The split began when the Democrats began to call county conventions in preparation for the election. Pro-Nebraska men in Madison County, for example, refused to allow opposition leaders to speak in the party's local convention. As soon as the Congressional convention met in Carlyle, the depth of the division in the party became known. William H. Bissell, who had voted against the Kansas-Nebraska Act in Congress, had been forced by illness to retire from office, leaving the nomination wide open. Philip B. Fouke, Bissell's old enemy, hoped to capture the nomination as a Nebraska man. He was opposed by Lyman Trumbull, former Illinois Supreme Court Justice. The convention was so badly divided that it adjourned without making any nominations. The party organization was completely destroyed, as Fouke and Trumbull carried on an extremely bitter campaign. Trumbull won the election in the fall but the struggle had been so divisive that the anti-Nebraska Democrats were forever cut off from the old party.[26]

There were other anti-Nebraska Democratic movements in Illinois, but they failed to achieve the same strength as the Alton group. The anti-Nebraska Democrats around Springfield were kept in the regular party by John A. McClernand, who carefully kept the party focused on the old issues, ignoring the Nebraska question even though he was a strong Douglas supporter. The Chicago district also had an anti-Nebraska Democratic movement that failed. The Congressional district was heavily Yankee and pietistic. A radical movement quickly developed in which the Republicans were joined by a number of Democrats led by Ebenezer Peck and Norman B. Judd. John Wentworth, the Congressman, however, remained silent on the Nebraska issue in hopes of preserving his alliance with Douglas. Eventually, Wentworth was forced to show his opposition to the Nebraska Act and Douglas forced him out of the regular organization. Not allowed by his old enemies, Peck and Judd, to join with the other anti-Nebraska forces who were now calling themselves Republicans, Wentworth formed an anti-Nebraska Democratic faction that was badly defeated in the fall elections.[27]

Against this array of anti-Nebraska factions, representing groups ranging from those who wished to preserve the old parties to those who welcomed the confrontation with slavery, stood Douglas and the Nebraska Democracy. Douglas had an almost impossible task before him in countering the various opposition factions. He clearly saw, however, that in order to stand any chance, the Democratic party would have to be united. For Douglas that meant that the party must avoid the quirks of personalities and rely on principles for its strength. "The only way to avoid a division of the party," Douglas wrote, "is to sustain our principles . . . [and] the principles of this Bill will form the test of parties. . . . We shall pass the Nebraska Bill in both Houses by decisive majorities & the party will then be stronger than ever, for it will be united upon principle."[28]

Because of Douglas' immense popularity and prestige, he was able to preserve the bulk of the Democratic party in Illinois. But the base of the party changed. The Democratic Congressional candidates in 1854 received their votes almost exclusively from the Baptists, Southerners, and Illinois-born voters (see Table 9). Even many of these voters were lost to the various anti-Nebraska factions and the Democracy also lost some of its support among the Germans who had been loyal party members. The most interesting aspect of the Democratic vote is the complete absence of the pietists. Religion had not previously been a major factor in the party coalitions of the Whigs and the Democrats, but now the pietists were solidly aligned against the Democracy, although they did not focus their support on any one particular anti-Nebraska faction.

Table 9. Regression: 1854 Congressional Democratic Vote

	Multiple R	R Square	RSQ Change	Simple R	B	Beta
Value Produced	.473	.223	.223	-.47	-0.0001	-1.74
Pietist	.620	.384	.160	-.45	-14.42	-0.42
Liturgical	.699	.489	.104	.09	2.43	0.10
Percent English	.715	.512	.022	-.29	0.79	0.17
Percent Canada	.736	.542	.029	-.32	-11.40	-0.33
Average Acre Value	.757	.573	.031	-.23	-0.08	-0.16
Percent Yankee	.771	.594	.021	-.39	-4.15	-0.88
Capital Investment	.792	.628	.033	-.37	0.0001	0.98
Percent German	.795	.633	.004	.12	-2.41	-1.19
Percent French	.801	.642	.009	-.09	-7.52	-0.26
Baptist	.803	.645	.002	.14	-1.11	-0.05
Percent Illinois	.804	.647	.001	.33	-3.09	-1.24
(constant)					87.55	

Indicating the extent to which the composition of the Democratic coalition had changed, the correlations with the previous party elections were extremely weak. The 1854 vote, for example, correlated at -.09 with the Congressional election of 1850 and at -.35 with the State contest. Democratic Congressional supporters represented only a part of the coalition that had voted for Franklin Pierce in 1852; their vote correlated at only .48 with the Democratic vote in the Presidential contest. That Douglas drew many former Whigs into the party on the Nebraska question is demonstrated by the .35 correlation between the Congressional vote and the 1850 Whig State coalition. In fact, the Democratic coalition was such a blur of ethnic and religious groups in 1854 that the Congressional election had a positive correlation of .11 with the anti-Nebraska Whigs and only mild negative correlations of -.44 with the Fusionists and -.30 with the anti-Nebraska Democrats.

The new divisions in the electorate can be seen more distinctly in the contest for State Treasurer in 1854, which was held at the same time as the Congressional elections. The various anti-Nebraska factions were able to muster considerable combined strength in the State-wide contest. Opposing the Democratic candidate for Treasurer, John Moore, was James Millar, a Know-Nothing, temperance advocate and anti-slavery man. Millar officially ran as a Fusion candidate, although in reality there was no state-wide Fusion organization. The remnants of the Whig State party had nominated Millar and he adopted the Fusion label in order to attract more support. For the most part, the anti-Nebraska groups combined to show impressive strength behind Millar, and even though he lost the election to Moore, the margin of defeat was only two percent, the closest any man had ever come to defeating a Democrat for a major office in Illinois. The vote showed, however, the inability of the anti-Nebraska forces to present a united front.

Many of the groups who supported anti-Nebraska Congressional candidates split their tickets and voted Democratic in the Treasurer's contest. The Southerners, for example, who were divided in the Congressional contests, voted Democratic in the State election. An examination of the groups not voting, however, provides a better illustration of the confusion and shifting of the voters. Almost 49 percent of the Illinois-born voters failed to vote in the Congressional election, but virtually all of them voted in the Treasurer's contest. Likewise, 26 percent of the "other"-born and 14 percent of the Germans did not vote in the Congressional contest, while these groups participated more heavily in the State-wide election.[29] The Kansas-Nebraska Act caused an explosion in the electorate, but the disruption of the old coalitions confused many voters and they responded by refusing to vote. Overall, 55 percent of the voters did not go to the polls in 1854.

When the issue had been clearly drawn between a former Whig, who was a temperance man and a Know-Nothing on an anti-slavery platform, and an old Democrat, who ignored the Nebraska question, many anti-Nebraska voters returned to the Democracy. This is demonstrated more precisely by examining the correlations between the

Treasurer's vote and other elections. The Moore supporters correlated at
.10 with the anti-Nebraska Democratic Congressional voters and at .70
with the Nebraska wing of the party, an indication of how much the
coalition had changed. Most of the correlations to previous Democratic
contests were only moderately strong at best. Democratic voters in the
1850 state contest, for example, correlated at -.16 with the Moore voters.
Likewise, the Fusion vote for State Treasurer had only moderate correlations to previous elections, including the 1854 Congressional vote. Millar
supporters correlated with the anti-Nebraska Whig electors at only .05
and the Fusion Congressional voters at a mild .47. The Whig State vote
in 1850 had a Pearson correlation of -.18 with the Millar supporters in
1854, and the Scott vote of 1852 a correlation of .64 with the Millar people. Clearly then, the Treasurer's contest resulted in a different shuffling
of the electorate than did the Congressional elections, and in all cases,
the 1854 campaign brought into existence new combinations of voters.

Although new coalitions were not yet firmly established, a major
division in the Illinois electorate was apparent. Except for the
conservative wing of the Whigs, all the anti-Nebraska factions
represented voters who, without regard to cultural or ethnic differences,
were united against the Southerners. The Democracy, which had once
been a pluralistic coalition of voters, was reduced to a party of
Southerners.

Since 1850, the voter coalitions in the Second Party System had not
been stable, but by taking the 1852 Presidential vote as typical of the
groups supporting the parties and by comparing that election to 1854, the
amount of change among the voters can be assessed. The vote for Pierce,
for example, drew liturgical and very mild Baptist support while the
pietists weakly opposed him. Economically, the Democrats were
predominantly from the poor farm and industrial regions. Ethnically,
Democratic voters included about 90 percent of the Germans, almost all
of the Irish, Canadians, Scandinavians and French, 69 percent of the
Illinois-born and 54 percent of the Southerners.[30] In the 1854 contests,
the Democrats were still concentrated in the poorer economic areas, but
every other aspect of the coalition changed. Southerners voted between
80 and 90 percent Democratic and the Illinois-born voters responded
almost unanimously for the Nebraska Act. The Democratic vote,
however, now included only 30 percent of the Germans, 13 percent of
the "other" U.S.-born, and 40 percent of the Scandinavians while the
French and the Canadians broke completely out of the coalition.[31] This
shift in the ethnic composition of Democratic support resulted in the loss
of almost all of the pietists. The Democratic party in 1854 was firmly
based on Southerners, Baptists and liturgicals.

The Whig party was shattered by the Kansas-Nebraska Act. In 1852, Scott received the votes of virtually all the Yankees, 70 percent of the English, "other"-born and Scandinavians, and about half of the Southerners. The Whig party drew support from at least 30 percent of the Illinois-born and 46 percent of the Southerners.[32] Economically, the Whigs were the strongest in relatively wealthy communities. By 1854, however, only the areas with large farms still supported the Whigs. The coalition was so ripped apart that only a limited number of Southerners and Illinois-born remained in the party. About 35 percent of the Southerners and 15 percent of the Illinois-born voted Whig, giving the party a strong Baptist base.[33] All the other groups in the old Whig coalition were fragmented into the various anti-Nebraska factions.

The realignment in 1854 did more than destroy the old voter coalitions. It also undermined the personal alliance system that controlled politics. Personalities became less important once the voters were again motivated by principle. Most of the political bailiwicks were destroyed in 1854 and the old party leaders who resisted the movement of voters were soon deposed. William Pickering, a Southern Illinois Whig, expressed in a letter to his friend, Joseph Gillespie, the difficulty of deciding between principle and personality. Pickering struggled with the decision of voting for his old friend, E.B. Webb, a Whig who now supported Douglas, or for a Democrat who was opposed to the extension of slavery. The decision, Pickering wrote, "cost me a desperate struggle for 3 or 4 days in deciding. . . ." In the end, Pickering's desire to stop the extension of slavery was stronger than his friendship for Webb. "Private friendship & private preference, in this case, shall yield & give way to a strong sense of consiencious [sic] principle."[34]

John Wentworth of Chicago was one of the bosses whose political fiefdom was destroyed by the realignment of voters. In the middle of the storm over the Kansas-Nebraska Act, Wentworth remained silent. Having just secured his new alliance with Douglas, he did not want to jeopardize his future in the party. The problem for Wentworth was that his constituents demanded action against the Nebraska Bill and "Long John" could not satisfy the party and his voters at the same time. Wentworth's solution to his dilemma was to avoid the issue and hope that the protest against the Douglas Bill would soon die out. The Chicago *Democrat*, Wentworth's newspaper, made few references to the Nebraska question, and then only to declare its opposition to the renewal of the slavery agitation. Mostly, the *Democrat* concentrated upon discussing legislation for pensions for veterans of the War of 1812. Wentworth voted against the Kansas-Nebraska Act, but by remaining silent he hoped to preserve his alliance with Douglas. In Chicago, Wentworth came under heavy pressure from the Fusionists to declare himself emphatically against the Bill. The *Democrat* finally bowed under the pressure and made statements criticizing the Bill, but at the same time, it tried hedging on the question by declaring that there was no great damage to the nation. For Wentworth, even this mild statement was too much of a commitment and he wrote to his editor:

> [L]eave the whole negro & slavery question . . . to me. You know how difficult a question this is to manage. . . . [I]n my own District, the democrats are as wide apart as the poles & what will get me votes in Cook [county] will kill me in Rock Island. . . . In trying to kill Douglas, some of my indiscreat [sic] friends will bury me ten feet under ground.[35]

Wentworth, however, could not continue to straddle the fence. Douglas, hurt by the anti-Nebraska attacks, decided to punish all Democrats who refused to follow his lead. He considered even Wentworth's silence intolerable. The "Little Giant" removed all of Wentworth's patronage workers and created his own Chicago newspaper, the *Times*. To the editor of the *Times*, Douglas wrote, "Make war on Wentworth every good chance you get, for I shall attack him openly in my speech I make in his district [sic]. He must be beaten at all hazards."[36]

Douglas' attacks forced Wentworth to take a stand against the Nebraska Bill, but because he had straddled the issue for so long, "Long John" found that the Fusionists were not willing to trust him. Unwilling to face defeat and without a political home, Wentworth retired from public office, but he remained politically active by organizing an anti-Nebraska Democratic faction which supported Edward L. Mayo for Congress.[37] Mayo finished a poor fourth in the election, which was won by the Republican Woodworth. Wentworth's control of the district was destroyed. He no longer had a party, even though he continued to call himself a Democrat, and he no longer had a constituency.

Wentworth, of course, was not the only personality to have his political fiefdom destroyed. In the Congressional districts that produced an anti-Nebraska majority, all the bailiwicks, Democratic and Whig, were destroyed. Especially on the local level, politicians who were accustomed to politics by personality were overthrown. A survey of the local elites in the counties of Madison, Peoria, Rock Island, and Stephenson, each of which was in a different Congressional district, reveals that the anti-Nebraska leaders were new politicians.[38] Regardless of whether the movement was anti-Nebraska Democrat, as in Madison; Republican, as in Rock Island; or Fusionist, as in Peoria and Stephenson counties, only 12.4 percent of the leadership had been Whig politicians and 6.2 percent members of the Democratic political elite. An amazing 81 percent of the local anti-Nebraska leaders were men with no previous active party experience. Of the old Whig party, only 13.3 percent of the local leadership was active in the various anti-Nebraska movements. An incredible 86.7 percent of the local Whig politicians were not active in the anti-Nebraska movement in these counties.

Although it was evident in 1854 that the party system had been disrupted by the Kansas-Nebraska Act, it was not clear what would be the new shape of politics. The Whig party persisted as a viable organization in many areas, and the anti-Nebraska Democrats refused to believe that the old party could not be reunited on Jacksonian issues. The strength of old party loyalty, as well as the uncertainty of the voters, made it impossible for an anti-Nebraska party to form. More importantly, the inability to define anti-slavery principles prevented the anti-Nebraska forces from coalescing.

The Fusionists and the Republicans were the most active in attempting to form a new political party. A Republican convention in Geneva resolved to "waive all former party predilections and associations. . . ."[39] The Congressional convention that nominated James H. Woodworth for Congress declared: "the times imperatively demand the reorganization of parties and repudiating all previous party attachments, manner and predilections, we unite ourselves together . . . and will hereafter cooperate as the Republican party."[40] The Republicans argued that they could not join the Whig party as it was then constituted because it could never be the party of freedom. Instead, they hoped to draw the Whigs into a new party founded on the single issue of opposing the extension of slavery. In an attempt to form such a party, they called for a State convention of all those opposed to the Douglas Bill. Although there is no contemporary report of the proceedings, the Republican convention was apparently poorly organized and poorly attended. The Republicans made one final effort to unify the anti-Nebraska groups by placing on their central committee a number of prominent politicians representing all the factions of the movement. Among those appointed was Abraham Lincoln. Lincoln, like most, declined the honor.[41]

Fusion efforts to create a party were no more successful than the Republican attempts. There was, however, more response to the Fusionists' appeals, and all factions of the anti-Nebraska movement met in a mass convention in Springfield. In spite of the enthusiastic spirit shown at the rally, efforts to unify the factions failed. Old party loyalties were still too strong and the extension of slavery had not yet polarized all the voters.

The Whigs especially hoped to maintain the old party. Although against the Kansas-Nebraska Act, the Springfield *Journal*, the leading Whig paper in the State, wrote that "we cannot believe that any good can result to the country, by continuing to agitate the question of slavery."[42] Even David Davis, who would in the future play an important role in the formation of the Republican Party, found it difficult to give up the old party. Davis wrote to a friend pleading with him to "Try to save the Whig party. I don't fancy its being abolitionized."[43] The idea of joining the Republican or Fusion parties on the single issue of preventing the extension of slavery was absurd to most Whigs, since the result would be a sectional party and continued agitation. Eventually, many of these men came to oppose the Republicans and Fusionists as vigorously as they did the Democrats. In response to a call for fusion, the Springfield *Journal* wrote that "the Whigs should act as they always have, — together — we think we consult their permanent welfare as a party."[44] Rather than joining a new party, the Whigs hoped to revitalize their own party on the platform of restoring the Missouri Compromise. In the best tradition of Henry Clay, the Illinois Whigs saw themselves as defenders of the Union while the Democrats and the abolitionists tended toward sectionalism. The *Journal* declared that they would "cling to the Whig organization until [a party] shall be formed, which may be more American or national in its scope."[45]

Anti-Nebraska Democrats also resisted attempts to form a new party. The Democrats who opposed the Nebraska Act saw themselves as upholding the true party. "It is these [Nebraska] men who repudiate old and introduce new tests — who have violated not only the solemn compact of 1820, but the Democratic platform of 1852 . . . who have produced this disorganization and will continue it so long as they insist upon ostracising all who are true and steadfast in the old principles of Democracy."[46] Anti-Nebraska Democrats refused to join a one-idea party because they were "not willing to forsake every principle of the Democratic party."[47] John Wentworth declared in the *Democrat* that "we want no new party — no new names. We want an old party — a party that hung nullifiers and disunionists — the party of Andrew Jackson."[48]

Other Democrats refused to join a new party for personal reasons. Gustave Koerner, an old friend of Douglas, was against the extension of slavery, but he refused until 1856 to cut his ties with the party. Koerner wrote that to leave the party would destroy his own promising political future and result in social ostracism. After he finally did leave the Democracy, he wrote that, "I left my old party not without many pangs, and that it cost me much to burn my bridges."[49] John Palmer, on the other hand, did not think that the slavery question would persist, and therefore saw no point in bolting the party. "I was conscious that I had differed with my party upon the subject of the Kansas-Nebraska Bill, . . ." Palmer recalled, "but I did not then foresee . . . that the slavery question would not cease to disturb the country as long as that institution existed. I supposed that the Democratic party would again unite upon other issues."[50] Despite their hesitancy to leave the Democracy, Douglas systematically drove most of the anti-Nebraska wing out of the party. Their refusal to join a new party left these Democrats with no political home and they remained an independent faction until 1856.

The confusion in politics and the lack of cooperation between the anti-Nebraska groups were reflected in the election for the United States Senate in the Illinois legislature.[51] An anti-Nebraska majority had been elected to the Legislature in 1854, making the reelection of James Shields doubtful. It became apparent, however, that the anti-Nebraska men were divided and that they were unlikely to support a single candidate. The leading anti-Nebraska candidate, Abraham Lincoln, had the support of most of the Whigs. Because the anti-Nebraska movement was so fragmented and the elections for the legislature were so confused, the composition of the new Assembly was unclear, which hampered Lincoln's campaign. For example, Lincoln had difficulty learning who had been elected from Edgar county and on what platform. Lincoln wrote a letter to a friend asking for his aid: "I have a suspicion that a Whig has been elected to the Legislature from Edgar. If this is not so, why the *'nix cum arous'* [*sic*] but if it is so, then could you not make a mark with him for me?"[52] Relying upon the old method of electioneering through personal contacts, Lincoln depended on such men as David Davis to advance his campaign. In a letter to Lincoln, Davis reported on the efforts of Leonard Swett in gathering supporters for the election:

> Swett thinks he can do something with Strunk & Parks of Will [county] & with the member from Kendall [county]. He says Strunk is a Whig. He talked with Strunk about you before the election. Strunk was very favorable. Parks he also states, has been very Whiggish for some years and he knows him very well. He is confident in relation to those two. . . . Swett does not think that he can do any good with the LaSalle members. He does not know them.[53]

Davis became Lincoln's manager and attempted to unify the anti-Nebraska members of the Legislature in support of Lincoln. He advised Lincoln to stay clear of the Republican party, which was considered too radical, but did propose a compromise with that group in order to receive their support. Davis suggested to Lincoln that "it would be well enough, I think, to let the Republicans, as they call themselves, have all the offices of the House, if they would agree to let the Whigs have the Senator without the troublesome platform."[54]

Davis had managed to win the support of the Fusion and Republican members for Lincoln, but the five anti-Nebraska Democrats, who held the balance of power in the Assembly, refused to cooperate with the other anti-Nebraska groups. Lyman Trumbull, in a long letter to fellow Democrat John Palmer, wrote about the need for all anti-Nebraska men to cooperate to prevent the reelection of Shields. In the letter, Trumbull recognized that there was no middle ground for Democrats who opposed the Nebraska Bill and that they must join with other anti-Nebraska men or be defeated. The irony of Trumbull's letter was that he concluded by saying that "as for the Senate I am for any good anti-Nebraska Democrat."[55]

The balloting for Senator began in the first week of January, 1855. Lincoln had a clear plurality, but was just short of a majority, since the anti-Nebraska Democrats voted for Trumbull. As the balloting continued into the next week, numerous legislators changed sides, voting for Lincoln and then Shields, but Lincoln could not win a majority as long as Trumbull refused to yield. At different points, compromise candidates were brought forth, but that only confused the election. Then in a surprising move, the Democrats dropped Shields and threw their support behind the popular Governor, Joel A. Matteson. A number of anti-Nebraska men joined the Matteson move and the Governor received 44 votes while Lincoln, who had previously led with 45, was reduced to 38 votes. On the ninth ballot, Matteson was just 3 short of a majority and Lincoln could count only 15 votes. Trumbull, who had steadfastly remained in the contest, rose from 5 votes to 35. At this point Lincoln made a decision to withdraw and support Trumbull rather than see Matteson win. On the tenth ballot, Trumbull was elected to the Senate.[56] Lincoln's defeat made his supporters bitter and resentful, and left the anti-Nebraska forces more divided than ever, even though they had won a great victory.

The Kansas-Nebraska Act, which had introduced a new issue to politics and had begun to polarize the voters on the slavery extension question, destroyed the coalitions of the Second Party System, but nothing was found in 1854 to fill the political void. Although a new majority aligned against the Nebraska Bill carried the fall elections and captured the Senate seat, the anti-Nebraska movement lacked a stable coalition of voters and a party organization. The factionalism would continue until anti-slavery principles could be defined to stabilize the realignment.

In a post mortem on the elections, the embittered Joliet *Signal* wrote that the Democracy had gone down "before a torrent of abolitionism, whigism, freesoilism, religious bigotry, and intolerance all joined in a wild and wicked foray upon the democratic party and the constitution."[57] Of these "isms," Know-Nothingism and temperance proved to be the greatest threats, but not to the Democrats. Know-Nothings and temperance became roadblocks to the formation of an anti-slavery party.

4

The Realignment Stalled

Recently, historians examining the transformation of politics in the middle 1850s have concluded that Whiggery combined with anti-Catholicism, temperance, nativism, and anti-slavery into a new Protestant coalition – the Republican party.[1] A close examination of voting patterns reveals, however, that this was not the case in Illinois. The realignment on the slavery issue begun by the Kansas-Nebraska Act was jeopardized, not aided, by the rise of temperance and nativism as political issues. Ironically, these crusades which were built upon the same pietistic tradition that had motivated radical anti-slavery men forestalled the realignment on slavery and stood as roadblocks to the formation of an anti-slavery party.

The anti-slavery passions raised by the Kansas-Nebraska Act began to cool after the election of Lyman Trumbull to the Senate in early 1855. It had been almost a year since the passage of the Act, and it had not yet resulted in any catastrophe in the new territories. The bloody struggles in Kansas between the free soilers and the slavery men were still a number of months away. Without the impetus of an energetic slave issue, and with no major election for another two years to serve as a rallying point, the anti-Nebraska forces began to lose focus. Large segments of voters, who were dislodged from the old parties by the Nebraska controversy, became attracted to a number of side issues. In 1855 and much of 1856, temperance and nativism took precedence in the public mind. Neither of these were new developments, but both temperance and nativism as political movements had been previously kept in check by the Whig and Democratic order of politics. The Nebraska controversy had broken down that order and the intensely moralistic passions of a large segment of voters, which were unleashed by the anti-slavery campaign, found comfort in temperance and Know-Nothingism. These two crusades captured the imagination of the moralist after the slavery issue subsided and, in the confusion of the realignment, emerged as powerful forces.

The intellectual impetus behind the temperance and the Know-Nothing crusades came from the pietistic sects born out of Calvinism. Originally, the doctrines of Calvin stressed the concept of a spiritual elite who would overcome all difficulties to glorify God. An integral part of this concept was the idea of the "calling." A few chosen men received a "calling" from God as a sign of their salvation, and in order to demonstrate His grace, they devoted their entire lives to that "calling." Calvinism was initially hostile, or at least indifferent to, the secular world; the entire thrust of its theology was directed toward the inward search for signs of grace. The revivalism of the 1830s and the 1840s and the role of the churches on the frontier transformed the social and theological heritage of Calvinism into a dynamic ideology for reform.[2]

Evangelism in the Jacksonian period was based upon Calvin's theory of individual regeneration. The revivals, however, stressed not just the spiritual elite, but the salvation of all men through instantaneous conversion and sanctification. Now every man had a "calling." The Calvinistic idea that only a select few were predestined for salvation was modified into the belief that all men were capable of perfection. Since salvation meant perfection, which in theological terms was the absence of sin, then this new doctrine implied that all evil could be conquered. Because all men received grace, no man could escape or ignore his duty to God. All were personally responsible for their conduct and for the pietists, failure meant eternal damnation. Moral complacency then became a distinctive sin.

The concept of man's perfectibility is the theological transformation that separated the pietistic sects from all other religious groups, including the Calvinists. The idea that perfection was not only an attainable goal, but also a responsibility, meant that the pietists had internalized the notion of God's grace. Instead of man waiting for God to give His grace, God was now waiting for man to manifest his perfection. Because man carried the entire responsibility for his own salvation, pietists believed that man could be free from sin; hence, the effect of failing to be perfect was shame. Strict Calvinist and liturgical denominations, on the other hand, accepted man as imperfect. The individual had no choice with sin. Consequently, liturgicals felt guilt, not shame. Certainly liturgicals must repent their sins, but there was nothing they could do to prevent themselves from sinning again. Imperfection was the natural order of mankind, and therefore, there was no sense of individual responsibility for personal, much less social, sin.

The spread of revivalism onto the frontier brought an additional change in the Calvinistic tradition. The churches in the west, as the dominant social institution in the newly settled areas, served a central function in the community. Through their voluntary but extensive and intimate fellowship, they provided direction and standards for the settlers and, in doing so, created social conformity in the atomistic communities by regulating the personal, social, and economic life of the members. Public as well as private behavior of men became the concern of the church. The result was that Calvinism became more anxious about this world.

Armed with the idea of a "calling" for all men and a concern for the affairs of this world, the pietistic religious sects in the mid-19th century began their quest for perfection. They found that a number of obstacles in the world blocked the path to salvation, but instead of withdrawing from society, the pietists attacked these conditions as vigorously as they did individual sins. The pietists reasoned that if personal sin precluded man's perfection, then malfeasance in society prevented the millennium. It was the duty of man to rectify sin immediately or be held responsible by God. If, however, the sins of society were of such magnitude that a few men could never hope to eradicate them, then the only recourse for the pietists was to divorce themselves from the evil. Consequently, many pietistic churches in the 1850s prohibited fellowship with individuals and institutions which they deemed sinful. The *Western Citizen* spoke for most pietists when it declared:

> [I]t is not 'God's method of procedure' to allow national and organic, anymore than individual sins in the church; and so long as this course is pursued in the missions of the Protestant church, the Gospel can never have free course, and the 'latter-day glory' can never dawn upon the world. . . . [There must] be a complete divorce of the church and of missions from national sins [which] will form a new and glorious era, . . . the precursor of Millennial blessedness.[3]

Withdrawal from social sins did not mean the abandonment of attempts to improve conditions. Since moral complacency could not be tolerated, the pietists devoted much of their attention toward reforming society. They turned to politics as a tool in their mission.

It was not difficult for pietists to make a connection between religion and politics. Typically, pietists declared that "men's conduct in the political relations is no less moral and accountable than in any relation of life." One religious newspaper stated that "in proportion as men are religiously honest in politics in that proportion our government will assume its proper form."[4] The First Presbyterian Church of Chicago captured the pietist notion of religion and politics in a resolution which declared that "we recognise [sic] civil government as an institution ordained by God for the welfare of society."[5]

Once it was recognized that politics was a legitimate means for religious ends, the pietists began to agitate for a number of reforms. The list of offenses against God was quite long. One of the evils in society that the pietists hoped to destroy was land monopolies. These were said to be "one of the greatest sources of human misery," and their reform would bring about "the fulfillment of [God's] prophecy . . . that *every man* shall sit under his own vine." Licentiousness was another sin which required the attention of the pietists. One church conference declared it the duty of all "to enforce in our public teachings, strict obedience to the spirit and letter of the 7th commandment."[6] But of all the numerous sins which the pietists identified in American society in the 1850s, the most damnable was intemperance. Although there was much debate among the pietists on whether slavery was sinful or whether it was in fact sanctioned by the Bible, there was no such ambiguity about liquor.

Early temperance groups relied upon moral suasion to eliminate the evil of liquor in society. By the 1850s, however, Illinois prohibitionists became bolder and, encouraged by the passage of prohibitory liquor laws in Maine, they agitated for a political solution to intemperance. "We have tried all the varied phases of 'moral suasion' with but only partial success," complained one temperance advocate. "We are now willing and desirous to see if the evil can be reached and remedied by law."[7]

The temperance crusade was all but forgotten during the realignment over the Kansas-Nebraska Act, but once the slavery question lost its energy early in 1855, the liquor question once again surfaced. The crusade reached its political zenith in Illinois in the spring and, under pressure from prohibitionists, the legislature ordered a referendum on temperance for the summer of 1855.

Temperance men worked vigorously in the months preceding the referendum. They organized conventions, mass meetings, stump speakers, publications and correspondence committees. The pietists approached the referendum with great expectations and with a sense of relief that another sin against God would be removed from society. "Illinois is about to throw off the yoke of bondage which the arch enemy of mankind has for long years imposed," declared one temperance newspaper, "and step forth in the majesty of a sovereign people, declaring that rum shall no longer be an article of legal traffic." "We rejoice," the paper concluded, "that this is the fact, that the day star of temperance will soon dispel the night of sin."[8]

To the great disappointment of the temperance advocates the prohibitory law was soundly defeated. An examination of the referendum vote reveals the depth of the crusade and the character of the people to whom temperance appealed (see Table 10).[9] As expected, voters in communities where pietistic churches dominated provided the heaviest support for the prohibitory referendum. The regression shows that as the strength of the pietistic churches increased, so did the temperance vote. Of the ethnic groups, the Yankees were the strongest supporters of the temperance law. The category of "percent other," those voters born in the mid-Atlantic states, Ohio and Indiana, was also a major explanatory variable, with about 94 percent voting for temperance. This group had no distinctive ethnic character, but a partial explanation of their coherent support of the referendum was that many of these people were second-generation Yankees and heavily pietistic. The Canadians and the English were also nearly unanimous in favor of prohibition. Finally, temperance attracted close to 25 percent of the Southerners, 34 percent of the Scandinavians, and 36 percent of the French.[10]

Table 10. Regression: Vote for the 1855 Prohibition Law

	Multiple R	R Square	RSQ Change	Simple R	B	Beta
Percent Other	.640	.410	.410	.64	.487	.569
Percent Yankee	.809	.654	.244	.59	2.712	.744
Pietist	.838	.703	.048	.45	4.233	.162
Capital Investment	.856	.733	.030	.11	-.0001	-1.268
Average Farm Value	.890	.792	.058	.59	.010	.381
Value Produced	.893	.798	.006	.14	.00005	1.098
Percent English	.898	.806	.008	.10	-1.300	-.370
Percent Scandinavian	.904	.817	.011	.20	-7.400	-.225
Percent Illinois	.909	.827	.009	-.57	.537	.277
Percent French	.917	.842	.014	.08	4.846	.222
Average Acre Value	.918	.844	.002	.09	-.042	-.101
Liturgical	.919	.845	.0009	-.26	2.125	.121
Percent German	.920	.847	.001	-.14	-.103	-.066
Percent Canadian	.920	.847	.0002	-.02	.958	.036
Baptist	.920	.847	.0003	-.23	.785	.049
Average Farm Size	.920	.848	.0001	.33	-.009	-.020
(constant)					-10.508	

Voters who opposed the prohibitory law included, besides liturgicals and those Baptists who were anti-prohibition, many of the immigrant groups. The Germans and the Irish were virtually unanimous in voting against the liquor law. Close to 65 percent of the French and 66 percent of the Scandinavians were also against prohibition. Of the native voters, only about 5 percent of the "other"-born, but close to 73 percent of the Southerners and all of the Illinois-born stood against temperance.[11] Clearly, then, the temperance vote was narrowly based upon native-born pietists.

An important feature of the election in 1855 was the behavior of the Baptists. The Baptist vote shows a mild negative correlation with the overall referendum results, even though the group was generally pietistic. Apparently Baptists were cross-pressured by the liquor issue. There is little evidence to support any explanation for this behavior, but possibly the congregations in the southern part of the State were skeptical of the motives of the Yankee-backed proposal. Many of the Baptists remained fundamentally Calvinistic and still harbored hostilities to anything outside their particular community. A large number of these Baptists were also Democrats, and since that party opposed the referendum, loyalty to the party must have influenced many voters. Some Baptists resolved their dilemma by not voting at all in the election. Overall, the Baptist variable correlated at .23 with the non-voters.

An examination of the non-voting groups adds further to understanding the character of the temperance coalition. About 18 percent of the Illinois-born and 8 percent of the Southerners refused to vote.[12] More importantly, the Yankees, like the Baptists, were highly inclined to stay away from the polls, even though they were an intensely pietistic group. Apparently, the New Englanders did not universally accept a political solution to intemperance but, rather than vote against the liquor law, they abstained. The Canadians also were disposed not to vote. An incredible 62 percent stayed away from the polls.[13] No liturgical or immigrant groups opposed to the temperance law, however, failed to vote. The non-voters were basically pietistic, indicating that while virtually all who supported the referendum were pietistic, not all pietists voted.

The reason for the behavior of the Baptists and for the lack of unified support among the pietists for temperance lies in the fact that the liquor issue had become intertwined with anti-slavery and nativism. Because so many of the pietists had been opposed to the Nebraska Bill, temperance became tainted with anti-slavery, driving the Baptists, who were predominantly Southerners, away from the prohibition crusade. On the other hand, many anti-Nebraska Yankees, English, and Scandinavian pietists refused to support temperance because of its connection to nativism. Many temperance men blamed the foreign-born for the excessive evils of liquor in American society. In reference to a prohibition meeting that was disrupted by a number of Germans, one newspaper wrote that the German citizens were "completely under the influence of men whose base motives are so plainly to be seen." The men who led the Germans were the "brewers, and the keepers of the lowest, filthiest, dram-shops that disgrace our city. . . ." The implications were obvious: "[How] can the Germans hope to become worthy citizens . . . while they permit themselves to be used, *as they now are*, as pliant tools of such men?"[14] The conclusions were that the foreign-born needed more education in American principles and more time to learn the ways of American life. Such declarations by temperance advocates drove foreign-born pietists to oppose the referendum, while keeping some of the Yankees away from the polls.

The confusion of temperance with other issues was inevitable in the chaotic political climate of early 1855. The lines between prohibition, anti-slavery, and nativism were strong, especially in that all three movements were supported by many pietists. The connections between these movements, however, have been exaggerated by a number of the ethno-cultural historians.[15] Although many groups of voters responded favorably to all three movements, the degree and depth of the voter reaction differed in each circumstance. The vote for the prohibitory referendum in 1855, for example, correlates no higher than .62 with any Whig election prior to 1854. More typical was the Presidential vote for Winfield Scott in 1852, which correlated at only .42. A comparison of the voter coalitions explains these mild correlations. In the 1852 Presidential election, the Whigs carried some 18 percent of the Yankees, 51 percent of the Southerners, 65 percent of the Illinois-born, 51 percent of the "other"-born, and 25 percent of the English. The temperance supporters, however, captured nearly all of the Yankees, Canadians, English and "other"-born while losing half of the Southern Whig vote and all of the Illinois-born voters.

A regression of the prohibition vote by the previous elections demonstrates exactly the difference between the Whig and the temperance voters. The anti-liquor coalition was such a conglomeration of Democratic and Whig voters that the computer could not correlate a linear relationship with the Whig elections. It did show, however, that the temperance question had mobilized nearly all of the non-voters in the 1850 and 1852 elections. Clearly, then, temperance and Whiggery were not part of the same continuous evangelical or cultural impulse.

The introduction of the slavery question produced a remarkable effect upon the correlations between temperance support and the Whig vote. The anti-Nebraska Whig voters correlated at -.15 with the temperance supporters. Interestingly, however, the temperance men had a moderate .37 correlation with the 1852 Free Soil vote, indicating that the early anti-slavery men were more likely to be temperance men than the voters who supported the anti-Nebraska position of the Whigs in 1854. Anti-slavery and temperance were of the same pietistic impulse, but again the connection was not overwhelming. The highest correlation of the temperance referendum with an anti-slavery vote was a .78

correlation with the Fusion election for State Treasurer. James Millar, the Fusion candidate for Treasurer, however, was a known temperance advocate, which accounts for the strong correlation. If the anti-slavery position of the Fusionists was the reason for the high correlation, then a strong correlation would be expected with the Congressional election. In fact, the temperance vote correlates with the Fusion Congressional vote at a much weaker .55. These correlations, however, are misleading. The regression of the temperance law to the anti-Nebraska elections again could not be calculated, indicating very little connection between the two. The anti-Nebraska coalition included Germans, French, and Scandinavians, who were all opposed to temperance, while the Southerners who favored prohibition voted Democratic.

The lack of strong connections between Whigs, temperance supporters, and anti-Nebraska voters is confirmed by the corresponding weak correlations between the anti-referendum vote and the Democratic elections. The highest correlation with an election prior to 1854 is .52 with the vote for Franklin Pierce. In the elections of 1854, the correlations are .60 with the Democratic Congressional vote and .78 with the State Treasurer's election. Again, with the exception of the Treasurer's election in 1854, none of the elections displayed an overwhelming connection with the anti-temperance vote. Certainly, many pietists were Whigs, anti-slavery men, and temperance advocates, but it is equally clear that not all prohibitionists were Whigs or opposed to slavery.

The defeat of the prohibition referendum in 1855 left the temperance forces disillusioned with politics. Temperance crusades did not end after 1855, but they did return for a number of years to the moral suasion tactics of the earlier days. Temperance men were so concerned with divorcing their crusade from politics that they suspended activities altogether during election campaigns. "As we are unwilling to have the cause of Temperance identified with any political party," declared a leading prohibition newspaper, "it was deemed unwise to attempt to interest the public mind upon the subject either by Convention or lectures during the Presidential canvass."[16]

The brief political existence of the temperance movement in 1855 had an important effect upon the realignment of the voters. Temperance cut across the polarization of the voters on the slavery issue and drew together a new combination of voters. The confusion in politics was completed by the emergence of a second political crusade led by pietists which was in many ways allied to prohibition – that of nativism.

The pietistic drive for perfection necessarily involved an insistence on social conformity. Freedom from sin meant correct behavior, and it was generally expected that such behavior would be uniform. Diversity was not by definition sinful, but it did present an obstacle to perfection. The pietists, in blaming the Germans and other foreign-born for the defeat of temperance legislation, accused them not of being innately evil people, but of being ignorant and misled. Many pietists found the Know-Nothings attractive because that group sought conformity through the regulation of the immigrant. Once homogeneity was achieved in America, the pietists believed, the task of rooting out sin would be much easier.

The Know-Nothing movement, however, was not concerned with mere social reform. It was no less than an attempt to preserve America in the face of change. In a remarkable document, Henry Winter Davis, David Davis' famous cousin who was a Whig, a Know-Nothing and, later, a Republican, outlined the principles and purposes of the Know-Nothings.[17] Simply stated, the purpose of the Know-Nothings was "to vindicate the fundamental principles of the republic sacrificed by worn out parties to personal and factious ambition."[18] The Americans, as the Know-Nothings came to call themselves, believed that the government had become a tool of special interests that were undermining the foundation of the republic. As a result, the rights of the citizens were endangered. The Americans saw themselves as guardians of "the right of the American people to have their Government freed from foreign sympathies, from sectional factions, and from sectarian intrusions."[19]

The cause of the corruption of American liberty was political parties. Politicians, seeking only private gain, captured public offices under the guise of serving the public interest. According to Davis, "measures around which parties rallied have ceased to be controlling, new measures attract primary attention, and the old parties have fallen to pieces in the hands of party leaders in the vain effort to maintain unity of thought and action on those novel topics." In a very accurate depiction of the state of politics, Davis declared "*party names have ceased to describe the actual relations of men to measures.*" "New principles divide the people by lines not coincident with former party divisions."[20] Davis argued that the great men, who for 30 years had been the symbols of the party principles, were dead and, along with them, all the old Jacksonian issues. New questions had arisen first with the Mexican War and then the annexation of Texas and California, and the "parties organized exclusively with reference to a previous state of things, no longer coincided on these new questions."[21] Yet, Davis complained, the people were forced to elect men who still argued these old principles. The result was that the "voice of the people has not been expressed directly on any great public measure . . . for ten years." Elections had "degenerated from an open inquest for the opinion of the people, to the simple question of who shall have the office."[22]   In this scramble by personalities, every passion, special interest, and sectarian influence was arrayed against the peace of the nation. The corrupt bidding by politicians for power had destroyed freedom of opinion and substituted private gain for public interest.   The purpose of the American party, according to Davis, "is to redress these evils by substituting government by the *people* for Government by a *party*." The Americans "will recall to the minds of the people the long neglected principles of the primitive republic. . . ."[23] The restoration of the early republic was their goal.

The definition of the principles of the republic made up the platform of the American party. First, all special interests were to be rooted out of government. Second, only Americans could rule America. Davis believed that the immigrants were ignorant of the duties of freedom and that they had no loyalty to this country. America's freedom was built upon "character" which experience had shown to be lacking in the immigrant. Davis pointed to the Negro and the Indian as proof that all men could not handle freedom. White Europeans could develop the proper character, but it would take a long period of probation. After all, the immigrants were "the enslaved millions of Europe . . . [who] proved their incompentency for self-government."[24] Davis argued that America gives the immigrants freedom and then they "abuse it by selling themselves as a mercenary army to decide our elections."[25] The inability of the immigrants to handle freedom and their effect upon American elections constituted a serious danger to the nation's liberty. Unless the situation was corrected American freedom would be turned "into the likeness of the bloody and drunken . . . French and German liberty," which was in reality nothing more than anarchy.[26]

The third principle that the Know-Nothings hoped to preserve was the neutrality of the state in religious matters. For Davis, the guarantee of freedom of religion also meant that the citizen must be protected from religion. No church should be allowed to accumulate much property. Public schools, where American principles were taught, must be kept clear of religion, and no denomination or sect should be able to exempt its children from a public education. The problem, according to Davis, was that in the past ten years the principle of separation of church and state had been violated. Mormons had systematically violated the laws. Ministers had become involved in politics to protest the Kansas-Nebraska Act. The Catholics had sought to exclude the Bible from public schools and had demanded private schools supported by public funds to instruct their own children in the Catholic doctrines. The Catholics also had garnered large tracts of lands, giving them despotic power in the nation.

According to Davis, the papists desired to control the civil government of America as they did in Europe. Their flagrant violations of American principles and their intrigues and conspiracies to establish a religious monarchy in America constituted a particular threat to the nation's freedom.

Finally, Davis argued that the Constitution was neutral on the question of slavery. The problem was local and the agitation of the issue, he believed, was a conspiracy by ambitious men to gain office. According to Davis, slavery "is an unfit topic of discussion in federal politics. We therefore are resolved to exclude from office . . . any person who shall appeal . . . to the sympathies or antipathies of any person on that subject."[27]

Once America had been restored to the true principles of the republic, political parties could be dissolved. The will of the people would again be free and the government would accurately reflect their desires. This new "era of good feelings" would be marked by a President who would refrain from interference in the legislative process and confine himself strictly to the duties of the office as outlined by George Washington. American freedom would be preserved and the nation would be restored to the pure and simple virtues of the old republic under Jefferson.

Although the Know-Nothings had an ambitious program outlined by 1856, little is known about the group in Illinois prior to 1854.[28] Initially, the Know-Nothings were pledged to promote longer periods of naturalization for immigrants and to oppose any Catholic for public office. In 1854, the secrecy of the group began to break down as the organization expanded and began to adopt a more active political role. As the campaign over the Kansas-Nebraska Act reached its peak, increasing references to the Know-Nothings appeared in the press. The *State Register*, for example, warned that "the Know-Nothings are suspected of being about, but no one knows anything of them or what they design."[29]

After the election of 1854, the Know-Nothings rapidly expanded and organized their secret clubs into a political party. The political chaos and the high emotions of the pietists in 1855 provided fertile ground for the American party. Its leaders were mostly old Whigs. Joseph Gillespie, Stephen T. Logan, James Millar, Ozia M. Hatch, William Jayne, and W. W. Danenhower became the guiding lights of the Illinois branch of the American party. Most observers of the day believed that the Know-Nothings consisted completely of old Whigs who were deprived of a party after the Nebraska controversy. Historians have generally agreed with this contention and have argued that the American party was another link in the chain between the Whigs, anti-Nebraska groups, temperance men, and the Republicans. The Yankees and the pietists in this view were the mainstays of each of these organizations.[30] A close examination of the voters in the 1856 election, however, reveals that this was not the case in Illinois and that the Know-Nothings appealed more to Southerners than to pietistic Yankees (see Table 11).[31]

Table 11. Regression: 1856 Know-Nothing Presidential Vote

	Multiple R	R Square	RSQ Change	Simple R	B	Beta
Percent Illinois	.778	.605	.605	.77	-1.31	-.826
Percent Yankee	.795	.632	.027	-.60	-2.95	-1.350
Farm Size	.811	.658	.025	.31	.29	.729
Percent French	.834	.696	.038	-.12	3.13	.878
Pietist	.857	.735	.038	.45	11.19	.595
Baptist	.887	.787	.052	.24	7.84	.390
Percent Irish	.893	.798	.010	-.46	-1.12	-.519
Percent German	.901	.812	.014	-.10	-2.25	-2.23
Acre Value	.912	.833	.020	-.16	.36	.441
Percent Scandinavian	.917	.840	.007	-.44	-5.53	-1.129
Capital Investment	.921	.848	.007	-.18	.004	.709
Percent English	.926	.856	.008	-.42	-.56	-.180
Farm Value	.929	.864	.007	.01	-.007	-.614
Percent Southern	.931	.867	.002	.44	-1.75	-2.082
Percent Other	.932	.868	.001	-.09	-1.54	-1.586
(constant)					3.93	

The vote for Millard Fillmore as the American candidate for President in 1856 shows that the Know-Nothings received heavy support from the pietists. The Yankees, however, were strongly opposed to Fillmore. More surprising than this opposition was the support given by Southerners and Illinois-born voters to the American party. The Illinois-born voters, a strong Democratic and anti-temperance bloc, alone explained 60 percent of the variance in the Know-Nothing vote. Both this group and Southerners were generally Baptists and in uniting them with other pietists, the Know-Nothings accomplished something the temperance movement had failed to do. Amazingly, the Know-Nothings had wedded Democrats and Whigs together. Equally important was the fact that, although there was a strong pietistic character to the movement, they failed to attract much Yankee support. Just as the pietistic Southerners refused to join the temperance movement because of its control by the Yankees, the Yankees voted against the Know-Nothing party because it was dominated by Southerners.

A curious feature of this election was the religious division. A breakdown of the Know-Nothing support by religion shows more clearly the influence of the pietists, Baptists, and liturgicals upon the election (see Table 12).[32] The pietistic support for Fillmore was straightforward. As pietism increased in the communities, so did the Know-Nothing vote. The problem, however, is in the Baptist variable, which has a curvilinear relationship to the American party. The highest Know-Nothing vote came in districts which were only medium in the size and number of Baptist churches, while the sample community with a high Baptist concentration gave minimal support to Fillmore. This pattern, however, could be an accident, resulting from some local influence entirely independent of religion. A larger sample might well have produced a linear pattern.

Table 12. Breakdown: Percent Know-Nothing Vote by Religion

	Number of Churches			
	None	Low	Medium	High
Pietist	1.00	1.66	10.00	17.70
Liturgical	14.78	16.60	7.00	10.40
Baptist	9.16	12.78	22.85	2.00

Another puzzle in the Know-Nothing vote was the liturgicals. Their vote also had a curvilinear relationship to Fillmore support, but the shape of the curve is nearly the opposite of the Baptist pattern. The American party vote was at its weakest in the medium-ranked liturgical communities and strongest in those with low and high liturgical rankings. The five high-ranked liturgical areas had a mean Know-Nothing vote of 10.4 percent, which caused the curvilinear pattern. Of these areas two were Chicago wards and three St. Clair county townships. The relatively high mean percent of the American party vote in these liturgical areas was the result of the St. Clair County returns, as the Sixth Ward of Chicago gave only 2 percent of its votes to Fillmore and not one man voted for the Know-Nothing ticket in the Ninth Ward. Each of the sampled townships in St. Clair had a large foreign-born population dominated by Germans, but each area also had a significant Southern and Illinois-born group. Even though the three areas were dominated by liturgical churches, there were a number of pietistic and Baptist congregations. Consequently, the increased percentage of Know-Nothing votes in these areas occurred not because the liturgicals, safe in a relatively homogeneous township, were less inclined to oppose Fillmore, but because the pietistic minority was more enthusiastic in support of the American party.

The vote for Fillmore in 1856 clearly shows that Know-Nothingism was more than an expression of frustration by old Whigs. Large groups of Democrats were also drawn into the movement. While pietism was certainly the backbone of the American party, the Know-Nothings lacked the messianic zeal that characterized the temperance movement. The Fillmore campaign attracted voters who wished to correct the abuses in society by restoring America to the simple virtues of the Jeffersonian era. The political movement of Know-Nothingism was a reaction to the changes in the party structure brought about by the Kansas-Nebraska Act. Reacting to the slavery realignment, the Southerners in Illinois responded heavily to the Know-Nothing appeal to reinstate the old republic. It was for that reason that the New Englanders were so strongly opposed to the American party. The Yankees sought to save society by reform, not by restoration.

The fact that the American party attracted more than just former Whigs and that Know-Nothingism was not a link between Whigs, temperance and anti-slavery is demonstrated by the correlations between the Fillmore vote and later Republican and Democratic elections. The antipathy between the Know-Nothings and the Republicans is particularly revealed in these correlations. The 1856 Fillmore vote showed a strong -.68 correlation with the Fremont supporters. This negative relationship persists in every Republican election, reaching a high of -.54 with the 1864 Lincoln vote. On the other hand, the Know-Nothings had a positive correlation with every Democratic vote, showing the strength of those former Democrats who voted for Fillmore. In 1856, the American party had a remarkable .20 correlation with the Democrats in a head-on contest. Again in 1858, the correlation between the two groups was .38, and by 1864, the Democratic vote was correlated at .55 with the Know-Nothings. The only other positive association the Fillmore vote had was a .38 with the Constitutional Union party in 1860. Clearly then, the Know-Nothings were not a halfway house for Whigs before they become Republicans, and the American party was not simply another expression of a continuous pietistic impulse motivating Whiggery, temperance and anti-slavery equally.

Politically, the Know-Nothing movement was less harmonious than the temperance crusade. When the American party was launched in Illinois in the summer of 1855, the group was already divided. One wing of the Know-Nothings, called "Sams," were anti-Catholic and anti-immigrant, while the other wing, called "Jonathans," were anti-Catholic and anti-slavery, but not necessarily anti-foreign. The first American convention in Illinois showed that the "Jonathans" had carried the party, as the platform called for a restoration of the Missouri Compromise and resistance to the corrupting influences of Catholicism.[33] The party, however, slipped into almost immediate decline. In preparation for the Presidential contest in 1856, the American party convention, meeting in Philadelphia, split over the slavery issue and, in Illinois, a badly divided convention was thrown into complete confusion when all the men slated for offices declined their nominations. A second state convention was later convened to find new candidates, but the proceedings were poorly attended and the men nominated were all political unknowns. The State ticket ran far behind Fillmore in the balloting and, after the defeat in 1856, the Know-Nothings ceased to operate as an organized political party in Illinois.

Although temperance and Know-Nothingism had brief political lives in Illinois, each played an important role in the realignment over slavery. The Kansas-Nebraska Act had split the electorate into a new pattern, with slavery as the line of demarcation between the voters. Before this new configuration could be firmly established, the issues of temperance and Know-Nothingism cut across the realignment. The anti-Nebraska coalition was based mainly upon Yankees, Germans, Canadians, English, and "other" U.S.-born. However, once temperance became a primary issue, the Germans and the Scandinavians broke away from the anti-slavery combination and the remainder of the coalition was joined by a number of Southerners in support of temperance. This configuration was then altered by the Know-Nothings. Basically, Southerners and Illinois-born voters joined with a portion of the "other"-born to vote for Fillmore (see Table 13).[34] Pietism was the basic strain in all three movements, but in each case, different groups of pietists combined to form a new pattern.

Table 13. Percentages Comparing Whig, Fusion, Temperance, and Know-Nothing Voters

	1852 Whig Presidential	1854 Fusion Treasurer	1855 Pro Temperance	1856 Know-Nothing
Yankee	18	100	100	0
Southern	51	12	25	42
Illinois	65	0	0	68
Other	51	86	94	11
German	04	70	0	0
English	25	100	100	0
Irish	0	0	0	0
Scandinavian	0	61	34	0
Canadian	0	100	100	0
French	0	100	36	0

The division created by the Kansas-Nebraska Act was too profound to be completely nullified by the issues of temperance and nativism. The original anti-Nebraska coalition, however, could not be reconstructed until the antagonisms caused by temperance and Know-Nothingism were healed. As long as nativism or prohibition was the issue, Yankees, English, Scandinavians and segments of the other ethnic groups would not cooperate against slavery.

The realignment on the slavery issue stalled, but more than just voters opposed to the Democracy were divided by the issues. All of the voters were confused, including the traditional Democratic supporters. One newspaper speculated that the foreign population and the Catholics refused to vote because they were "fearful they might vote for some Know-Nothing candidate. Everyone was charged with being Know-Nothings, and everyone denied the charge."[35] Lyman Trumbull summarized the problem of the anti-slavery forces when he wrote that the anti-Nebraska forces could not fuse because the anti-slavery Democrats would not join with temperance men and Know-Nothings. The only chance of success, according to Trumbull, would be to call a convention of men who were "opposed equally to the spread of slavery, to abolition, & to Know-Nothingism . . . ." "In order to carry this State," Trumbull wrote, "we must keep out of the pro-slavery party a large number of those who are democrats. There would be no difficulty in doing this were it not for old party associations & side issues, such as Know-Nothingism & the temperance question."[36] Trumbull recognized that cohesion could come only if anti-slavery could be presented as the single issue.

In 1855, however, the slavery issue was entangled with temperance and nativism. The result was political chaos. Factions and political organizations proliferated so quickly that one newspaper saw fit to print a list of the various parties so that the voters could see what was available. According to the *Ottawa Weekly Republican* in 1855, there were Republicans, Whigs, Wooly Heads, Silver Greys, Prohibitionists, Stringent Licensers, Moral Suasonists, Tee-totallers, National Democrats, Hunkers, Barnburners, Hard Shells, Soft Shells, Half Shells, Know Nothings, Know Somethings, Americans, Choctaws, Hindoes, Sams, Jonathans, Liberty Party, and Templars, to name a few.[37]

The problem for the anti-slavery men was immense. In order to overcome Douglas and the Democracy in Illinois, most of the various factions had to be united. The only means to accomplish this task was as Senator Trumbull had clearly seen—the presentation of the single issue of slavery.

5

Republicans

At the end of 1855, the anti-Nebraska movement offered only a pale reminder of its former strength and vitality. The various factions opposed to the extension of slavery still could find no common ground upon which to unite. The Fusion movements began to melt away as some of the Whigs persisted in trying to revive the old party while anti-slavery Democrats steadfastly adhered to their organization in hopes of returning to the Democracy on the traditional Jacksonian issues. The diminutive Republican party, completely in the hands of radical abolitionists, had no hope of attracting support from the more conservative anti-slavery advocates. What remained of the anti-Nebraska appeal was endangered by the emergence of temperance and Know-Nothingism as political issues, which began to reshape the realignment and threatened to alienate irrevocably the different groups of anti-Nebraska voters from each other.

A new sense of urgency, brought to the slavery question by the developments in Kansas in early 1856, prevented a complete dissolution of the anti-Nebraska factions. The territory had become a festering problem with two Legislatures and two Governors; one free soil and the other pro-slavery. The sporadic violence between the two camps erupted into a full-scale war when the Missouri "border ruffians" attacked the free soil town of Lawrence in May. In retribution for the "sack of Lawrence," John Brown led a foray into the Pottawattomie Creek area, killing five pro-slavery settlers. The Missouri men retaliated by burning the free-soil settlement at Osawatomie and killing one of Brown's sons. As if "Bleeding Kansas" were not enough to arouse anti-slavery passions, Senator Charles Sumner, after delivering a particularly invective speech entitled "The Crime against Kansas," was beaten unconscious in the Senate Chamber by Congressman Preston Brooks of South Carolina. The realignment of the voters on the slavery question, which had stalled in 1855, was revived, and the process was accelerated by the events in Kansas and the attack upon Sumner. Lyman Trumbull wrote that "the outrage upon Sumner & the occurrences in Kansas have helped us vastly." The anti-slavery forces revitalized; one anti-Nebraska editor prophetically declared that "the Kansas question will do what the Nebraska question did not."[1] This time the realignment would not be stopped or delayed. The formation of the Republican party reflected the coalescing of the realignment. Each step the Republicans took in creating a party was a step towards the completion of the realignment.

The approach of the Presidential election in 1856 made the need for unity among the anti-Nebraska factions more vital than ever. Most of the leaders understood that they could not expect to defeat Douglas a second time without cooperating in solid opposition to the Democracy. William Jayne wrote to Trumbull that "Illinois can only be carried by a combination of the opposition to Douglass [*sic*] . . . but the trouble is can the opposition unite[?]"[2] The task of creating an anti-slavery party was an imposing one. Besides the logistics of building an organization, old party loyalties had to be overcome, individual politicians used to politics by personalities had to be forced to cooperate, and voters, antagonistic to each other on the questions of temperance and Know-Nothingism and in the degree of their opposition to slavery, had to be forged into a coalition united on principle.

Ethno-cultural historians have viewed the new party as a Protestant Party, but this characterization is misleading. The process of forming the Republican party involved more than just uniting different evangelical groups into an anti-Democratic coalition. While Protestantism was an important aspect of the party, the Republicans formed no alliance with Know-Nothingism; and in Southern Illinois, the pietists, not the liturgical immigrants, were the backbone of the *Democratic* party. The realignment divided the electorate on slavery, not religion. The ultimate victory of the Republicans resulted from the successful definition of anti-slavery principles and not the exploitation of religious tension.

Initially, the main problems of organizing the new party lay in overcoming old loyalties and in convincing the factions to sacrifice their independence for cooperation. The first attempt to deal with these problems came in the winter of 1854 when 16 leading anti-Nebraska newspaper editors in the State agreed to meet in Decatur and to discuss plans for cooperation in the elections of 1856. Even this simple declaration that the Decatur convention would discuss future cooperation, however, met with suspicion from most anti-Nebraska men. The skepticism displayed by all the factions stemmed, in part, from their anxiety over the threatened loss of independence. Whigs, in particular, still nourished dreams of revitalizing the old party, and anti-Nebraska Democrats refused to give up the belief that the party of Jackson could be restored. The factions also were nervous about cooperating with the radical group who called themselves Republicans.

As the anti-Nebraska factions cautiously watched, 12 of the editors eventually assembled at Decatur and called for a general meeting, to be held at Bloomington in May, 1856. The call was issued to men who were opposed to Know-Nothingism, in favor of the restoration of the Missouri Compromise, against the introduction of slavery into the territories of Kansas and Nebraska, and opposed to interference with slavery in States where the institution already existed.[3] The resolutions of the Decatur convention were met with a sense of relief. The staunchly Whig *Illinois State Journal* wrote that the Decatur resolutions were "neither 'Know Nothing' nor 'Republican' but take a firm and emphatic ground against . . . the Kansas-Nebraska act." The anti-Nebraska Democratic *Belleville Advocate*, pleased by the Decatur convention, declared that "every plank [of the platform] is composed of sound Democratic timber — good hickory." The call for another convention, however, the *Advocate* found entirely unnecessary, but allowed that "no harm can result from the assembly." The radical *Rockford Republican* was disappointed in the timidity of the anti-Nebraska editors at Decatur, but did concede that at least the meeting would begin the process of thoroughly organizing the state for the coming election.[4]

Although the Decatur meeting had been moderate in tone, most anti-Nebraska men remained hesitant about joining the Bloomington convention. All realized that the Bloomington meeting would be a wide-open affair in which anything could happen. Previous attempts to organize had ended in failure and there was little reason to believe that this would be any different.

The local elections in the spring resulted in a number of Democratic victories which made the need for some kind of organization more pressing. The anti-Nebraska men found themselves in a dilemma. The political situation demanded some sort of action and they all knew that they could not effectively oppose the Democrats without coopera-tion. Yet forming a new party involved sacrifices from each faction. Whigs, Democrats, Know-Nothings, and temperance men would have to put aside their former differences and antagonisms. Their only bond was opposition to the extension of slavery, but even that issue was in dispute, especially with the radical faction of the Republicans. To remain as they were meant political defeat, but cooperation would by no means be easy and was no guarantee of future success. Ebenezer Peck doubted the wisdom of a convention since old loyalties remained strong and the anti-slavery groups were divided over temperance and nativism. "I fear a state convention of the anti-Nebraska people of the State," he wrote, for the reason that "it would tend rather to disunite them not amalgamate."[5]

The leading anti-Nebraska men eventually decided to risk the consequences of cooperation. The anti-slavery Congressmen from Illinois agreed to support the Bloomington convention simply because there was no alternative. Elihu Washburne explained, in a letter to Richard Yates, the Congressional delegation's belief that politically there was no choice but to cooperate.

> Trumbull, Know, Woodworth, Norton and myself have consulted as to what is best to be done in our state in regard to the approaching election. We are all agreed that all our folks . . . should go into the Anti-Nebraska Convention called at Bloomington. . . . Under that call, Republicans, Americans, Old-Line Whigs, Anti-Nebraska democrats can assemble . . . . If we do not take hold of this Bloomington Convention, what shall we do? We all think it is the only way.[6]

William Herndon, Lincoln's law partner, also wrote to Yates explaining that there was really no alternative but to attend the convention. "If you do not go," Herndon wrote, "you, Lincoln, and all others will be buried politically forever."[7]

Once the anti-Nebraska leaders decided to participate in the Bloomington convention, they confronted the problem of finding an acceptable basis for cooperation. Most anti-Nebraska men feared, above all, Owen Lovejoy, leader of the Republicans. Peck worried that "the ultras would insist upon something more than an avowal of hostility to slavery," which would give them all the odor of abolitionism.[8] Trumbull took the lead in arranging a plan of action among the moderates to prevent the Republicans from controlling the convention.

Carefully preparing the groundwork, Trumbull had his close friend, Peck, meet in Springfield with the State's leading moderate anti-Nebraska politicians. At that meeting, Abraham Lincoln and Jackson Grimshaw, representing the Whigs, Joseph Gillespie, speaking as a Know-Nothing, and Gustave Koerner and Peck, as the anti-Nebraska Democratic voices, agreed on a strategy. "We have all united in opinion," Peck reported to Trumbull, "that it is best to run [William H.] Bissell for Governor. The old whig party will go for him . . . and so will very many of the Southern democrats. The only trouble is, that the know nothings may bring out a candidate."[9] Besides candidates, the group also agreed upon a platform to present to the convention.

With accord among the leading moderates, Trumbull and the others vigorously moved ahead with their plans to control the Bloomington convention. Lincoln convinced a number of old Whigs including Yates,

Orville H. Browning, and Richard Oglesby to attend the convention, and Gillespie managed to ensure the presence of some anti-slavery Know-Nothings like Ozias M. Hatch and Jesse K. Dubois. Peck, Bissell and Norman B. Judd, following the lead of Trumbull, promised to attend, but a number of Democrats refused to participate in any effort for cooperation.

John M. Palmer, like many anti-Nebraska men, feared Lovejoy and the Republican label that was being attached to the convention. Palmer endorsed the feelings of a fellow Democrat who had written saying, "I have but little faith in the permanent success of the Republican Party. If we go with them on this election will they not ask us to go farther next time & claim our adherence now as an adherence to the party that shall take the place of whiggery[?]"[10] Trumbull wrote Palmer a series of letters trying to convince him to attend the Bloomington convention. Pointing out that the Democrats had gone completely pro-slavery and that there was no hope of saving the party, Trumbull assured Palmer that the Republican convention would be moderate.

> When I speak of the Republicans I do not mean as have assumed that name in Illinois & who oppose the fugitive slave law, the admission of any more slave states under any circumstances but I mean all those who on the slavery question simply make this issue, opposition to its spread into free *Territory*. The republicans will I think be willing to abandon their ultraisms & stand upon this one issue....[11]

Although Palmer finally relented and joined the Bloomington convention, another Democrat, Gustave Koerner, did not. Koerner typified the anti-slavery men who refused to give up hope that the old parties could be restored. Koerner had been appointed to a State Central Committee by the Decatur convention, but he declined, and continued to resist all efforts to get him to join in the Bloomington meeting. Holding steadfastly to the hope that the Democratic party would repudiate the Kansas-Nebraska Act, he refused to entertain the idea of leaving the party until the Democracy emphatically declared itself. Only after the nomination of James Buchanan in June did Koerner finally, and reluctantly, leave the Democracy.

By March, however, most anti-Nebraska politicians had agreed to attend the Bloomington convention, even though they were aware that the endorsements and promises of cooperation from the moderate leaders were not enough to insure that the convention would be conservative. Trumbull and the others realized that Lovejoy and the Republicans would be at Bloomington. The moderates understood that in order to assure their control of the convention, they would have to control the delegations. Conventions were usually convened in a haphazard manner, with many of the delegates being self-appointed. While moderates could easily pack the meeting, they understood that such action might result more in disruption than in harmony. Confident that a vast majority of the voters would support them, they organized local delegate conventions. This tactic not only prevented the Republicans from packing the convention, but also involved more people in the movement and built much needed local interest in the Bloomington convention.

The month of April was a time of great activity in preparation for the convention. Local meetings and rallies were organized to arouse enthusiasm and to allay the fears of the voters that the Bloomington meeting would be a radical one. One of Trumbull's close advisors wrote that he was "getting the surrounding counties organized so as to make the Bloomington affair as respectable as possible."[12]   Anti-Nebraska moderates carefully disassociated themselves from the Republicans in the preliminary meetings. The *Belleville Advocate*, for example, absolutely denied that the Bloomington gathering, and even the national meeting at Philadelphia, would be Republican conventions.

> Some of the Nebraska papers are endeavoring to create the impression that the coming conventions of Bloomington and Philadelphia are to be meetings merely of the Republican party; and we also notice, with regret, that many of the Republicans so understand it, and have called meetings to appoint delegates to those Conventions. By this means they would, without intending it of course, exclude all other men who are opposed to slavery extension from meeting with them; and there are many of this latter class who are not Republicans. The object of the Conventions . . . as we understand it, is to unite and concentrate the force of all men opposed to the extension of slavery into our national territories, and to organize this force for the coming contest. The address of the National Committee expressly repudiates and ignores all existing party names; and the call attached to it is addressed to men of all parties.[13]

Typical of the moderates in planning for the convention, William Herndon sent a long letter of instruction to Richard Yates.

> I want to know whether Morgan County intends to send delegates to Bloomington or not, and what is to be their stripe, their distinctive name. Will you send Whigs, Republicans, or simply Anti-Nebraska? My individual opinion is that Morgan, Sangamon, others below us . . . had better send simply Anti-Nebraska delegates. . . .   You know that old Sangamon is tender-footed, cannot be pushed or ridden too hard, faint on the way she is, and we must act prudently. . . .   If the people could only see the question beyond the cry of niggers, there is no earthly doubt that nine out of ten would be against democracy, i.e., Nigger driving despotism. . . .   I

think the only way for us to act is this; if you do not go, the whole affair
will be wild, fanatical, crazy, and . . . the field will be free. . . .[14]

When the convention assembled at Bloomington on May 29th,
1856, it was clearly controlled by the moderates. Palmer was elected
chairman of the proceedings and the prearranged nominations were made
by acclamation. The platform was simple and moderate. The
convention resolved that "foregoing all former differences of opinions
upon other questions, we pledge ourselves to unite in opposition to the
present administration." The delegates declared that Congress possessed
the power to prohibit slavery in the territories and that the Missouri
Compromise must be restored. Finally, after professing devotion to the
Union, the convention resolved that "we will proscribe no one by legislation or other wise on account of religious opinions, or in consequence
of place of birth."[15]

Most anti-Nebraska men, while satisfied with the proceedings of the
Bloomington convention, were still reluctant to call themselves
Republicans. The *Urbana Union* called the meeting the Anti-Nebraska
State Convention and referred to the new party as an "auxiliary to the
national Anti-Slavery extension party." Even Lincoln refused to accept
the Republican label. In a letter to Trumbull, in which he urged the
Senator to attend the national convention at Philadelphia, Lincoln
referred to the party holding the convention as the Anti-Nebraska party.[16]
Even after John C. Fremont was nominated at Philadelphia as the first
Republican Presidential candidate, the new party name was not widely
accepted in Illinois. Those involved in meetings, rallies, and clubs on
behalf of the candidate referred to themselves as "Fremont supporters"
rather than Republicans.

The forging together of the anti-Nebraska factions in 1856 resulted
in a turnover of politicians on the local level. The anti-Nebraska
movement in 1854 had cleared away most of the personalities on the
local level, and for the most part, new men took over the leadership of
the factions.[17] These new politicians, after two years of political
independence, were an obstacle to the formation of the Republican party.
They feared affiliation with the new party not only because they realized
that it would mean the loss of much of their power, but also because a
new party would demand regularity, which would diminish their ability
to bend the issues to please the local voters. The Republicans found that
they had to replace these local anti-Nebraska men in order to create an
effective party organization. Consequently, only 30 percent of the 1854
anti-Nebraska leaders survived the transition into the Republican party.
Of the old Whig leadership, 27 percent became active Republicans.[18]

Just as the initial realignment in 1854 caused a turnover of local politicians, the coalescing of the realignment formalized by the creation of the Republican party forced another change in the local leadership. The new leaders of 1854, many of whom had never before been active in politics, were replaced in 1856 by another set of new men. This new leadership allowed the Republicans to bypass many local political problems and, at the same time, it helped to create loyalty to the organization by making the political careers of a number of men dependent upon the party.

Trumbull, Lincoln, and a few others had accomplished much in building the new party. They had managed to win the grudging acceptance of most of the anti-Nebraska politicians, but the party still lacked real cohesiveness. Old loyalties and antagonisms persisted and there was no certainty as to how the voters would respond. The means of overcoming these difficulties lay in the issues. In 1856, Trumbull wrote that the "next canvass is to be fought more on principle than men" and it was the principles set forth at the Bloomington convention that became the key to the growth of the party and the cement which held the organization together.[19]

The single issue of non-extension of slavery united the anti-Nebraska factions. The force of that issue did more to win acceptance for the party than all the promises and cajoling of the moderate leaders. Gustave Koerner was one who was finally won over to the new movement. He expressed, in a speech to a number of Democrats, the importance of the slavery issue. "I have been a Democrat all my life and am yet one," Koerner declared. "I am with you on all points in the Democratic catechism and mean to stay with you, except on one, which is an entirely new one, of which you knew nothing a year or two ago. I am opposed to the repeal of the Missouri compromise, and to the reopening of the slavery agitation."[20]

The single issue of non-extension of slavery and the intensity of the campaign in 1856 made most anti-Nebraska men forget their fears of cooperating and they gradually began to call themselves Republicans. By the end of the year, the party was a distinct organization. The Republican party in 1856 was different from the 1854 faction. This second Republican party in Illinois was created with new men and moderate principles. Unlike the earlier group, the unifying cause of the new Republicans, as the *Quincy Whig* stated, was "*freedom*, not of the black but of ourselves."[21]

Once the politicians committed themselves to the new party, the Republicans were able to deal with the problem of building a stable coalition of voters. Until 1858, they attempted to draw new groups into the party by exploiting religious tensions and by making special appeals to particular groups. The Republicans found, however, that this tactic perpetuated old divisions in the electorate and lost for them as many voters as it gained. The course of events and the need to expand the coalition forced a change in tactics. In the campaign in 1858 and for the next two years, the Republicans, under Lincoln's direction, concentrated upon defining their anti-slavery principles and projecting a distinct image of the party. The special appeals remained a part of politics, but it was the successful definition of principles that brought victory to the party in 1860.

The election in 1856 demonstrated to the Republicans the problem of building a coalition. Bissell and the entire State ticket were elected—a remarkable achievement and cause for major celebrations—but Fremont lost the State. The base of the Republican support was very narrow. An examination of the multiple regression table for the Presidential contest in Illinois indicates the problems the Republicans faced in building a coalition (see Table 14).[22] The Fillmore candidacy as a Know-Nothing hurt the Republicans. Many of the former Whig voters supported Fillmore, and more importantly, the bulk of the pietists also did so. The

Table 14. Regression: 1856 Republican Presidential Vote

	Multiple R	R Square	RSQ Change	Simple R	B	Beta
Percent Southern	.822	.677	.677	-.82	-2.416	-1.463
Percent Yankee	.895	.801	.124	.76	2.105	0.491
Percent Illinois	.911	.830	.028	-.74	-1.170	-0.375
Value Produced	.914	.836	.006	.09	-0.001	-0.481
Percent Other	.921	.848	.011	.16	-1.731	-0.908
Percent French	.930	.866	.017	.28	-11.735	-1.674
Percent German	.944	.891	.025	.30	0.451	0.228
Acre Value	.947	.897	.006	.24	-1.967	-1.208
Farm Size	.949	.901	.003	-.08	-.885	-1.100
Farm Value	.964	.931	.029	.27	0.031	1.395
Percent Scandinavian	.973	.948	.017	.40	3.635	0.378
Capital Investment	.979	.959	.011	.14	0.0009	0.072
Baptist	.981	.963	.003	-.26	-7.300	-0.185
Pietist	.988	.976	.013	-.41	-13.574	-0.368
Liturgical	.989	.979	.002	.17	-5.540	-0.201
Percent English	.990	.981	.001	.52	-3.723	-0.609
Percent Canadian	.991	.982	.001	.55	-4.240	-0.239
Percent Irish	.992	.984	.002	.48	-2.801	-0.658
(constant)					305.679	

Republicans received overwhelming support only from the Yankees, the English, and the Scandinavians. Fremont also attracted close to 51 percent of the "other" U.S.-born, 72 percent of the Germans, and about 25 percent of the Irish.[23] The Irish support for Fremont was the direct result of the work of John Wentworth. The large Irish voting blocs in Illinois were concentrated in the Chicago wards where Wentworth had flourished as a Democrat for over a decade. After Wentworth's conversion to the Republican party, he labored hard in the Irish districts and through chicanery, fraud, and patronage, he brought many of the Irish into the Republican column. Basically, however, the Republican coalition was a narrow alliance of Yankees, Germans, English, and Scandinavians.

   Not surprisingly, the Southerners and the Illinois-born voters went unanimously against the Republicans, which resulted in a sectional division in Illinois. Geographically, Fremont received 74 percent of the vote in the northern districts of Illinois. In central Illinois, the mean Republican vote dropped to 37 percent while, in the southern part of the State,

Table 15. 1856 Republican Geographical Comparison

Northern Townships

	Multiple R	R Square	RSQ Change	Simple R	B	Beta
Farm Size	.93	.87	.87	.93	.642	1.531
Capital Investment	.97	.95	.07	-.73	.215	0.413
Percent Canada	.99	.98	.02	.10	-1.934	-0.282
Farm Value	.99	.99	.01	.35	-.331	-0.261
Percent Illinois	1.00	1.00	.0008	.25	-4.27	-0.033
(constant)				42.735		

Northern and Central Townships

	Multiple R	R Square	RSQ Change	Simple R	B	Beta
Percent Southern	.79	.63	.63	-.79	-4.03	-2.12
Percent Yankee	.87	.76	.13	.77	-1.21	-0.33
Percent French	.92	.84	.08	.29	4.31	0.59
Percent Scandinavian	.95	.90	.05	.33	-.51	-0.07
Percent Illinois	.95	.92	.01	-.71	-1.20	-0.32
Farm Size	.96	.93	.01	-.32	-.33	-0.46
Percent German	.97	.94	.01	.27	-8.59	-2.76
Percent Irish	.98	.96	.02	-.27	-.20	-0.05
Baptist	.99	.98	.01	-.24	16.45	0.44
Percent Other	.99	.99	.01	.06	-3.20	-1.50
Value Produced	.99	.99	.003	-.02	-.86	-1.50
Farm Value	.99	.99	.00006	-.13	-.66	-0.02
(constant)				349.08		

Southern Townships

	Multiple R	R Square	RSQ Change	Simple R	B	Beta
Liturgical	.95	.89	.89	.94	32.29	1.83
Scandinavian	.97	.94	.05	.63	-22.60	-1.06
Acre Value	.99	.98	.03	.11	-0.79	-0.53
English	.99	.99	.008	-.26	1.26	0.10
French	.99	.99	.002	.85	0.10	0.02
Farm Size	.99	.99	.002	-.29	0.68	0.11
Other	.99	.99	.001	-.34	-0.10	-0.08
(constant)				18.9		

Fremont captured only 23 percent of the voters and most of them were confined to the German communities surrounding St. Louis. The geographical imbalance was so great that in one southern county, Fremont received but two votes, and according to Koerner, "one of these voters, a schoolmaster, was driven out of the county after the election."[24]

The solid anti-Republican stand of the Southerners profoundly influenced all other considerations in the voting pattern (see Table 15).[25] Significantly, Fremont received exceptionally higher support from liturgicals and immigrants in Egypt than he did in the rest of the State. For example, the liturgicals in southern Illinois correlated at an incredible .94 with the Fremont vote, while the total State correlation was only .17. The economic pattern in the 1856 vote was also affected by this sectional division. In the northern townships, the Fremont vote correlated highly with farm size and value. In Egypt, however, these variables had little explanatory value. The presence of Southerners, then, and not religion or economics, determined the political response in 1856. The more Southerners there were in the area, the more Republican were all the other economic, ethnic, and religious groups.

The sectional division of Illinois and the presence of the Know-Nothings produced an interesting effect upon the voting pattern among religious groups. For the State as a whole, the liturgicals had an extremely weak association with the Fremont vote while the Baptists were negatively correlated. The pietists, in spite of historians' claims to the contrary, were strongly opposed to the Republicans. The Germans and the Scandinavians accounted for the mild correlation of the liturgicals with the Republican vote. On the other hand, the support of the Southerners, Illinois-born, and "other" U.S.-born for Fillmore and Buchanan explains the strong negative association of the pietists. A breakdown of the 1856 Republican vote by religion illustrates the pattern more clearly (see Table 16). The Fremont vote drops from a mean 74 percent in areas with no pietists to 36 percent in highly pietistic communities. The effect of the liturgicals is negligible. As liturgicals increase from areas with no churches to communities with a high concentration of churches, the Fremont vote rises 8 percent.

Table 16. Breakdown: 1856 Percent Republican Vote by Religion

Number of Churches

	None	Low	Medium	High
Pietistic	74.0	55.3	52.5	36.4
Liturgical	42.4	34.8	56.4	50.6
Baptist	53.4	42.2	33.7	47.0

The Republicans' biggest problem after 1856 was the need to appeal to more voters. The obvious group in the electorate that might be swayed to the Republican side was the Know-Nothings. Lincoln wrote that "until we can get the elements of this organization there is not sufficient materials to successfully combat the Nebraska Democracy with."[26] But Lincoln rejected any plan for outright fusion with the Know-Nothings, as had happened in many other States. He wrote that "as to the matter of fusion, I am for it, if it can be had on republican grounds; and I am not for it on any other terms. A fusion on any other terms . . . would be as foolish as unprincipled. I would lose the whole North, while the common enemy would still carry the whole South."[27] Know-Nothings had to be drawn into the Republican party in some less compromising manner, but the game was a dangerous one. Lincoln clearly saw that the "inherent obstacle to any plan of union, lies in the fact that of those germans which we now have with us, large numbers will fall away . . ." if an outright appeal were made to the Americans.[28]

As one tactic, the Republicans tried to convince the Know-Nothings that their votes for Fillmore would be wasted and would help Buchanan in the Presidential election. The Republicans prompted Joseph Gillespie, Ozias M. Hatch, and Jessie K. Dubois, all Know-Nothings, to try to persuade the American party not to run a candidate for Governor and to support Bissell and Fremont. Lincoln wrote numerous Fillmore supporters urging them to go with Fremont, but he admitted that "the great difficulty with anti-extension Fillmore men, is that they suppose Fillmore as good as Fremont on that question; and it is a delicate point to argue them out of it."[29]

Another method the Republicans used to attract Know-Nothing voters, while not offending the foreign-born Republicans, was to attack Catholicism. Since the Catholics voted Democratic, nothing could be lost. Koerner remembered that the "Catholic element in many places was very strong, and the stand they took for the Pro-Slavery Democracy impaired the strength of the Republican party very greatly."[30] Consequently, an assault upon popery in America would not hurt the Republicans and it would appeal to the Nativist vote.

The *Chicago Tribune* took the lead in attacking the Catholics. Stephen A. Douglas' tour of Europe was widely reported in the press, but the *Tribune* dwelled upon his visit to Rome in particular. It was not enough that Douglas had married a Catholic; now he had entered into a holy alliance with the Pope. According to the *Tribune*, Douglas had exchanged money for the promise of Catholic support. The *Tribune* concluded that this alliance was a threat to American liberty.

> It is the Senator's right to be a Catholic. But as Catholicism and Republicanism are as plainly incompatible as oil and water, it is the right of the American People to refuse to entrust him with power whereby Protestantism and Freedom may be beaten down, and Popery and Slavery built up. The nation needs no Jesuit in the White House.[31]

The attacks upon the Pope also were designed to draw into the party the Protestant immigrant vote. William Pickering advised Joseph Gillespie to talk to the "Lutheran priests" and convince them that in supporting the Democracy they were aiding the Pope.[32] The Republican strategy was expressed in a speech given by a Republican at Crete, Illinois during the 1856 campaign.

> There are 300 Protestant Dutchmen [Germans] in the three eastern towns of this county. Let us publish and circulate amongst these Protestant Dutch, pamphlets in the German language about the Pope of Rome and the Catholic religion, and we shall have every man of them vote the republican ticket. They have imbided [*sic*] strong prejudices against the Pope of Rome and the Catholic religion in Germany; let us now stir up their *prejudices* anew, and by the right kind of representations, bring them all round to go republicanism.[33]

Another Republican tactic for winning over the Know-Nothings was to charge that the American party was a tool of the Democrats. There was in fact, much evidence to support the accusation. In southern Illinois, one of the Presidential electors for Buchanan was Charles H. Constable, a former Whig and avowed Know-Nothing. W. W. Danenhower, the leading Know-Nothing editor in the State, actually received financial support from Douglas, and Danenhower's paper, the *Native Citizen*, was printed by Douglas' *Chicago Times*. Buckner S. Morris, the American candidate for Governor, wrote a public letter in which he viciously attacked Bissell and Fremont but did not mention one word about the Democratic candidates. The Democratic strategy, according to the Republicans, was to divide the anti-slavery vote so that Buchanan would carry the State. "Funds have been raised in Chicago to start a Fillmore paper," declared one Republican newspaper, "in the hope that Know Nothings in northern Illinois may be fooled to vote for him, while those in Egypt go strong for Buchanan and thus secure to him the State."[34] Trumbull charged that the "Nebraskites [sic] are acting in concert with the Know Nothings" and that Douglas was "evidently hoping for salvation through the Know Nothings."[35]

By accusing the American party leaders of being tools of Douglas and by appealing to the anti-Catholic sentiment of the pietists, the Republicans hoped to draw the Know-Nothings into their coalition without accepting the nativist program or offending the foreign-born voters. The great advantage the Republicans had beyond their special appeals was that the Know-Nothing program, by trying to avoid slavery, was fast becoming irrelevant. One Republican wrote to Palmer that "the Fillmorites are in a state of *solution* . . . [and] in the present unsettled state of affairs they cannot move unless they wish to separate the Fremont strength from them, and this they cannot afford to do."[36] By 1859, the Know-Nothings had ceased to be a factor in the elections. Koerner correctly wrote that "it is time we should quit the absurd hope of gaining converts from the Know-Nothings. . . . In our state they have taken their sides. They do not pretend to exist as a party. This policy pursued by some of our friends . . . has been from the start fatal to us. For every Know-Nothing we gained we lost two Republicans."[37]

Besides the Know-Nothings, the Republicans also attempted to draw old Whigs into the party. After the Bloomington convention, many of the Whigs who had not joined the Know-Nothings sided with the Democracy. Whigs with Southern antecedents in the downstate counties were especially quick to affiliate with the Democratic party. Led by Don Morrison, E.B. Webb, Robert S. Blackwell and James W. Singleton, these Southern-born Whigs were primarily attracted by Douglas' appeal for Union. So many Whigs became Democrats that Koerner wrote that "with the exception of Lincoln, Judge [David] Davis and a few other prominent Whigs, the other leaders of the old Whig party became most ardent Douglas men."[38] The Republicans, relying heavily upon such men as Lincoln, argued that they were the true party of the Union and that the Democrats were in reality the sectionalists. The old Whig paper, the *Springfield Journal*, captured the essence of this appeal when it stated that "the Republican Party is essentially a conservative and defensive party — that it was born and lives to prevent innovations, not to make them."[39]   The chief innovation that the Republicans sought to prevent was the Democratic intention of spreading slavery into the territories ordained free by the Missouri Compromise, the sacred document of Henry Clay.

Despite the appeals of Lincoln and David Davis, many of the Whigs stayed with the Democracy, especially after the publication in 1858 of a letter from John J. Crittenden, Henry Clay's son-in-law, endorsing Douglas.[40]   The intransigence of the old Whigs so infuriated Davis that he wrote, "the Pharisaical old whigs in the central counties, who are so much more righteous than other people, I can't talk about with any patience."[41]   Lincoln termed the former Whigs who supported Douglas the "exclusive silk-stocking whiggery," but he did not believe that all hope of winning their votes was lost.   As William Herndon wrote, the old-line Whigs were "timid shrinking, but good, men."[42]

After the elections in 1858, the Republicans made fewer direct appeals to the old Whigs.   They realized that special appeals to specific groups of voters could not sustain the party, and in fact only seemed to keep alive old animosities.   Two Republicans writing to Lincoln understood exactly the problem.

> Our party is a composite one and has diverse elements whose tastes and feelings ought to be carefully handled until time renders us a homogeneous mass.   Such arguments, or rather such appeals to old prejudices that ought to be forgotten, only serve to perpetuate our original diversities and to retard very much the complete fusion which must take place before we can hope to become a power in the land.[43]

Similarly, David Davis wrote that "the Republican party is a confederation — not a consolidated party — sympathy is one of the main elements of strength in a party — and never before have I known of such a favor simply because members of a party preferred one man to another."[44]

Instead of special appeals, the Republicans concentrated on creating a distinct party image.   The party leaders recognized that their coalition could only be expanded by one strategy, and that was to draw an emphatic line between themselves and the Democracy on the slavery question.

The Dred Scott Decision, which declared that Congress could not prohibit slavery in the territories and that the Missouri Compromise was unconstitutional, along with the administration's acceptance of the pro-slavery Lecompton Constitution for Kansas, propelled the Republican party into a broader attack upon slavery.   It was this wider anti-slavery appeal that attracted more voters to the Republicans, and not the emphasis on the party's conservative character or the exploitation of cultural tensions. On the question of how to expand the coalition, Lincoln wrote that the "danger will be the temptation to lower the Republican Standard in order to gather recruits. In my judgment such a step would be a serious mistake—would open a gap through which more would pass *out* than pass *in*."[45]

As the Republicans pursued their anti-slavery program, they were suddenly pushed into a more radical position by the maneuverings of Douglas. In 1857, President James Buchanan, hoping to defuse the Kansas question and thereby undercut an important aspect of the Republican platform, accepted the pro-slavery Lecompton Constitution and recommended immediate Statehood for Kansas. Because the Lecompton Constitution was so flagrantly fraudulent, however, many northern Democrats refused to support Buchanan. Led by Douglas, the anti-Lecompton Democrats voted with the Republican members of Congress to block the admission of Kansas as a slave state. Buchanan was furious and he began to strip the anti-Lecompton Democrats, especially Douglas, of patronage. Douglas became a hero for many Republicans. There was much talk that the "Little Giant" would in fact become a Republican. Horace Greeley, the editor of the *New York Tribune*, heralded Douglas as a new champion in the battle against slavery. Greeley even suggested that the Republicans of Illinois should help re-elect Douglas to the Senate in 1858.

The Illinois Republicans were at first confused over how to react to Douglas' stand against the Lecompton Constitution. Lincoln wrote to Trumbull asking "what think you of the probable '*rumpus*' among the democracy over the Kansas constitution? I think the Republicans should stand clear of it."[46] Trumbull cautiously wrote that "what Douglas will do, or where he will go I know not . . . [but] he must take several more steps yet before he can be fellowshiped [*sic*] by Republicans."[47] Greeley's praise for Douglas and his suggestion that Republicans support him in the next election added to the confusion of Illinois Republicans. Lincoln demanded to know from Trumbull what Greeley was planning.

> What does the New-York Tribune mean by its constant eulogising, and admiring, and magnifying Douglas? Does it, in this, speak the sentiments of the republicans at Washington? Have they concluded that the Republican cause, generally, can be best promoted by sacrificing us here in Illinois? If so we would like to know it soon; it will save us a great deal of labor to surrender at once.[48]

For Lincoln, the solution to the problem of Douglas was clear. The issues had to be distinctly drawn. Douglas had co-opted the middle ground and unless the Illinois Republicans moved farther in their opposition to slavery, they would become nothing more than a tail to Douglas' kite. In his famous "House Divided" speech, delivered at the Republican State Convention in 1858, Lincoln emphatically took issue with Douglas. After his declaration that the nation could not endure half slave and half free and that it must become "*all* one thing, or *all* the other," Lincoln questioned where Douglas' policy would lead. Douglas' doctrine of caring "not whether slavery be voted *down* or voted *up*," Lincoln stated, "is all [that slavery] now lacks of being alike lawful in all the States." According to Lincoln, Douglas could not possibly oppose the advance of slavery because he cared nothing about it; all the Senator's efforts were aimed at reducing the question to one of property rights. If that is all the problem of slavery is concerned with, Lincoln warned, then there is no means of stopping its expansion.[49] The "House Divided" speech was a declaration of war against Douglas. It clearly defined the slavery issue for the Republicans.

The Republican stand against slavery was based on the pietistic notion of perfection. One Republican saw the 1858 election of "no less than a contest for the advancement of the Kingdom of Heaven or the Kingdom of Satan."[50] A Republican newspaper declared that "the doctrine of non-intervention with slavery in the States is inconsistent with our allegiance to God. . . ."[51] Quoting the Scriptures, Lincoln, in a speech in Chicago, said, "As your Father in Heaven is perfect, be ye also perfect." Although he did not believe all men could indeed be perfect, Lincoln thought that every man should have the chance. "If we cannot give freedom to every creature, let us do nothing that will impose slavery upon any other creature."[52]

In taking the position that slavery was morally wrong, Lincoln and the other Republicans opened themselves to the charge that they were in favor of Negro equality and that they would interfere with slavery in the Southern States. Lincoln went to great lengths to deny both of these charges. In the fourth debate with Douglas, held at Charleston, Lincoln declared:

> I am not, nor ever have been in favor of bringing about in any way the social and political equality of the white and black races . . . and I will say in addition to this that there is a physical difference between the white and black races which I believe will for ever forbid the two races living together on terms of social and political equality.[53]

The black man, however, had "the right to put into his mouth the bread that his own hands have earned," and in that respect, "he is the equal of every other man. . . ." All that Lincoln asked for in regard to the Negro was "that if you do not like him, let him alone."[54] As for the charge that the Republicans intended to abolish slavery in the South, Lincoln issued numerous denials. "I have declared a thousand times, and repeat that, in my opinion," Lincoln wrote, "neither the General Government, nor any other power outside of the slave states, can constitutionally or rightfully interfere with slaves or slavery where it already exists."[55]

Although the Republicans declared that slavery was morally wrong because it deprived God's creatures of the opportunity to be perfect, they also stated that the question of Negro equality was irrelevant. They wanted to link the question of slavery with the interest of the white man, and they were able to do so through their definition of freedom. Free labor was the bulwark of American liberty, according to the Republicans. Every man had the right to the goods his labor earned and this economic independence guaranteed the individual political freedom. Economic freedom was assured through the opportunity available in the new territories. Free Men, Free Soil, and Free Labor were a trinity; each separate and distinct, yet one and the same. Free men could not exist without free labor which, in turn, depended upon free soil. Slavery was a threat to this freedom. Slave labor degraded free labor and destroyed competition.[56] According to Lincoln, "Free labor had the inspiration of hope; pure slavery has no hope."[57] If allowed to expand into the territories, slavery would destroy the opportunity for free labor to improve itself and hence jeopardize economic independence. Slavery was morally wrong because it prevented the white man from achieving perfection. As for the black slave, he too had the right to his own labor, but all the Republicans asked, as Lincoln stated, was that the Negro be left alone. The question, one Republican explained, was not Negro slavery, but "whether those vast and beautiful Territories now free, shall be preserved to the free labor of white men, or whether they shall be surrendered to the blight of slavery."[58]

The Republicans, by broadening their principles and mounting a frontal assault upon the institution of slavery, achieved immediate benefits in the election of 1858. Although Lincoln was defeated for the Senate, because a Democratic majority had been elected to the Legislature, the State Republican ticket received 15,000 more votes in 1858 than Bissell had received two years earlier.

A regression of the vote in 1858 indicates the degree of change that had occurred within the Republican coalition (see Table 17).[59] The State vote carried at least 91 percent of the 1856 Fremont supporters and attracted an additional 7 percent, and possibly as high as 16 percent, of the Buchanan voters.[60] The Yankees, the English, and the Scandinavians remained the backbone of the Republican party, which slightly increased its support among the "other" U.S.-born voters from 51 to 63 percent. The Republican also made some outstanding gains in 1858. The French and the Canadians had not supported Fremont, but in 1858, close to 41 percent of the French and 32 percent of the Canadians voted Republican. While gaining these new voters, the Republicans were also able to maintain their German support. The only group to drop out of the coalition was the Irish. Apparently, Wentworth could not work a miracle twice with the Irish in Chicago.[61]

The shift in the Republican support provided by each ethnic group caused a change in the religious makeup of the party. The Republicans made significant gains among the pietists. In 1856, the pietists had been strongly for Fillmore, correlating at -.41 with the Fremont vote. In 1858, the pietists had only a -.09 correlation with the Republicans. The gain among the pietists, however, caused a corresponding decrease in liturgical support, to the point that there was virtually no correlation at all. These religious and ethnic changes in the Republican coalition signify the hardening of the lines of the realignment following the demise of the Know-Nothings. Republicans had brought the realignment into focus through their definition of the anti-slavery principles. They realized,

Table 17. Regression: 1858 Republican State Vote

	Multiple R	R Square	RSQ Change	Simple R	B	Beta
Percent Southern	.676	.457	.457	-.67	-3.332	-3.154
Percent Irish	.765	.585	.127	-.003	-3.459	-1.900
Percent Yankee	.817	.668	.083	.59	-1.148	-0.380
Pietist	.831	.691	.022	-.09	-0.487	-0.027
Acre Value	.844	.713	.022	.03	-0.694	-0.583
Farm Value	.850	.723	.010	.17	0.007	0.467
Capital Investment	.862	.744	.020	-.007	0.006	0.706
Liturgical	.872	.761	.017	.007	-3.535	-0.224
Percent Canadian	.874	.765	.003	.12	-2.300	-0.810
Baptist	.876	.767	.002	-.27	2.426	0.104
Percent Scandinavian	.878	.771	.003	.23	-2.284	-1.019
Value Produced	.880	.774	.003	.02	-0.001	-0.378
Farm Size	.881	.776	.002	.09	-0.045	-0.084
Percent French	.882	.778	.001	.27	-2.914	-0.569
Percent Other	.883	.781	.002	.21	-2.532	-2.250
Percent German	.884	.781	.0004	.22	-2.427	-1.918
Percent Illinois	.884	.782	.001	-.45	-2.376	-1.091
Percent English	.890	.793	.010	.36	-2.492	0.586
(constant)					322.516	

however, that their continued success depended upon a thorough organization that would ensure party regularity. The Bloomington convention in 1856 had authorized the formation of a State Central Committee charged with organizing the campaign. The Central Committee set up county committees in the manner of the old Whig and Democratic parties, but there were a number of innovations. The most important was that the Central Committee was made a permanent feature of the party. The party then was kept active and coordinated, and the Republicans did not have to recreate a new organization at every election. Another innovation the Republicans made was to extend party lines to the local level. Contests for town and county offices had formerly been carried on without reference to party names. The Republicans, however, made all elections a party affair and in doing so, brought more unity to the party.

A further change in party structure occurred when, in preparation for the 1858 campaign, Lincoln hired a professional party manager. Little can be determined about the man or what his exact duties were, but this was the first known time a man was employed in Illinois solely for the purpose of organizing a campaign.[62]

Probably the most significant change the Republicans brought to politics in the State campaign of 1858 was the unprecedented declaration that Lincoln was their choice for the Senate. Since a Senator was chosen by vote of the Legislature, the State elections had been conducted without reference to the Senate seat, and candidates were discussed only in the Legislative party caucus after the State campaign was concluded. The Republicans, however, realized the importance of having a publicly announced candidate before the elections. Gustave Koerner wrote that "to have a name to rally around at the commencement of a struggle is worth thousands of votes. . . . It will not do at this time, where the opponents have an idol which they at least pretend to worship, to meet with them with a possible contingent man."[63] The resolution that Lincoln was their candidate for the Senate bound the party closer together in 1858 and ended intrigues among the party's personalities before they began.

After the elections in 1858, the Republicans tightened their organization and created a far more unified and efficient structure than the Whigs or Democrats ever had. Instead of relying upon personalities, the Republicans depended entirely upon committees to conduct the campaigns. Rather than the local areas acting independently and creating their own organization in whatever form deemed necessary, the Republicans required each community to follow a uniform order. This regular and semi-permanent organization minimized haphazard arrangements and confusion.

The Central Committee took the lead in organizing the party. Declaring that "all that is needed to ensure our complete ascendency in every department of the State Government, is a proper organization . . ." the Republicans organized in every county an executive committee whose function was to create sub-committees in each precinct.[64] The county committee also was charged with collecting campaign funds to be turned over to the Central Committee. The Central Committee would direct workers to the county if needed, and send speakers and documents during the campaign. The party also instructed the local areas on the form of their organization and the procedure each area was to follow in calling for conventions and conducting campaigns.

By 1860 the State Committee was much more than a clearinghouse for information. The committee was completely in charge of the campaign. Accordingly, it sent circular letters to the county committees directing the entire organization.[65] The State Committee arranged for voter registration drives, supervised fund raisings, scheduled speaking engagements, and published campaign documents. In some cases where the local organization was divided over choice of candidates, the Committee even ordered primary elections. Although the local committees were still not a permanent feature of the party structure, the Republicans had managed to unify and bring regularity to the party.

Despite their strong organization, the Republicans were still plagued with the problems of personalities. Individual politicians had dominated the Whigs and the Democrats in the early 1850s to the point where personalities were more important than the party. Politicians created their own organization, made their own issues, and commanded the loyalty of the voters. Although personal political power was restricted by the importance of principles after 1856, individual politicians still could disrupt the party and damage the coalition. To insure the success of the party, the Republicans had to force the personalities to cooperate. It is a testimony to Lincon's political ability that the Republicans were not severely hurt by the struggles between personalities.

One of the disputes between personalities that threatened the Republican coalition was the battle David Davis waged against Owen Lovejoy for control of the Third Congressional District in Illinois. Lovejoy was one of the original Republicans in the State, having declared himself in 1854, but the Bloomington Republicans greatly feared his radicalism. Davis and a number of old Whigs conspired to defeat Lovejoy's nomination for Congress in 1856 by fielding their own candidate, Leonard Swett. When Lovejoy was nevertheless nominated by the Congressional convention, Davis gave no indication that he would accept the verdict. In fact, he planned to hold another convention to nominate Swett. With the local party about to be destroyed, Lincoln intervened and persuaded Davis to accept Lovejoy's nomination for the sake of unity.

> When I heard that Swett was beaten, and Lovejoy nominated, it turned me blind. . . . However, . . . seeing the people – their great enthusiasm for Lovejoy – considering the activity they will carry into the contest with him – and their great disappointment, if he should now be torn from them, I really think it best to let the matter stand.[66]

Without Lincoln's support, Davis quickly abandoned any plans he may have had of splitting the party with his own candidate. Much to Davis' credit, after receiving the letter from Lincoln, he did his best to smooth over hurt feelings, but much of the bitterness of the incident remained. One county committee issued a letter to the other committees in the district with a warning.

> We are sorry to say that some leading and influential Republicans are in the league to defeat Mr. L[ovejoy] and to such we can say that if they succeed in their plots it *must* and *will* forever damn them in this county should they hereafter be proposed as candidates for any office. . . . Now we think that personal prejudices or preferences should weigh nothing in a contest in which so much is involved as there is in the present – Defeat now in this matter will be defeat hereafter. Mark that![67]

Although a party split had been averted, the dispute between Davis and Lovejoy was not settled. In 1858, there was another move to dump Lovejoy. Davis and the old Whigs again thought about running an independent candidate. Ward H. Lamon explained the feelings of these men to Lincoln.

> I fear that Lovejoy's election a second term will put this congressional district irredeemingly in the hands of the abolitionists. . . . We all here, who were opposed to Lovejoy in convention feel a little *sore*. It is proposed by some of our friends to run an independent candidate.[68]

Lincoln had suspected that another attempt would be made to overthrow Lovejoy. Lovejoy was very popular with the voters in the district and Lincoln realized that if he were pushed aside in favor of someone else, the Republican cause would be damaged. Lincoln, consequently, warned Lovejoy early in March that he should prepare for opposition in the Congressional convention, but not wanting to offend the old Whigs, Lincoln remained apart from the contest. Upon receiving

Lamon's letter, however, he responded immediately. After again convincing Davis to accept Lovejoy's candidacy, Lincoln pressured all the dissident Republicans in the district to accept the verdict of the convention.

Two or three days ago I learned that McLean [county] had appointed delegates in favor of Lovejoy, and thenceforward I have considered his renomination a fixed fact. My *opinion* . . . remains unchanged that running an independent candidate against Lovejoy will not do — that it will result in nothing but disaster all round. In the first place whoever so runs will be beaten, and will be spotted for life; . . . and will in the end lose us the District altogether. There is no safe way but a convention; and if, in that convention upon a common platform, which all are willing to stand upon, one who has been known as an abolitionist but who is now occupying none but common ground, can get the majority of the voters to which *all* look for an election, there is no safe way but to submit.[69]

Ignoring Lincoln's advice, a number of old Whigs, led by T. Lyle Dickey, bolted the party and ran an independent candidate for Congress with Democratic support. But because of Lincoln's efforts, the vast majority of the Republicans, including David Davis, remained with Lovejoy. Although Davis never reconciled with Lovejoy, Lincoln kept the personalities from disrupting the party.

A far more serious threat to the Republicans than the Lovejoy-Davis dispute was the feud between John Wentworth and Norman B. Judd. The conflict had begun in the late 1840s, when both men were Democrats. After they became Republicans in 1856, their battle to control Chicago politics continued. In 1857, Wentworth won the Republican nomination for mayor after a long struggle against Judd and his friend, Ebenezer Peck. "Long John" went on to win the election but Judd and Peck continued their fight against him, and they were joined by Joseph Medill and Charles H. Ray, editors of the *Chicago Tribune*. Daily attacks upon Wentworth appeared in the *Tribune* and, by 1858, the Judd faction was accusing "Long John" of seeking to steal the Senate seat away from Lincoln. This charge was carefully calculated to bring Lincoln into the battle, but Wentworth headed off a confrontation with Lincoln by denying the charge. Wentworth hoped to earn the favor of Lincoln by informing him that Congressman Elihu Washburne was secretly in favor of Douglas. Once Washburne learned of Wentworth's accusation, he immediately joined the Judd faction in attempting to politically destroy the mayor. The conflict in Chicago was broadened even further when, after the election in 1858, Wentworth informed David Davis that Judd, as Chairman of the State Central Committee, was responsible for Lincoln's defeat. Wentworth charged that Judd had unwisely spent the party's treasury and that he had sacrificed Lincoln for his own ambition. Davis, convinced that Wentworth's assessment of Judd was correct, sought to impress Lincoln with the importance of removing Judd from the Central Committee. Although Lincoln tried to remain neutral in the struggle, he was finally forced into the fray when Wentworth charged that Lyman Trumbull had been unenthusiastic in his support of Lincoln. Reminding Davis of the Senatorial contest in 1854, Wentworth hinted that Trumbull again had subverted Lincoln.

The lines were clearly drawn. On one side stood Wentworth, Davis, and Swett. On the other was the *Tribune* clique: Judd, Peck, and Trumbull. In 1859, Wentworth, in the *Democrat*, began unceasing attacks upon Judd's financial honesty. At the same time, he started a whispering campaign that Judd was conspiring against Lincoln and wanted to be the next Governor. Furious, Judd reproached Lincoln for not stopping Wentworth and demanded that "Long John" be driven out of the party. Lincoln did admonish William Herndon and others to cease attacking Judd, but beyond that, he did nothing. Finally, Judd brought a $100,000 libel suit against Wentworth that forced Lincoln to try to settle the feud or watch the whole party be destroyed. Wentworth, in one last attempt to draw Lincoln to his side, asked Lincoln to represent him in court in the libel case. Lincoln refused, but he did offer to mediate the dispute.

Lincoln moved to bring peace to the party by drafting a public letter in support of Judd. He declared in the letter that Judd was not guilty of any treachery in the 1858 campaign and that his conduct as Chairman of the Central Committee deserved only praise. Lincoln also convinced Judd not to press his libel suit against Wentworth. After a long correspondence between Lincoln, Judd, and Wentworth, a truce was drawn. The peace, however, was short-lived. The battle erupted again over the gubernatorial nomination and the Cook county convention. Wentworth successfully blocked Judd's nomination for Govenor, but the *Tribune* clique carried the county convention. The feud continued through the National Republican Convention in Chicago and into the campaign of 1860. Even after Lincoln's election to the Presidency, the factions battled for cabinet positions, patronage, and influence. There appeared to be no solution to the problem. The Illinois Republican party was on the verge of an irreconcilable split when the firing upon Fort Sumter diverted all attention to the national crisis. Wentworth and Judd temporarily forgot their feud as the struggle for the Union took precedence.[70]

Despite the deep-seated personal hostilities, the party held together. Lincoln persuaded the personalities to cooperate during the campaigns and he kept most of them from bolting the party. Although the voters were now aligned by principle and not by loyalty to a particular personality, individual politicians still wielded a great deal of political power. Their battles for patronage and elective offices could still disrupt the newly formed party. Lincoln's genius was his ability to mediate the disputes; in doing so, he insured a united effort for the party at election time.

The election results in 1860 demonstrated more than anything else the success of the Republicans in building the party. Old loyalties had been overcome, voters had been unified by principle, and an efficient party structure had been erected to enforce regularity. All of these factors contributed to the Republican victory as Lincoln and the entire ticket swept the State. Douglas had finally been defeated and for only the second time in Illinois history, an opposition majority was elected to the Legislature, ensuring the reelection of Trumbull to the Senate.

The Republican Presidential, Congressional, and State tickets showed a high degree of cohesion, correlating at .99. The 1860 vote correlated with the 1858 election at .92 and with the 1856 contest at .91, demonstrating that the coalition had remained intact over time and that there was little shifting among the voters. A regression of the Presidential vote by previous elections shows that the Republicans carried virtually every voter who supported Fremont in 1856, and approximately 97 percent of the 1858 coalition.[71] This type of consistency had been missing in the old Whig and Democratic parties due to the lack of party regularity and the weakness of sustaining principles.

Table 18. Percentages Comparing Republican Vote, 1856-1860

	1856 Presidential	1858 State	1860 Presidential
Yankee	100	100	100
Southern	0	0	0
Illinois	0	0	0
Other	51	63	66
German	72	71	68
English	100	100	100
Irish	25	0	0
Scandinavian	100	100	100
Canadian	0	32	63
French	0	41	100

A regression of the Lincoln vote shows that no major changes had occurred in the ethnic, economic, or religious composition of the

Republican coalition since 1858 (see Table 18). There were, however, a number of subtle shifts. As was the case in 1858, the Republican vote was strengthened within each ethnic group. The French, for example, showed a major increase, from 41 percent Republican to near unanimous support for Lincoln. The Canadian vote also rose sharply from 32 to 63 percent Republican. The Republicans lost support only among the Germans. The slight decline in German support, however, is within the range of error of estimate by the regression.[72]

The regression also indicates that there was no major change in the religious composition of the Lincoln vote as compared with the Republican support in the 1858 election. Yankee pietists were still Republicans but, overall, pietism was not a major explanatory factor. By comparing the 1856 and 1860 votes, however, a change in the religious composition of the Republican vote can be more clearly seen (see Table 19). The Baptists and liturgicals showed little difference over time, but the pietists made a definite shift to the Republican column. In 1856, highly pietistic areas gave only 36 percent of their votes to Fremont, but by 1860 these same areas supported Lincoln by 51 percent. Pietists, however, were still not overwhelmingly Republican, because of ethnic considerations.

Table 19. Percentages Comparing Republican Vote by Religion

	1856	1860
Pietists		
None	74.0	47.8
Low	55.3	50.2
Medium	52.5	58.6
High	36.4	50.9
Liturgical		
None	42.4	51.6
Low	34.8	46.3
Medium	56.4	59.4
High	50.6	52.4
Baptists		
None	53.4	55.9
Low	42.2	49.5
Medium	33.7	51.0
High	47.0	Missing Value

As had been the case since 1856, the Southerners greatly influenced the voting patterns (see Table 20).[73] The Republican correlations with immigrant groups were much stronger in Egypt than they were in

Table 20. 1860 Republican Geographical Comparison

Northern Townships

	Multiple R	R Square	RSQ Change	Simple R	B	Beta
Farm Size	.86	.74	.74	.86	.262	0.840
Capital Investment	.96	.93	.18	-.60	.818	2.110
Liturgical	.98	.97	.04	-.74	-21.652	-2.027
Percent Canada	.99	.99	.01	.19	-.570	-0.111
Percent Southern	.99	.99	.008	-.40	-.549	-0.144
(constant)					58.22	

Northern and Central Townships

	Multiple R	R Square	RSQ Change	Simple R	B	Beta
Percent Southern	.78	.61	.61	-.78	-2.323	-1.953
Liturgical	.87	.76	.14	-.24	-0.835	-0.049
Percent Yankee	.88	.78	.02	.74	0.224	0.098
Percent Scandinavian	.90	.81	.03	.31	-0.747	-0.164
Percent German	.93	.86	.05	.25	-4.882	-2.505
Percent Other	.96	.93	.06	.02	-2.206	-1.655
Baptist	.98	.96	.03	-.32	13.086	0.558
Percent French	.98	.97	.01	.30	2.575	0.564
Farm Size	.99	.99	.01	-.21	-0.190	-0.427
Pietist	.99	.99	.003	-.01	9.017	0.464
Percent Irish	.99	.99	.002	-.24	-0.622	-0.266
Percent Illinois	.99	.99	.0004	-.58	-0.456	-0.199
(constant)					210.76	

Southern Townships

	Multiple R	R Square	RSQ Change	Simple R	B	Beta
Southern	.91	.84	.84	-.91	-0.73	-0.72
French	.96	.92	.07	.71	8.37	2.32
German	.97	.94	.02	.75	-1.41	-1.68
Farm Size	.99	.98	.03	.15	0.15	0.28
Irish	.99	.99	.008	.07	0.70	0.07
Baptist	.99	.99	.002	-.35	-2.60	-0.10
Scandinavian	.99	.99	.001	.46	-5.77	-0.30
(constant)					54.77	

northern Illinois. The Germans, for example, correlated with the Republican vote in the southern counties at a strong .75, but in the northern and central parts of the State, at a significantly weaker .25. A similar pattern existed for other immigrant groups like the French and the Scandinavians. The correlations of the Lincoln vote to liturgicals shows to what extent the presence of Southerners pushed immigrant groups into the Republican camp. In the northern townships, the liturgicals were strongly anti-Republican, as indicated by a -.74 correlation. In the central counties, however, the correlation dropped dramatically to a -.24 correlation. When Egypt is added to the regression, the overall liturgical correlation to the Lincoln vote becomes an insignificant .08. Besides their effect on the vote of the liturgical immigrants, the Southerners in Illinois, most of whom were pietists, accounted for the weak correlation between the Republicans and pietism. The Republican coalition was a pluralistic combination of immigrants and native-born voters, pietists and liturgicals, united in their opposition not only to the slave power in the nation, but also to the Southerners in Illinois.

With the election of Lincoln to the Presidency, the Republicans had accomplished a major transformation in politics. They had overcome old party ties and had united the discordant elements of the anti-Nebraska factions into a new party. Voters divided by old animosities had been forged into a new coalition on the principles of anti-slavery. It was the Republicans, and not the Whigs, the anti-slavery Democrats, or any other faction, that had successfully defined the principles which brought the new coalition into existence. Lincoln wrote that the "party is newly formed; and in forming old party ties had to be broken, and the attractions of party pride, and influential leaders were wholly wanting. In spite of old differences, prejudices, and animosities, its members were drawn together by a paramount common danger."[74] The danger was slavery. Speaking at the Cooper Institute in New York, Lincoln declared that "their thinking it [slavery] right, and our thinking it wrong, is the precise fact upon which depends the whole controversy."[75]

This new coalition had been solidified by a vigorous party organization, and now, in 1860, the Republicans had become the majority party. This radical change in politics in the short span of four years prompted Horace White, editor of the *Chicago Tribune* to write, "We live in revolutionary times & I say God bless the revolution."[76]

6

Democrats

The rapid growth of the Illinois Republican party from 1856 to 1860 reflected the polarization of the voters. The realignment, originally a reaction to the Kansas-Nebraska Act, accelerated in response to the tumultuous events in Kansas, and the opportunity was not lost on the organizers of the new party. The Republicans were successful in building a coalition because they aggressively pursued the slavery question and because they accurately defined the stages of the anti-slavery sentiment.

The history of the Democratic party during these years stands in marked contrast to the Republican development. The Democrats had everything to lose by the polarization of voters, and consequently, they tried to forestall the realignment. Initially, they attempted to sidestep the slavery question by claiming that nativism was the real issue of the day. Failing in that strategy, the Democrats tried to straddle the slavery issue and proclaim themselves to be the moderates between two unreasonable extremes. While Lincoln declared that the nation could not endure half slave and half free, Douglas was saying that he cared not whether slavery was voted up or down. The Democratic strategy brought temporary success in 1858, but in the end the position was impossible to maintain.

Douglas, the architect of the Democratic policy, pursued his plan with determination and energy. The party, however, had been weakened by long years of his personal rule and it began to break under the tension of the realignment. Douglas found it increasingly difficult to maneuver his party on the nearly impossible course he had set for it. When war finally broke out in 1861, both Douglas and the Illinois Democracy were broken.

The elections of 1854 stunned Douglas. He expected that the Democrats would lose some ground, but he was completely unprepared for the magnitude of the defeat. Surveying the situation, he realized that unless something was done, the anti-Nebraska forces would coalesce into the majority party. In December, Douglas initiated the strategy he would follow for the next two years: he ordered his lieutenants in Illinois to attack nativism. By making that the central issue, he hoped to neutralize the divisiveness in his own party on the Nebraska question and to divert public attention away from the slavery problem. "The Nebraska question is over," Douglas wrote, "and Know Nothingism has taken its place as the chief issue in the future."[1] In a letter to the editor of the *Chicago Times*, Douglas explained his future strategy. "We will gain more votes than we will lose on Nebraska and No Nothingism. You ought to publish the exposition of No Nothingism . . . and charge into them every day boldly and disputedly. That will bring the Germans and all other foreigners and Catholics to our side."[2] Before the 1855 election for the Senate in the Legislature, Douglas began to put his plan into operation by attacking as nativists those who opposed the reelection of James Shields. "At all events our friends should stand by Shields and throw the responsibility on the Whigs of beating him *because he was born in Ireland* . . . [and] it will be apparent . . . to the whole country that a gallant Soldier and a faithful servant has been stricken down because of the place of his birth."[3]

In 1855, a lull in events agitating the public on the slavery issue and the growth of the temperance and nativist movements, made the Democratic strategy successful. The anti-Nebraska forces became hopelessly divided, and many of the moderate anti-slavery men returned to the Democracy. Every time an anti-Nebraska newspaper tried to raise the Kansas question, the Democrats responded with charges of deception. In reaction to an editorial on the growing violence in Kansas, for example, the Democrats accused the *Illinois State Journal* with duping the public.

> Ignoring the prominent issues now before the country in regard to the rights of conscience and the proscription of foreign-born, the Illinois Journal, conscious of the whig and abolition character of the Thug [Know Nothing] organization, attempts to smother these questions with columns about 'outrage in Kansas'. For weeks its columns have teemed with twaddle on this subject while it even affected not to understand the issue involved between the Hindoes and the democracy! The Journal will find that it cannot blink the question which its party friends are making by hugging the nigger, while it winks at the Thug.[4]

The eruption of violence in Kansas, however, nullified the Democratic tactic of deflecting attention away from the slavery issue. As the shootings and burnings progressed into full scale warfare, it became impossible for the Democrats to ignore the slavery question. Douglas was forced to change his strategy, but because the attacks on the Know-Nothings had restored some unity to the Democracy and had kept the anti-Nebraska forces divided, he decided to confront the renewed anti-slavery agitation by combining nativism and anti-slavery into a single issue.

The abolition fanatics, Douglas charged, were nothing more than sectarian zealots. "In the future," the Democrats declared, "the Know-Nothings will fight under the banner of abolition but at heart they are still hindoos because all abolitionists hate catholics and foreigners."[5] In contrast to this band of fanatics, the Democrats portrayed themselves as defenders of the Union. "The only questions now presented," declared one Democratic newspaper, "are the stability of the constitution, and the right of the people to self-government."[6]

In allying the "isms," Douglas expected to dislodge the foreign-born voters and the old Whigs from the anti-Nebraska factions. Charging the anti-Nebraska groups with nativism, he hoped, would draw the immigrants into the Democratic party, while the attack upon the anti-slavery advocates as disunionists was calculated to capture the old Whigs by appealing to their sense of patriotism. The *Register* declared that the Whigs "will not swallow rank abolitionism and black intolerance simply for the purpose of putting demagogues in office."

> The future will show that the old Henry Clay national whigs . . . have cut loose forever from the abolition know nothing alliance which was got up by demagogues as a substitute for the old whig party. These leaders will find that their old followers prefer to take refuge in the democratic ranks rather than aid such a cause.[7]

As proof that an alliance of threatening "isms" existed, the Democrats pointed to the call by the anti-Nebraska newspaper editors to meet at Decatur to discuss plans for cooperation in the 1856 election. In reference to the Decatur convention, the *Joliet Signal* wrote: "It was a zebra affair, indeed, comprising abolitionists, ex-whigs, renegade democrats, and renegade know-nothings, antagonistic in everything, except hatred of Douglas and democracy."[8] Again, the Democrats viewed the move to form the Republican party at Bloomington as nothing more than a fusion of nativists, temperance men, and abolitionists, uniting for the purpose of gaining public office. One Democratic newspaper wrote a parody of the proceedings.

> Know Nothingism said: 'Foreigners must be kept out of the country.' The Prohibitionists replied: 'We agree with you, cut off the supply of beer and whisky, and the Dutch and Irish will keep out of the State.' Good! but how are we to get the abolitionists, without whom we can do nothing? Easy enough, they are proverbially *moral* men, naturally inclined against drinking, they will readily go with us, if we will aid them in their war upon the slave States. The bargain was struck, the *fusion* completed and an

> alliance formed between the K. Nothings, abolitionists, and Maine Law
> men, who prostituted the name of 'Republican' to the base purpose of
> representing their coalition. Their organization embraced *five* points:
> Hatred to Foreigners! Down with Catholics! No more Slave States! Trial
> by jury for fugitive slaves! And no more spiritous or malt liquors, but for
> mechanical, medicinal or sacramental purposes![9]

All that was lacking from this new party, according to another paper, was
"woman's rights . . . to make it a complete hotchpotch of all sorts of
loose-ended and straggling doctrines."[10]

One benefit the Democrats hoped to gain by identifying the
Republicans as a combination of anti-slavery, temperance, and Know-
Nothing fanatics was to capture the German vote. William A. Richardson
wrote to Douglas that "time is thrown away upon any other Germans
except Catholics" unless the Know-Nothings were tied to the Republican
party.[11] Toward that end, the Democrats labored hard in the campaign.
The *Register* declared that "the vile projects of the corrupt clique of
combined know-nothings and abolitionists . . . are without a parallel in
partisan corruption. They one day appeal to German prejudices and
another to that of nativism." The Germans were being duped, the
Democrats charged, because if the Republicans win they will "be cheated
and the proscription of know-nothingism . . . is to be carried out."[12]
Gustave Koerner remembered that during the campaign he came upon a
Democratic rally in the heavily German St. Clair county where the
speaker was attacking the Republicans as "long-faced, white-livered,
hypocritical Yankees" who cheated honest men. "They would not allow
a man to cook meals on the Sabbath, or kiss his wife, or take a walk for
pleasure," Koerner reported the speaker to have said, and the man
continued that the Republicans would not allow the Germans to drink or
sing and dance.[13]

The final note of the Democratic appeal to the immigrants was the
charge that the Republicans, at the same time they desired to deny
foreigners their rights, intended to elevate the Negro.

> All the abolitionists, from Garrison to Lovejoy, support Fremont, and that
> means up with the *Darkies.* Col. Fremont was nominated by the Northern
> Know-Nothing Convention, . . . on a pledge to the Massachusetts
> delegation that he would carry out their policy in regard to foreigners.
> This is a pretty 'kettle of fish' truely. Imagine a big, burly, thick-lipped
> African crowding Gen. Shields away from the polls on election day. That
> is the practical working of the Fusion policy.[14]

While hoping to draw the immigrants back into the party, the
Democrats in 1856 were also attempting to prevent the old Whigs from

joining the Republicans. Although the party appealed outright for former Whig support, Douglas believed that the best he could hope for was to keep the Whigs in an independent American party. Confident that a large Fillmore vote would result in a Democratic victory, Douglas emphasized the abolition character of the Republican-Know Nothing alliance in order to frighten moderate anti-slavery Whigs into maintaining their independence. At the same time, the argument that the American party had been captured by the Republicans would dislodge the "Sam" wing of the party and leave them with no political alternatives except to join the Democracy as the party of the Union.

To carry out their strategy, the Democrats gave financial aid to the "Sam" faction of the Know-Nothings. They publicized widely the letter written by Buckner S. Morris, the American party gubernatorial Candidate, attacking the Republicans as abolitionists. W.W. Danenhower's *Chicago Citizen*, financed by the Democrats and printed by the *Chicago Times*, was an important tool in Douglas' strategy. Each of its articles criticizing the "Jonathans" was reprinted across the State. Typical of these attacks by Danenhower was one charging that the "Jonathans" designed to commit the American party to the "ultraism of anti-slavery" while ignoring the real sentiments of the Know-Nothings.[15] Thus while the Democrats were supporting the "Sam" faction in order to keep the Whigs from joining the Republicans, at the same time, they were attacking the Know-Nothings as a tool of the abolitionists. The *Register* warned the Whigs that the American party "is the wooden horse, to be used in Central and Southern Illinois, where abolitionism is at a discount, to effect the purposes openly avowed by 'black republicanism' in the northern section of the state."[16]

The strategy of characterizing the Republicans as nativists to draw the foreign vote, and of charging the Know-Nothings with abolitionism to attract the old Whigs, represented only part of the Democratic appeal in 1856. Combining the "isms" into a single enemy had benefits as a specific political tactic, but it also functioned as a unifying symbol of all that the Democratic party was against: the violation of American freedom by fanatics. In particular, the Democrats stood against the introduction of religion into politics, viewing the combination as a kind of moral imperialism that threatened to destroy individual freedom. The Democrats regarded society as requiring a balance between liberty and religion.

> Religion is a powerful instrument in restraining the excesses of liberty, and liberty in combating that disposition to encroach on human rights which seems almost an instinct of the state church. In this way, when properly balanced, they maintain a due equilibrium between the despotism of one

> and the licentiousness of the other.   Liberty without religion is an unbridled savage; religion without liberty is an unmitigated tyrant. . . .[17]

The Democrats believed that the "isms" had prostituted religion and morality for political purposes and that they had consequently upset the balance in society. The Democrats sought to restore the balance by preserving liberty against the political priesthood of the fanatics.

The pietistic doctrine of perfection, with its corollary of rooting out sin by legislation, was the antithesis of the Democratic ideal of a balance between liberty and religion. That is why the Democrats opposed liquor legislation, although they felt that intemperance was a terrible evil. Nothing could be more dangerous to freedom than moralistic politics. The petition by 3,000 clergymen in New England against the Kansas-Nebraska Act, and the letter signed by 25 Chicago clergy condemning Douglas for his lack of reverence toward man and God, were viewed by the Democrats as the final assault upon liberty by pietistic fanatics. The Chicago clergy had declared:

> We protest against it [the Kansas-Nebraska Bill] as a great moral wrong; as a breach of faith eminently injurious to the moral principles of the community, and subversive of all confidence in national engagements; as a matter full of danger to the peace, and even existence of our beloved Union, and exposing us to righteous judgments of the Almighty.[18]

Douglas' response to the Chicago clergymen stands as a complete statement of the Democratic position. He expressed astonishment that these clergymen had presumed to be authorized by God to make judgments upon political questions. "I fear," Douglas wrote, "that it is your purpose to claim and exercise this prerogative of the Deity upon legislative and political questions." If the claims of the clergy that "the ministry is the divinly [sic] appointed institution for the declaration and enforcement of God's will upon all points of moral and religious truths" were accepted, Douglas argued, then there would be no limit to their temporal power. The claims of the clergy to divine authority, Douglas pointed out, were subversive of the principles of the republic, just as the Mormons' had been.[19] If the clergy were allowed to judge legislation, then there was no need for Congress. Why not, Douglas argued ironically, dispense with government and let this divinely appointed group supervise the secular as well as the spiritual interests of the people? The reason was that history had shown a church with secular power to be the most fearful and corrupting of all forms of despotism. Douglas declared that America's forefathers had understood the need for a balance between church and state, and for that reason had provided for a separation of the two powers.   He concluded his response to the Chicago clergy with a question.

> Do you wish to have the people of this country to understand that you claim the Divine authority for saying that it is 'a great moral wrong,' a violation 'of God's will,' and an infringement of His Holy Law, for Congress to allow the people of the Territories to enact and establish for themselves their own laws and institutions, in obedience to the Constitution their fathers have made, and to remove all legal obstructions in the way of the exercise of such rights?[20]

Temperance, Know-Nothingism, and anti-slavery were different expressions of the same intent of certain denominations to interfere with politics and, hence, freedom. "The Cross of Christ," declared one minister in a sermon, "is taken down from its high place as the crowning glory of the sanctuary, and in its stead — as an engine of reform — is lifted the ballot box; and the popular passions are lashed into storm, that with their suffrage as freemen they may carry a Main law or defeat a Nebraska bill." All of the aims of these religious groups were worthy objectives, but, according to the minister, they were a part of a moral logrolling for "ruffian demagogues seeking preferment and place."[21] Many Democrats spoke out in the sincere belief that the nation was endangered by a political priesthood.   John Reynolds, the old Governor of Illinois, declared that "it is the imperious [*sic*] duty of every patriot without looking to the consequence, 'to cry aloud and spare not,' until a religious fanatical sect of Puritans in New England, who are undermining the Union, are prostrated and annihilated as a party."[22]

The image of the Democrats as defenders of freedom against the allied "isms" of the fanatics was a powerful one in the campaign of 1856, but an examination of the voting returns reveals that Douglas' strategy missed the mark (see Table 21).[23]   While Buchanan carried Illinois in the Presidential contest, the entire Democratic ticket for state offices went down in defeat.

Historians have long recognized the difficulty the Know-Nothings posed for the Republican party, but the effect of the American party upon the Democrats has been ignored.   In Illinois, the nativists were pietistic, but also Southern-born.   While Fillmore's candidacy deprived the Republicans of many pietists, it also drew many Southern and Illinois-born voters away from the Democratic camp.   Know-Nothingism cut across the realignment on slavery and, consequently, Douglas' attempt to manipulate the issue cut into his own voter base as well as the Republicans'.   Douglas calculated that the issue of nativism would divide the Republican party, but in fact, the Know-Nothings hurt the

Democracy. The Southerners and the Illinois-born were the mainstays of the Democracy in 1856, with the Southerners alone explaining 69 percent of the variance in the vote. Douglas' strategy, however, caused a decline in Democratic support from these two groups. The issue of nativism attracted many of these voters to Fillmore.

Table 21. Regression: 1856 Democratic Presidential Vote

	Multiple R	R Square	RSQ Change	Simple R	B	Beta
Percent Southern	.830	.690	.690	.83	4.124	3.494
Value Produced	.864	.748	.057	-.007	0.002	0.746
Percent Other	.883	.780	.032	-.16	3.234	2.376
Acre Value	.904	.818	.037	-.22	1.592	1.368
Farm Value	.909	.826	.008	-.38	-0.024	-1.509
Farm Size	.927	.860	.033	-.10	0.583	1.014
Percent French	.941	.886	.026	-.31	8.608	1.719
Percent Canadian	.947	.897	.010	-.41	5.750	0.453
Percent English	.953	.908	.011	-.43	4.264	0.976
Liturgical	.961	.924	.015	-.09	6.825	0.346
Percent Scandinavian	.970	.942	.017	-.24	1.812	0.263
Capital Investment	.974	.949	.007	-.06	-0.005	-0.596
Percent Yankee	.976	.952	.003	-.63	0.761	0.248
Percent Irish	.983	.967	.014	-.34	3.923	1.289
Percent Illinois	.986	.973	.005	.48	2.443	1.097
Pietist	.987	.974	.0003	.25	2.237	0.084
Percent German	.987	.975	.001	-.35	1.748	1.237
Baptist	.987	.975	.0001	.20	-0.525	-0.018
(constant)					-325.895	

Avoiding the slavery issue and charging the Republicans with nativism failed to dislodge many foreign voters from the anti-slavery camp. Although the French and the Canadians were drawn into the party, the more important German bloc still voted only 22 percent Democratic. The other part of Douglas' strategy, charging the Republicans with abolitionism, also failed to bring many new voters into the party. Of the old Whigs, the Southerners had already joined the Democracy, and all but 20 percent of the "other" U.S.-born supported either Fillmore or Fremont.[24]   Finally, despite Douglas' stand against pietistic intrusion into politics, the Democrats received more support from the pietists and the Baptists than they did from the liturgicals. Slavery overshadowed the other issues in 1856 and it left the Democracy with a southern-based coalition. Egypt became the stronghold of the Democratic party, so much so that one Republican paper claimed that when "Douglas takes snuff, Egypt sneezes."[25]

Douglas was quick to realize that his strategy of ignoring the slavery issue was a disaster. Unless he changed his campaign tactics, Douglas knew that the Republicans would win the coming election in 1858. Realizing, further, that his own Senate seat would be in jeopardy, he abandoned his policy of covert aid to the Know-Nothings and moved to appeal directly for old Whig support. Toward this end, he portrayed the Democrats as the party of the Union, and therefore, the only party moderate enough to find a compromise to end the slavery issue. In effect, Douglas was now straddling the slave issue instead of ignoring it. In a letter to John A. McClernand, he expressed his hope for the new course.

> What course will the National Whigs pursue now that the issue is distinctly made up between Fremont abolitionism on the one side and constitutional-law-abiding-Union-loving men under the Democratic banner on the other side. So long as this issue is pending there can be no third party. Will not the Union men of the old Whig party go with us?[26]

Douglas' strategy won over some of the Old Whigs, but it brought him into conflict with his own party. In the end, Douglas' new policy was no more effective than the old one.

The first action Douglas undertook to broaden the Democratic appeal in Illinois was his stand against accepting the pro-slavery Lecompton Constitution for Kansas. Douglas' image was dramatically altered by his opposition to the Buchanan administration on this issue. Instead of being widely considered a pro-slavery demagogue who had despoiled the nation by repealing the Missouri Compromise, Douglas was now viewed increasingly as a defender of principles and the protector of the Union against extremists. Even many Republicans began to think of Douglas as a new anti-slavery champion. Douglas' strategy, however, was not to become an anti-slavery advocate, but to undercut the Republican strength by standing as a moderate between two extremes. The *Chicago Times* stated explicitly Douglas' policy in regard to Kansas.

> We know that any attempt to force a pro-slavery constitution upon the people without the opportunity of voting it down at the polls, will be regarded . . . as so decidedly unjust, oppressive and unworthy of a free people, that the people of the United States will not sanction it. . . . Kansas is to be a Free State! That fact being ascertained, let the Convention frame a Constituion to suit her best interests upon all other questions, and let the prohibition of slavery be put into it, clearly, and without quibble, plainly without disguise, explicitly, broadly, and firmly. Let the Convention then submit that Constitution to the people. If it be adopted, Kansas will come into the Union at the next session, and the Republican party will expire for want of sustenance.[27]

During the campaign in 1858, and particularly in the debates with Lincoln, Douglas expanded his new role as a moderate. Douglas identified himself with Henry Clay, the Compromise of 1850, and popular sovereignty, to substantiate his claim as a strong Union man devoted to solving the slavery crisis. The key to Douglas' stand was popular sovereignty, which he presented as the solution to the slavery question. The fraudulent Lecompton Constitution, he maintained, violated the principles of this compromise and therefore, forced the "Little Giant" to oppose its adoption.

Although Douglas' anti-Lecompton stand captured for him most of the middle ground on the slavery question, his position was precarious. The Dred Scott decision, the Republicans charged, had negated popular sovereignty by opening all the territories to slavery. In order to secure his stance as the new "Great Compromiser," Douglas was forced to move further away from the administration's position, which was expressed by the Supreme Court decision. The apparent contradiction between popular sovereignty and the Dred Scott decision compelled Douglas to argue for his own interpretation of the case.

In the second debate with Lincoln, at Freeport, Illinois, Douglas attempted to resolve the contradiction between his position on slavery in the territories and the Dred Scott case. Douglas declared that "if the people of the Territory want slavery, they will encourage it by passing affirmatory laws . . . [and] if they do not want it they will withhold that legislation and by withholding it slavery is as dead as if it was prohibited by a constitutional prohibition."[28] The "Freeport Doctrine" firmly established Douglas as a moderate by reconciling the inconsistencies between his support for the Dred Scott decision and his stand on popular sovereignty. Like Henry Clay, Douglas was willing to save the Union through compromise.

Besides presenting himself as a moderate, Douglas also hoped to attract the old Whigs by manipulating the Negro question. The Republican party, the Democrats warned the Whigs, was not anti-Nebraska but pro-abolition. It was "a nigger-stealing, stinking, putrid, abolition party, and has for its prime object the repeal of the Fugitive Slave law, and the placing of niggers above white men in legal rights, intelligence and everything else."[29] The Democrats constantly charged the Republicans with advocating Negro equality, playing upon the prejudices of the voters. As if equality with the Negro was not repulsive enough for most voters, the Democrats also attacked the Republicans as being less than men for advocating such nonsense.

The inhabitants of the northern part of the Sucker State . . . are universally known as the most moral, religious, respectable, intelligent and refined people on the face of the earth. It is no wonder that they have become so, for from their earliest infancy the children are trained to a life of morality and usefulness. They are fed entirely upon mush-and-milk and weak gruel, and kept in hothouses, that their brains and bodies may become soft and spongy, so as to be delicately susceptible of all humane emotions. At the same time their ears are stuffed with cotton, it being considered that the noise of the distresses of those around them might grate too harshly upon their susceptible nerves, and thus render them unable to hear the complaints of the suffering Feejee Islanders and natives of Congo and South Carolina. Their lungs, however, are trained to hard usage, the children being daily made to yell vehemently, and to imitate cats, crows, parrots and cur-dogs, so that they may be able to shriek lustily for freedom, and make abolition speeches. They are early taught to believe in God, who made man in his own image and the colored man a little more so, and whose chief occupation is to send slave-holders to the infernal regions, fight for freedom in Kansas, and aid their election of 'Republican' candidates.[30]

Another aspect of the Douglas strategy was to flatter the Whigs and to deify Henry Clay. The Democratic press constantly mourned the death of Whiggery. The Douglas newspapers always asked, where were the old Whigs to go? In answer to their own inquiry, the Democrats offered their own party as the only one which was truly national in spirit. "The disbanded Whig . . . is in a position to scrutenise [*sic*] impartially the principles and objects of all the parties which are now exist, and deliberately determine to affiliate with the one having the strongest claims to nationality. We think that the Democratic party . . . is the only one now, which has any respectable claim to that virtue."[31]

The Democrats hoped to influence undecided Whigs by reporting on how few of the old Whig party supported the Republicans. The *Joliet Signal* observed that in a recent Republican convention, only five old Whigs had been in attendance out of 41 delegates.[32] A related Democratic tactic was to publicize conversions of old Whig leaders to the Democracy. One of the more important old Whigs to become a Democrat was Don E. Morrison. Morrison had been an anti-Nebraska man but he could not tolerate the fanatics, the Democrats reported, and he was "compelled by his allegiance to the Union to turn around, be a Nebraska man, and support the principles of the bill as the final settlement of the slavery question."[33] E. B. Webb was another Whig to convert to the Democrats. In a public letter printed in the *Register*, Webb said that a Republican victory would end the Union. "I hate slaves and slavery," Webb wrote, and "I would do anything—pay heavily—to get rid of them." "But this *can't* be done," he continued,

"Our fathers found it, and were obliged to submit to it. We can do no better."[34]

Letters constantly appeared in the Democratic newspapers signed "An Old Whig Farmer" or simply "A Whig" telling of the writers' intent to vote for Douglas. One letter that Douglas personally received was typical.

> *Whig* as I am, it makes my heart glad to behold the defeat of fanaticism in the Republican ranks[.] That party has got filled up with a *swarm* of negro worshipers [*sic*] who base their political creed on that question *alone.* They had better read Henry Clay's speech to the fanatics of Indiana when they petitioned him to set his slaves free.[35]

The conversion of a Whig newspaper was a cause of great delight among the Democrats. The *Winchester Chronicle* was one such paper that declared for Douglas and the union party of the Democracy. "We have always been a whig," the newspaper stated, "but we must confess, that for the last few years, there has been little difference discoverable between the principles of the whig and the democratic party."[36]

By far the most important help Douglas received in his bid for old Whig support came from Senator John J. Crittenden of Kentucky. Crittenden, leaning toward Douglas after the Lecompton battle, urged Lyman Trumbull "to have no controversy with Douglas." Lincoln was aware of Crittenden's influence with Illinois Whigs and he warned the Senator "that you would better be hands off!" Late in the campaign in 1858, Crittenden wrote a public letter endorsing Douglas. He explained to Lincoln that the "Little Giant's" reelection was necessary as a "rebuke to the administration, and a vindication of the great cause of popular rights & public justice."[37] The Democrats were ecstatic over Crittenden's support; Thomas L. Harris claimed that it would bring the party "20,000 American and old line whig votes in the center & the south[ern counties]."[38]

Harris' estimate of the effect of the Crittenden letter was probably exaggerated, but overall the Douglas strategy was successful in the election of 1858. Although most historians have emphasized the significance of the Know-Nothing-Republican alliance, most of the former Fillmore supporters in Illinois voted Democratic. This resulted from Douglas' appeal to the old Whigs, his characterization of the Republicans as fanatics, and his straddling of the slavery issue which brought many of the Southern and Illinois-born nativists into the party. Overall, the Democrats attracted approximately 27 percent of the Fillmore voters, while the Republicans gained virtually no Know-Nothing support.[39]

The ethnic divisions in the electorate remained basically the same (see Table 22)[40] as they had been in 1856, except for the increased Democratic strength among the Southern and Illinois-born voters. Many of

Table 22. Regression: 1858 Democratic State Vote

	Multiple R	R Square	RSQ Change	Simple R	B	Beta
Percent Southern	.676	.457	.457	.67	3.846	3.527
Percent Irish	.766	.587	.129	.005	4.025	2.142
Percent Yankee	.827	.685	.098	-.61	1.469	0.471
Pietist	.841	.708	.023	.09	0.040	0.002
Acre Value	.851	.724	.015	-.06	0.649	0.528
Capital Investment	.855	.732	.008	.0009	-0.007	-0.736
Farm Value	.869	.755	.022	-.18	-0.006	-0.390
Liturgical	.876	.768	.012	-.01	2.920	0.179
Percent Canadian	.877	.770	.002	-.11	2.842	0.970
Baptist	.879	.772	.002	.28	-2.615	-0.109
Value Produced	.880	.775	.002	-.02	0.001	0.395
Percent Scandinavian	.881	.777	.002	-.22	2.816	1.217
Farm Size	.882	.779	.001	-.08	0.016	0.029
Percent English	.883	.779	.0007	-.36	3.075	0.700
Percent French	.883	.780	.0005	-.29	3.315	0.628
Percent Other	.884	.782	.001	-.20	3.050	2.626
Percent German	.884	.782	.0002	-.23	2.937	2.249
Percent Illinois	.894	.799	.017	.46	2.912	1.296
(constant)					-271.668	

these people had been Whigs and had voted for Fillmore, but in 1858, they were solidly Democratic. Douglas also attracted more of the "other" U.S.-born voters. In 1858, the "other"-born voted about 36 percent for the Democrats, while in 1856 most had been either Republican or Know-Nothing. The party, however, lost 31 percent of the Canadians and 41 percent of the French.[41]

As for the effect of religion upon the Democratic vote, only the Baptists provided substantial support. The moralistic appeal of the Republicans had drawn to that party almost all of the pietists who were not Southern or Illinois-born, while at the same time maintaining the support of many of the liturgical immigrants. The 1858 Democratic vote did show a slight increase in liturgical support but the overall correlation remained very low. The increased Democratic support among the liturgicals came from the Irish and the Germans. The Irish, almost all of whom lived in Chicago, had been tricked by John Wentworth in 1856 into voting Republican, but in 1858 they avoided "Long John" and carefully cast their ballots for the Democratic party. The return of some of the German voters in 1858, however, was a different matter. Douglas' policy of straddling the slavery issue in combination with the Republican attacks upon Catholicism brought a number of the Germans back into the Democracy.

Although the State ticket again lost in the election, the Legislature was returned with a Democratic majority that insured Douglas' reelection to the Senate. Charles Lanphier fired off a letter to Douglas proclaiming a great victory: "Glory to God and the Sucker Democracy. Douglas 54, Lincoln 46." To which Douglas responded: "Let the voice of the people rule."[42] Douglas believed that he was vindicated by the people, and therefore was convinced that he should pursue to the end his course of straddling the slave issue. Of Douglas' arguments during the campaign, the "Freeport Doctrine" in particular had saved Illinois for the "Little Giant," by firmly establishing him in the middle ground on slavery. But as Lincoln astutely pointed out after the election, Douglas' strategy could bring only temporary success. "Douglas had the ingenuity to be supported in the late contest as the best means to *break down* and to *uphold* the slavery interest," Lincoln wrote, but "no ingenuity can keep those antagonistic elements in harmony long."[43]

All of Douglas' efforts after the election in 1858 were directed toward that impossible task of maintaining the middle ground. However, he found himself irretrievably cut off from the administration. Douglas' anti-Lecompton stand so provoked Buchanan that the President began to strip Douglas of all of his patronage and to build his own party in Illinois. The Danites, as the Buchanan party in Illinois was called, posed a severe problem for Douglas, and this split in the party aggravated existing tensions. With all the resentments built up over the years of Douglas' domination exploited by the split, the weakness of the party stemming from personal rule was never more apparent.

Douglas' decision to oppose the Buchanan administration on the Lecompton Constitution surprised most of the party in Illinois. Characteristically, the "Little Giant" mapped out his own strategy without consulting his followers. The implications of Douglas' action were so drastic that the party was thrown into confusion and even John McClernand, the Senator's chief spokesman in the House of Representatives, had to write Douglas for a clarification and an explanation of what the party should do. In his response, Douglas wrote that "we must stand firmly by the principle of t[he] Kansas organic act, which guarantees the right of t[he] people . . . to form and regulate their own institutions in their own way."[44] The Lecompton Constitution was a fraud, Douglas argued, and hence violated the principle of the Kansas-Nebraska Act. The anti-Lecompton stand helped Douglas establish himself nationally as the leading moderate on the slavery question, but the Senator found that it was not so easy to bring his own Illinois party into line.

President Buchanan's determination to build a loyal party in Illinois in retaliation against Douglas' anti-Lecompton stand provided an opportunity for a number of politicians to challenge the Senator's rule. One of the more spectacular personal feuds intensified by the Douglas-Buchanan split was the battle between James W. Sheahan, editor of the *Chicago Times,* and Isaac Cook, postmaster of Chicago. Sheahan and Cook had been struggling since 1856 for control of the *Times* and the party in Chicago. Through Douglas' efforts, Cook was eventually eased out of the *Times,* but the rancor of the feud persisted.[45] In 1858, when Buchanan was searching for men to organize the Danites, he found Cook a willing supporter. Cook was re-appointed postmaster of Chicago, and he directed all of Buchanan's efforts to upset Douglas' control of the State. Sheahan became Cook's special target, the object of a constant barrage of attacks.[46] The loss of patronage and of government printing contracts drove the *Times* to the brink of bankruptcy, which threw the whole party in Chicago into chaos.

Douglas found his personal rule challenged in other districts as well. In one area, a loyal Douglas supporter wrote to the Senator complaining that the newspaper and the post office had been captured by the Danites and were being used to rule the party.

> For the last two years, Stevens & Pine, self-constituted leaders, or rather dictators, having in view their personal, rather than the political welfare of the party, have inaugerated [sic] a different policy. All who could not be used as willing tools have been put under the ban [i.e., kept out of office]—all who were supposed to be in their way have been attempted to be read out of the party. . . .[47]

Such disruptions in the party happened so frequently that one man was moved to declare that the whole battle with the Danites was "all a *personal* fight."[48]

Nearly all of Douglas' old enemies seized the chance for revenge against him and joined the Danite movement. Sidney Breese was no exception. The old Senator and boss of southern Illinois had harbored jealousy and hatred of Douglas since his defeat for the Senate in 1848. With his old ally Don Morrison, Breese schemed to upset Douglas' reelection in 1858. He found another willing conspirator in Phillip B. Fouke, who had long been ignored by Douglas in his bid for control of the Alton Congressional district. Breese's plan was to control the nominations in the Legislative districts, with Morrison and Fouke as candidates ostensibly pledged to Douglas. But when voting for Senator was held in the Legislature, Morrison and Fouke would go for Breese, creating a deadlock and thereby a Danite victory. The plan, however, was discovered by Douglas supporters and they easily controlled the local conventions which nominated loyal men.[49]

The loss of patronage hampered Douglas in his efforts to dominate the Illinois party. Buchanan gave Isaac Cook and Dr. Charles Lieb control of the appointed offices in the State as a means of building the Danite organization. The two men quickly began to remove some of Douglas' postmasters, not only depriving the Senator of a source of money but also making it impossible for him to send campaign documents to his workers. Cook and Lieb pressured all office holders to declare themselves and if they failed to support Buchanan they were threatened with removal from office.[50] Although Buchanan did not carry out the wholesale removal of Douglas supporters that was recommended by Cook and Lieb, enough damage was done to prevent Douglas from using patronage as a tool to keep all the politicians in line.

The years of personal rule by Douglas had weakened the party organization to the extent that it was virtually useless as a means to ensure support against the Danites. Unlike the Republicans, who had spent a great deal of energy in developing a unified and sound party structure, the Democrats still labored under the haphazard arrangements of the early 1850s. Consequently, Douglas found it much more difficult to marshal the strength of the party and control the personalities than did the Republicans. The problems Douglas faced in focusing the attention of the party against the Danites as well as the Republicans were expressed in a letter from a local politician:

> I have had some trouble in several of our representative districts in guarding against the danger of local questions, and personal rivalries, that have to some extent endangered the success of our cause. In Wayne and Edwards [counties] they have a 'railroad question' to which with personal rivalries has caused a good deal of trouble . . . White and Wabash [counties] is [sic] still a more important district that . . . requires more especially to be looked after. A good many in Wabash are dissatisfied that the Democracy of White did not concede the candidate to them, as White had had the representative for the two previous terms.[51]

Without patronage and an effective oganization, Douglas could barely manage to control the personal feuds exploited by the Danites. Exasperated, Douglas wrote that "if our friends would cease their personal quarrels and fight the common enemy of our principles with the same zeal & energy that they now fight one another, our party would be in the ascendant." The battle in Chicago was particularly disturbing to the Senator. "It is a melancholy spectacle," Douglas wrote, "to see the party . . . so totally disorganized and demoralized, that they are afraid to hold a convention or make a nomination at this time." The consequences were clear. "Unless our friends will be more forbearing and conciliatory, and exert themselves to promote the unity & harmony of the party and the success of our principles, as predominant to all personal prejudices and jealous victory," Douglas warned, "the party will lose every election and we will have nobody to blame but ourselves."[52]

The problem the Danites caused for Douglas was more the threat of party disruption than that of a loss of voters. The Danite state convention held at Springfield was a miserable failure. Despite all of Cook and Lieb's cajoling, only 30 counties sent delegates and all of these men were office holders. The Danites tried to endorse the Douglas-nominated candidates for State Treasurer and Superintendent of Public Instruction, William B. Fondey and August French, in hopes of later claiming that their victory was in reality a Danite success, but the Douglas convention forced all their nominees to repudiate such endorsements. The Danites eventually nominated their own candidates and adjourned without much enthusiasm. The election results confirmed their pessimism. They received only 5,000 votes in the entire State, and Douglas was easily re-elected to the Senate. As the composition of the Danite vote reveals, the Buchanan men did not even draw upon the same groups that Douglas did (see Table 23).[53]

Table 23. Regression: 1858 Danite State Vote

	Multiple R	R Square	RSQ Change	Simple R	B	Beta
Percent Yankee	.503	.253	.253	.50	-.275	-1.155
Acre Value	.575	.331	.078	.37	.056	0.603
Percent French	.648	.420	.088	.40	-.372	-0.921
Pietist	.681	.464	.044	-.01	.489	0.345
Farm Value	.692	.479	.015	.18	-.001	-0.928
Liturgical	.701	.492	.012	.12	.711	0.571
Percent Irish	.720	.519	.027	-.03	-.540	-3.755
Percent Scandinavian	.736	.542	.022	-.06	-.504	-2.850
Farm Size	.743	.553	.010	-.16	.038	0.880
Value Produced	.752	.566	.013	.001	-.00007	-0.292
Percent English	.756	.572	.006	.09	-.549	-1.635
Percent Illinois	.762	.580	.008	-.29	-.500	-2.906
Baptist	.764	.584	.003	-.13	.294	0.160
Percent Other	.766	.586	.002	-.06	-.482	-5.425
(constant)					-3.25	

The Danites drew most of their strength from the Yankees, the Germans and the French. All the other ethnic groups were negatively correlated with the vote for Danite candidates. The Danites posed no real threat to Douglas as a voting bloc, but the split left the party weakened.

The Danites acted as a wedge, widening the cracks between personalities in the Democratic party. As a practical political movement, they were dead after 1858, but the personal rivalries aroused by the party split continued. One faction or another was always being charged with being Buchanan supporters by an opposing group hoping to win control of the local party. Murray McConnell, for example, aspired to win the Congressional nomination in the Springfield district, but he was accused of being a Danite. "This was a false and groundless charge against me," McConnell explained to Douglas, and "it was encouraged by the two contending factions in Sangamon [county]. The one [was] headed by Lanphier & the other by John A. McClernand." McClernand captured the nomination because McConnell was discredited by the Danite charge. McConnell reluctantly supported the party in the election but he never forgave McClernand, whom he characterized as "a very selfish vindictive [and] unacceptable person."[54]

Despite all the factionalism. the loss of patronage, and the weakness of the party structure, Douglas was able to hold the Illinois Democracy together fairly well. He accomplished this through the force of his personality. During the struggle with the Danites, Douglas worked tirelessly to bolster his friends and assure them of his support. Douglas warned McClernand, for example, that "we are now engaged in a great struggle for principle which calls for all our energies and powers." Trying to comfort his friend, he wrote that "I am with you heart and soul in this great struggle, and you may rest assured that I will take no steps backwards and abate not one iota."[55] After McClernand defeated McConnell for the party's nomination to Congress, Douglas offered more assurances. "I trust that there are no defections or dissentions [*sic*] growing out of the disappointments of unsuccessful rivals," Douglas wrote. "If I can be of further service to you," he continued, "you can command my services in any way you may indicate."[56]

Beyond offering assurances and services, Douglas also became directly involved in many local struggles in order to keep harmony in the party. In some cases, he even mediated the writing of convention resolutions before the meetings were convened in order to avoid public dissension from the platform. In other instances, the "Little Giant" virtually picked the candidates for elective offices by personal endorsements. Such endorsements were so important that one local Democrat wrote to Douglas complaining that a man named Henderson claimed to have the Senator's approval and demanding to know if it were true.[57]

Douglas was successful at holding the party together because of his tremendous popularity. The Senator was deluged with correspondence from admirers either singing his praises or begging for a favor. One man wrote saying, "I do believe that God intended to bless this world when Stephen A. Douglas was born. . . ." The letter was unexceptional in its praise when the man stated that "You are with them [the people] when the Proud Bird of Liberty from [*sic*] soaring in upper air to gaze upon the sun looks down to cheer you on as the mighty Standard bearer of the 'Stars and Stripes' this glorious Republics ensign. Yes Sir you are with them when their '*hearts*' *pure devotion goes up to Heaven*' working the Almighty's blessing on the *Douglas*, the *Democracy* and for . . . the *Union*." Only when the writer concluded that the letter was "but a meagre expression of the feelings of *genuine* admiration I have for you," did it become outstanding from the numerous other letters the "Little Giant" received.[58]

Douglas' course after the elections of 1856, to stake out for himself the middle ground on the slavery question, produced uneven results for the party in Illinois. He had captured many of the old Whig and Know-Nothing voters in his successful bid for reelection to the Senate, but at the same time he had cut himself off from his own party's administration. By mapping out his own strategy and defining his own issues, Douglas had strained the bonds of the Illinois party. The Danite movement, although attracting few supporters, aggravated the tensions in the party. While Douglas almost single-handedly held the Illinois Democracy together, the personal rivalries had become so divisive that even the slightest jolt to the party might cause its complete dissolution. Despite the disruptions, Douglas' strategy had brought success in 1858, so he continued to pursue his own strategy. In a letter to an old friend, Douglas wrote, "I am determined to stand firmly by my position and vindicate my principles and let the consequences take care of themselves [and] if the Party is divided by this course it will not be my fault."[59]

With the approach of the elections in 1860, Douglas doubled his efforts to establish himself as a moderate on the slavery question. In his self-appointed role as savior of the Union, the "Little Giant" attacked the extremists both in the North and in the South and argued for non-intervention in the territories as the only solution to the slavery question. "We must meet the issue boldly which has been presented to us by the Interventionists from the North and from the South," Douglas wrote, "and maintain with firmness a strict adherence to the doctrine of popular sovereignty and non intervention by Congress with slavery in the

Territories as well as in the states." "I do not intend to make peace with my enemies," Douglas continued, "nor to make a concession of one iota of principle, believing that. . . neither can the Union be preserved or the Democratic party maintained upon any other basis."[60]   For Douglas, intervention meant disunion, and the Southern and Northern extremists were the same in principle, each against the right of self-government.[61]

Douglas argued that the Supreme Court should decide the question of the powers of Congress in the territories. Since the meaning of the Dred Scott case was highly disputed, another ruling was needed. The only political question involved with slavery, Douglas argued, was that "the whole question of slavery must be banished from the Halls of Congress, and referred to the people of the States and Territories interested in and to be effected by them."[62] In taking the position that slavery was not really a political question, but a legal one, Douglas was trying to make the issue one of State's rights. The *Register* said that "the Abolitionists care nothing for slavery—they seek only to make use of it for the purpose of diminishing the force and efficacy of state rights."[63] The Republicans were really Federalists. All the talk that slavery was the main issue was false. The vital question was "shall we elect a *sectional* president, a *sectional* Congress . . ." or the party of the Union, the Democrats?[64] Like the early Federalists, the Republicans sought nothing less than the destruction of freedom, which was rooted in local self-government.

> It is not whether Kansas or any other territory shall be free . . . [or] whether the slave trade shall be reopened or a slave code adopted for the territories—these are side issues thrown in and harped upon by the Republicans to divert attention from the infinitely greater and more desperate and treasonable object at which they are aiming,—the subversion of our present system of independent States with local customs and institutions as diverse as the climate of our broad Union, and the forcible introduction of *uniformity* in laws, customs, and institutions among the States.[65]

Douglas pursued his strategy nationally as well as in Illinois. On the larger scene, however, his moderate position on slavery was less successful. At the National Democratic Convention, held at Charleston, South Carolina, the party split with Buchanan supporting John C. Breckinridge and the Southern wing. After the Southerners walked out of the convention, the remaining delegates reconvened at Baltimore and nominated Douglas.[66] Douglas' strategy had reached its end point. He had cut himself off from the South without attracting major Republican support. He had secured the middle ground on the slavery question, but that ground was fast becoming untenable.

At the same time that fewer voters were willing to compromise on the slavery question, Douglas in 1860 found his appeal to the remaining moderates challenged by the appearance of the Constitutional Union party. Douglas, however, instead of seeing the Constitutional Unionists as a threat to his own position, believed that the John Bell and Edward Everett ticket would somehow help him. To Lanphier, Douglas wrote, "we must make the war boldly against the *Northern Abolitionists* and the *Southern Disunionists,* and give no quarter to either. We should treat the Bell & Everett men friendly and cultivate good relations with them, for they are Union men."[67] Some Democrats even believed that the Bell vote would aid Douglas' election. One man wrote to Douglas that he "was in Egypt last week [and] the Bell & Everett ticket will help you there."[68]

In accepting the Bell men as allies, Douglas was apparently planning well beyond the election. The struggle at the Charleston Convention and his uncompromising stand against Breckinridge was a battle more for the control of the Democratic party than for the Presidency. According to the *Illinois State Journal,* "the struggle between the Democrats and the Douglasites is one not for the Presidency, but for the heirship. The question between them is which of the two factions is the legitimate head of the party."[69] Douglas may have realized late in the campaign that Lincoln would be elected, but he was secure in the knowledge that he would defeat the Buchanan-Breckinridge wing of the party and win control of most of the party machinery. By not taking issue with the Bell men in 1860, Douglas hoped to draw them into a new coalition—a new party of the center. If union Whigs and Democrats could be united, Douglas figured that the Presidency would be in easy reach in 1864.[70]

The election results in Illinois showed the impossibility of Douglas' strategy. Douglas carried virtually every Democratic voter from 1858 in addition to about 43 percent of those who had voted for the Danites, while Breckinridge was able to garner only 2,000 votes, far less than one percent of the total. As the summary table indicates, the Democratic coalition had not changed significantly since 1858 (see Table 24). The Democrats were still basically Southern- and Illinois-born with a mixture of liturgical immigrants. The Irish remained almost unanimously Democratic and the "other" U.S.-born, as before, voted about 33 percent for Douglas. The only major changes were that Douglas attracted more German voters, but lost most of the French and the Canadians. Nearly 30 percent of the Germans voted for Douglas, an increase of 10 percent since 1856. The Canadian vote, however, dropped to 28 percent and the French fell completely out of the coalition.[71]

Table 24. Percentages Comparing Democratic Vote, 1856-1860

	1856 President	1858 State	1860 President
Yankee	0	0	0
Southern	100	100	100
Illinois	100	100	100
Other	20	36	33
German	22	25	30
English	0	0	0
Irish	100	100	100
Scandinavian	0	0	0
Canadian	100	69	28
French	100	59	0

Table 25. Regression: 1860 Bell Vote

	Multiple R	R Square	RSQ Change	Simple R	B	Beta
Percent Southern	.435	.189	.189	.43	.071	.837
Baptist	.517	.267	.078	.42	.546	.289
Liturgical	.584	.342	.074	.03	.921	.718
Farm Value	.651	.424	.082	.15	.00005	.038
Percent Irish	.662	.439	.014	-.16	-.023	-.158
Percent Yankee	.673	.454	.014	-.20	.068	.277
Percent English	.679	.461	.007	-.23	.057	.165
Percent Other	.687	.472	.010	-.10	.023	.260
Value Produced	.697	.486	.014	-.03	.00007	.303
Percent Illinois	.703	.497	.008	.27	.018	.103
Percent French	.706	.499	.004	-.07	.037	.088
(constant)					-6.081	

As for the expected aid from the Constitutional Unionists, Bell cut into Douglas' strength rather than adding to it. The two coalitions correlated at .28 with the composition of Bell supporters a weak reflection of the Democratic voters (see Table 25).[72] The only difference between the two groups was that Bell drew more pietists and richer farmers than did Douglas. Many of these voters were Know-Nothings, as shown by the correlation of Fillmore and Bell supporters at .38. In fact, John T. Stuart, the old Whig and Know-Nothing, was the leader of the Constitutional Unionists in Illinois and that party's candidate for Governor. Not all of the Know-Nothings went for Bell, however. The Douglas voters correlated at .39 with the Fillmore supporters.

Again, religion did not play a major role in the voting. Pietists, liturgicals, and Baptists failed to support overwhelmingly any one party.

Instead, the vote seemed to be more influenced by ethnicity. Pietistic Yankees were solidly Republican, but Southern pietists and Baptists were strong for Douglas. The Catholic Irish were almost unanimous in support of the Democracy, but the liturgical Scandinavians and French voted Republican. The Germans split their vote in 1860.[73] It cannot be denied that there were religious tensions among the voters or that those conflicts were exploited by the politicians, but it is impossible to describe the struggle in 1860 as a battle simply between pietists and liturgicals.

Slavery was the issue in 1860, and Douglas belatedly realized its effect upon the voters. After the election, the Senator understood that his plans for a new party of the center could not be accomplished as long as slavery persisted as a political question. "Nothing will do any good," Douglas wrote, "which does not take the slavery question out of Congress forever."[74] All of the "Little Giant's" efforts since the Kansas-Nebraska Act had been designed to remove slavery as an issue. After 1854, he tried to defuse the issue by attacking nativism, and in failing that, concentrated upon confronting slavery by compromise. Douglas believed that he could build a new coalition by standing on the middle ground. The voter polarization on slavery, however, left Douglas straddling the issue, a position that grew increasingly difficult to maintain. Nationally, he had lost the South without drawing new voters from the North. In Illinois, he was able to retain his position only by the strength of his personality. With secession becoming a reality, the impossibility of Douglas' strategy became more apparent. A letter from William A. Richardson to Douglas expressed not only the difficulty of maintaining the same ground but also the hopelessness of moving ahead.

> In this great emergency with events forcing all to change their opinions each day, I have determined to do as little as possible . . . . The great point now is to keep our ranks closed up and stand firmly by our guns, present as few new points as possible for fear that our friends will divide upon the new ones.[75]

The outbreak of war, however, made even this strategy impossible.

Toward the Third Party System

By 1860, the realignment of voters was virtually complete. The ethnic groups had been rearranged into new voter coalitions by the principles surrounding the slavery question. Although many of the old characteristics of politics continued, the Second Party System had collapsed. The years between 1861 and 1868 were a time of transition for the Democrats and the Republicans. Forced by the pressures of the war and Reconstruction to bring a more stable order to politics, the parties discarded the last vestiges of the emphasis on personalities, the campaign style, and the organizational techniques of the Second Party System.

The Republicans took the lead in developing the new style that would characterize the Third Party System. The battle to save the Union was a battle to save the party. The Republicans accordingly adopted new organizational features to maintain the coalition essential to the party's survival. Since the party could not tolerate factionalism, the power held by personalities was completely broken. By 1868, the Republican party was like an army, demanding strict discipline, unswerving loyalty, and rigid organization. The loss of any particular man might hurt the party, but would certainly not destroy it. The key to the success of the Republican transformation was voter loyalty. The crisis of war forged party loyalty and patriotism into one inseparable identity. This fusion allowed the Republican organization to transform the character of politics.

The complete bankruptcy of the Second Party System was evident when the South began to secede from the Union in the winter of 1860-1861. Symbolically, the death of the old party system coincided with the death of Stephen A. Douglas. The "Little Giant" had been the dominant figure in Illinois for over a decade. He had epitomized all the characteristics of the Second Party System. He enjoyed immense individual loyalty and he commanded the Democratic party in Illinois through personal alliances, manipulating policy at will. The issues that Douglas fought for in 1861, with the aim of banishing the slavery question from politics, were the same ones that he had presented in 1854. Like the Second Party System, Douglas was straddling the slavery issue and desperately trying to stop the realignment of voters. His death laid bare the instability of the system. Deprived of leadership and without realistic principles or a strong party organization, the Democracy floundered and split into contending factions.

After the election of 1860 in which he received around one and a half million votes nationally, Douglas planned to reorganize the Democratic party under his leadership and, by including the Bell supporters, to create a party of the center.[1] Ever optimistic, Douglas looked to 1864 with great expectations. Secession, however, upset his plans. The realignment had already made straddling the slavery issue extremely difficult and secession significantly reduced the possibilities that the strategy might succeed. Douglas, nevertheless, tried to steer the Democratic party through the crisis on the course he had chosen.

Douglas rested his strategy on two related points: a strong union and an end to the slavery agitation. He recognized that "no adjustment will restore & preserve peace *which does not banish the slavery question from Congress power* [sic] and place it beyond the reach of federal legislation."[2] He also saw clearly that the Democrats must support the Union. Reminding a fellow Democrat of Andrew Jackson's policy in the Nullification crisis, Douglas stated that "if we hope to regain and perpetuate the ascendancy of our party we should never forget that a man cannot be a true Democrat unless he is a loyal patriot."[3] John A. McClernand, carrying out Douglas' plans, wrote to Charles Lanphier that "our true and only policy is while denouncing their [the Republicans] fanatical policy, to stand for the Union, boldly & explicitly." The strategy was to charge the Republicans "with complicity with the fire-eaters and a design . . . to produce a separation of the slave from the free states." McClernand echoed Douglas' sentiments by stating that "*If we become entangled with disunion we will be lost as a party.*"[4]

Advocating pro-unionism and an end to slavery agitation, Douglas embraced nearly every compromise plan proposed in 1861. Although he proposed his own compromise program, Douglas eventually joined the majority of the moderates in support of the more popular Crittenden plan.[5] Of the many items in the Crittenden proposal, the most important called for an extension of the Missouri Compromise line to the Pacific, guaranteeing slavery in the territories to the south of the line and free soil to the north. The plan contained the elements essential to Douglas. The slavery question would be put to rest and the Union preserved. If the compromise were accepted, Douglas would then prepare for 1864. With the failure of this and all the other compromise plans, however, and the attack upon Fort Sumter on April 12th, any chance that Douglas might succeed and that the Second Party System might survive was lost.

Douglas' control of the Illinois Democracy began to break under the tension of the realignment. Douglas had to use every bit of his influence to hold the party together. In the hope of unifying the party, he called for a State convention to meet in January. Once the delegates assembled, however, they balked at two resolutions proposed by Douglas: one that denied the right of secession and the other that endorsed the Federal power to enforce the laws. The Chairman of the convention, Virgil Hickox, informed Douglas that he "must write immediately to all our leading men. Our friends are terribly disorganized."[6] The resolutions finally passed the convention, but only after Douglas had applied much pressure.

The tension, however, was too great to be calmed forever by Douglas' influence. The realignment had made the middle ground untenable and personal control impossible. The Democracy began to take sides. McClernand and Lanphier remained firmly behind Douglas, but William A. Richardson was conspicuously silent. John A. Logan and James C. Robinson wavered, disapproving of the strong union stand. Other Democrats like James Singleton, the former Whig, loudly denounced Douglas and sympathized with the South. The *Joliet Signal* declared that as "Democrats we claim exemption from service in this Black Republican war." Another paper stated that the South had "*justice and right on their side.* . . ." Especially in Egypt, Douglas' control broke down. The *Cairo Gazette* stated that "so far as our observations have extended, the sympathies of our people are mainly with the South."[7]

On June 3, 1861, Douglas died. Deprived of his leadership, and without realistic principles to follow, the Illinois Democracy broke apart. The essential ingredient for party durability, loyalty to the party, had been supplanted during the long years of personal rule by loyalty to Douglas. Without Douglas, the party lacked a strong bond to hold it together. His chief lieutenants, none of whom could hope to control the party, followed independent courses after the Senator's death. John A. McClernand, maintaining Douglas' strong union stand, resigned his Congressional seat and accepted a commission in the army. In sharp contrast, William A. Richardson drifted into opposition to the war. As a peace Democrat, he tried to maintain a position more impossible than the middle ground Douglas had occupied. After completing a term in the Senate in 1865, he never again played an important role in politics. John A. Logan, the third of Douglas' lieutenants, openly flirted with the Confederacy but, after a brief fling, made an about-face and joined the Republicans.

All the vestiges of Douglas' rule passed away with the "Little Giant." It was all the Illinois Democracy could do, by the fall of 1861, to maintain a distinct identity. The *State Register* frantically urged the Democrats to remain unified. *"It is the duty of the Illinois democracy to preserve their organization, nominate their tickets for the fall election,* and while they as ever stand by their country, should stand by their party principles and party organization." The principles of the party, the *Register* declared, were to "fight for the Union, *as it was,* and as it should be."[8] One newspaper even stated that slavery was irrelevant to the rebellion.[9] Nothing could have demonstrated the total bankruptcy of the Democratic party more than the principle of fighting a civil war to restore the Union as it had been. The voters had realigned on the slavery question, and secession and war turned on that issue. It was impossible to restore the Union as it had been. The Democrats collapsed under the weight of that principle, and by 1862, faced extinction as a political party.

Republicanism, on the other hand, grew and was transformed by the experiences of secession and war. The survival of the Republican party depended upon the preservation of the Union since the party would be blamed if the country should be irrevocably split by the slavery question. Even if the Republicans were able to overcome such a charge, a divided nation was incompatible with their doctrines of free men, free labor, and free soil.[10] In terms of practical politics and party principles, the Republicans were tied to the Union. Since the party depended upon the Union, the corollary became true for many Republicans; the Union relied upon the success of the party. Consequently, they viewed every compromise plan, armistice proposal, or Confederate victory in battle as an attack upon the Republican party.

The Republicans launched the campaign in 1860 well unified. According to Gustave Koerner, "no party ever entered upon a canvas with more devotion to principle than did the Republican party in 1860."[11] The enthusiasm and energy carried into the campaign were reflected in the Republican organization. Political clubs were formed in every district in Illinois. Throughout the nation, Koerner estimated, one and one-half million men belonged to the Wide-Awakes, as these clubs were called. Semi-military in nature, the Wide-Awakes performed an important function during the campaign. As Koerner noted:

> One of the most efficient agencies and one of the most characteristic of the people and the times, by which the canvass of 1860 was carried on, was an organization of the young men known as 'Wide Awakes.' They embodied nearly all the young men of the party, a semi-military organization, but without arms, wearing glazed caps and capes and at night carry torch-lights, and ready at all times for work – turning out at political meetings, escorting

speakers to and from the places of speaking, singing patriotic songs, circulating documents and canvassing votes.[12]

The Republican enthusiasm in 1860 developed into the "Spirit of '61" as the party faced its first challenge, secession. Acquiescence in the breakup of the Union was unthinkable. Compromise with the South presented an attractive alternative to war, but most Republicans believed that compromise would endanger both the nation and the party. One man wrote to Trumbull that "it is the veriest suicide for the party leaders to yield to the demands of the fire-eaters for it can only result in . . . rending the party into a hundred warring fragments and by so doing reinstate in power the slaveocracy."[13] Many Republicans saw that the real danger was not what the South would do, but what they themselves might do. These men exerted pressure through the entire organization to combat any thought of compromise. "The Republicans took ground in favor of free Territories, and the right and duty of Congress to exclude slavery therefrom," declared John Wentworth's *Democrat*. "On that ground it conquered, and its representatives should see to it that there is no flinching from that position—no surrender of principle."[14] Another Republican newspaper stated that it wished "the word compromise was stricken from the English language and [that] . . . every freeman would forget how to pronounce it."[15] When war finally broke out in April, the *Democrat* declared: "Never mind the past. Any reference to it will do no good. The war has been kept back too long. Everybody seems to admit this. But it is useless to talk now. Let the war now go on."[16]

The weight of the war was felt almost immediately in Illinois. As the State prepared for the conflict, trouble erupted in southern Illinois. Rumors flew throughout the state about divided loyalties and actual secession activities in Egypt.[17] Secessionists meeting at Marion on April 15th pledged to join the Confederacy. Another mass rally in Pope County also declared the right of secession. There was even talk of making Cairo a neutral city where both sides could trade freely. John Palmer recalled that "one member of the legislature handed me a scheme which proposed the division of the state upon the line of the National road which passed through Vandalia, and permitting the south part of the state to join the Confederacy."[18] A man frantically wrote to Governor Yates appealing for help.

[P]ay some attention to the Rebels in this End of the State. Some of them Say they are going to help Jeff Davis & others Say they are going to hang, cut throats, and shoott every Republican in egypt they say it will be sport at killing the Republicans as they are scatering. They have got a six pounder cannon belonging to the state. Also fifty stand of Arms which are

scatered. Among the people the canon is in charge of Kernall John
Dougherty. Rebellion is expected every day. [*sic*].[19]

The Republicans reacted immediately. The party tightened its ranks
to secure its hold on the State. In order to counter the threat from
Egypt, the Republicans began a campaign for the Union much as if they
were preparing for an election. Groups were organized to maintain
vigilance against treason, while the populace was whipped into a frenzy
by speakers sent into all parts of Illinois. Trumbull returned from
Washington to take the stump, but the most important Republican effort
to rally the people rested upon Douglas. Persuaded by Lincoln to go to
Illinois to participate in the campaign, the "Little Giant" delivered an
eloquent speech to the Illinois Legislature in support of the Union.[20]

Although there was little chance that Egypt could secede from
Illinois, the belief that rebellion was imminent kept the Republican party
in a state of readiness. In 1862 and 1863, a new threat challenged the
party. The war went unexpectedly badly, and the Democrats seized the
opportunity to disrupt both the Republican party and the Union cause.
Faced directly with the question of survival, the Republicans were forced
to make changes in the party organization in order to meet the challenge.

At a State constitutional convention in 1862, the Democrats
mounted the first in a series of attacks upon the Republicans. Since the
Illinois Constitution of 1848 was widely considered outmoded, the people
had voted in the election of 1860 to authorize a constitutional
convention. In response, the Legislature called for delegate elections in
1861. The Republicans supported the idea of framing a new government,
but they did not intend to make a partisan contest out of the delegate
selection. While the Democrats seemed to go along with the "no party"
idea, they quietly prepared slates of candidates. The sudden appearance
of Democratic candidates a few weeks before the election surprised the
Republicans, who had no time to counter with their own candidates.
The result was a Democratic victory. Of the 75 delegates elected, 45
were Democrats and only 21 Republicans, with 9 others being
independent.

The Democrats, using the convention as a political forum, quickly
seized the opportunity to attack the Republicans. The convention refused
to take the loyalty oath to the State and aggressively passed resolutions
defending States' Rights. The Democrats also refused to endorse the
President and the war effort, and they ratified a proposed amendment to
the U.S. Constitution guaranteeing the existence of slavery in the nation.
Even though there was no legal basis for such action the convention
began to repeal State laws and to appropriate money. Finally, the

delegates investigated Governor Yates' handling of military matters in Illinois. They searched through all the contracts and war expenditures in hopes of finding a scandal, and they began to study the treatment of Illinois troops in the field in order to embarrass the Republicans.

Although the Democrats hoped to humiliate the Republicans by these actions, the real thrust of the convention was to recreate the old Jacksonian issues as a basis upon which the party could strengthen itself.[21] The Republican *State Journal* accurately stated that the convention was "a mere machine for resuscitating and re-organizing the Democratic party in the State."[22] The convention drew up an article that prohibited the chartering of any State Banks or the renewal of the existing charters. This proposed that as of 1864 banks could issue no notes of less than 20 dollars, and by 1866, no bank notes at all. Another article stipulated that the Illinois Central Railroad could not be released from its obligations to the State. The convention also endorsed a general incorporation law which prohibited the chartering of corporations by special acts of the Legislature. A new Congressional and Legislative apportionment was drawn up giving representation to the smaller Democratic counties in Egypt equal to that of larger Republican counties, and attaching certain Republican districts to larger Democratic strongholds. Finally, the convention prepared a section that incorporated into the constitution the Black laws of 1853 prohibiting the immigration of Negroes into the State and the rights of citizenship to free blacks.[23]

In drawing up the new constitutional provisions for banking and corporations, the Democrats hoped to reshape the electorate. The *Register* stated: "We do not suppose it likely that old party lines can be drawn on the question of the adoption or rejection of this constitution. Many of the strongest republicans in the state have declared themselves for it."[24] By presenting old Jacksonian issues, the Democrats sought to cut across the slavery realignment and to restore the old party. One Democrat writing to Charles Lanphier bluntly stated "that if we are beaten [on the constitution] we are 'gave up' for years."[25] To carry out the Democratic plan, the convention called for a State election in 1862 if the constitution were adopted. With the proposed reapportionment, the Democrats could then capture a majority in the Legislature and, it was hoped, defeat Governor Yates.

The referendum on the constitution was scheduled for June, and the Democratic press campaigned hard. All the rhetoric was aimed against the banks and the corporations in the hope that the laboring class would be drawn into the party. The *Register* declared that the new constitution "guards the people against the villanies of designing persons, rascally corporations and huge monopolies. . . ." "All of the corporations in the state will make war upon it . . . ," the *Register* warned, and "the Illinois Central Road—a vast power in the state—will strain every nerve to defeat it. . . ."[26] The Democrats cautioned the people that the banks and railroads were scheming to suppress the popular will. "By the adoption of the new constitution laborers and others . . . ," the *Register* promised, "can no longer be cheated on their earnings."[27] The *Peoria Union* proclaimed, "The simple truth of the whole matter is this: the people may get for their labor and their produce *Gold*, and not rags."[28] The rallying cry became "*No more Banks and no more Negroes in Illinois.*"[29]

The Republicans understood perfectly the significance of the new constitution. At first, they tried to have the convention adjourned until after the fall elections. Failing that, they frantically attacked the constitution on every ground possible. The Republicans charged that the adoption of the document would increase taxes, enlarge the size and expense of the government, create more offices for patronage, disfranchise the northern districts of Illinois and, finally, introduce slavery into Illinois! The *Journal* declared that the new constitution usurped so much authority that "not only may they introduce negro slavery or interdict it, but they may even decree the slavery of white men for they have 'sovereign' power over the freedom of all white as well as black!"[30] The motives of such men were plain to see, argued the Republicans. "Such an outrageous piece of partisan gerrymandering and barefaced disfranchisement of the people could not have been concocted, except by demagogues bent upon acquiring political power by base and unholy means."[31] Who did this new constitution really benefit, the Republicans asked; certainly not the laborer. "The Constitution was made for the benefit of the Egyptian portion of the State," declared the *Aurora Beacon*, "and by it . . . we of the north will be held in vassalage for many years."[32]

The most effective of the Republican attacks upon the constitution, however, was their accusation that the convention sympathized with the Confederacy. Noting the delegates' refusal to take the loyalty oath and their resolutions against the war, the Republicans charged the convention with treason. The constitution, they maintained, was the Lecompton affair all over again, but this time in Illinois. The convention was composed of "sympathizers with the rebellion, rank secessionists at heart, who would be best pleased to carry with them all Egypt into the Southern Confederacy."[33]

The Democratic attempt to reshape the electorate by resurrecting the Jacksonian issues failed. The war proved to be the dominant concern of the people of Illinois, and the Republicans won their vote by presenting the issue as the Union versus the new constitution. The constitution was defeated along with the separately submitted sections on banking, railroads, and Congressional reapportionment. Only the articles restricting the immigration of blacks and prohibiting citizenship to freedmen won a majority of votes. The Democratic gamble for power had more than failed. It broke the party's already fragile coalition.

An analysis of the voting illustrates that the constitution was unsuccessful in attracting Republican voters, and more importantly, it did not even maintain the coalition that had voted for Douglas in 1860 (see Table 26).[34] In 1860, the Democrats had carried virtually all of the Southerners, the Illinois-born, and the Irish; 30 percent of the Germans; 33 percent of the "other" U.S.-born; and some 28 percent of the Canadians. The 1862 vote for the new constitution, however, did not draw significantly from any of these groups. Not even the Southerners contributed meaningfully to the overall pro-constitution vote. Only for the separate vote on the banking and reapportionment articles did the Southerners respond to the Democratic appeals, while the remainder of the 1860 coalition failed to follow the party.[35]

Table 26. Regression: Vote for the Constitution

	Multiple R	R Square	RSQ Change	Simple R	B
Farm Size	.69	.48	.48	-.69	-0.074
Percent Irish	.75	.56	.08	-.16	1.23
Percent French	.83	.69	.12	-.13	-23.45
Percent Yankee	.90	.82	.13	-.50	-5.74
Baptist	.93	.88	.05	-.12	-7.64
Percent Other	.95	.91	.03	-.45	-0.58
Value Produced	.97	.94	.03	-.17	0.004
Acre Value	.98	.97	.02	.31	2.16
Pietist	.99	.99	.02	.03	-21.70
Percent Scandi-navian	.99	.99	.003	-.32	2.55
(constant)					108.10

Although the articles prohibiting citizenship for blacks and restricting the immigration of freedmen won a large majority of votes, their popularity did not help restore the Democracy to power. The Republicans did not make the status of Negroes in Illinois into a party issue, as they had with the constitution. Therefore, the many Republicans who voted for these articles did not represent a defection from the party, and consequently did not help the Democrats.

The Republicans succeeded in defeating the new constitution, but the regular elections in 1862 loomed as an equally imposing threat to the party. A series of unfortunate circumstances made the party particularly vulnerable. The war had not gone well for the North. Attempts to capture Richmond failed miserably, first at Bull Run and then in the Peninsula campaign of May, 1862. Later in the summer, another Union army, led by Governor Yates' friend John Pope, was defeated at the second battle of Bull Run. Although the Union forces turned back the Confederates at Antietam Creek in the fall, the victory was marred by heavy casualties and lost opportunities. Just as the Union armies had met defeat on the battlefields, the Republicans at home were in retreat.

A number of other developments also hurt the Republicans. The Second Confiscation Act of 1862, declaring that all property belonging to persons supporting the rebellion was forfeited and that all escaped or captured slaves were free, aroused intense opposition. Lincoln's Preliminary Emancipation Proclamation, issued after the battle of Antietam, also proved to be very unpopular. Additionally, the threat of conscription to fill the Union ranks, and the suspension of the writ of habeas corpus, provoked strong reactions. The Republicans were clearly on the defensive.

In gearing up for the campaign, the Republicans tried to make the issue a simple matter of patriotism or treason. The State convention declared that "we acknowledge but two divisions of the people . . . in this crisis—those who are loyal . . . and those who openly or covertly endeavor to sever our country or to yield to the insolent demands of its enemies. . . ."[36] Trying to undercut the Democratic strength, the Republicans appealed for an end to party warfare. "It is the country that is at stake now, not party," stated one Republican paper, "and the man or men who cannot rise above party in such an hour—that cannot act together for the preservation of a free form of government, are unworthy to live under it."[37] Knowing that if they were successful in making the issue loyalty or treason they would benefit from a "no party" contest, the Republicans declared that only selfish men "howl for their con-temptible party organizations while the country is struggling in the throw [sic] of revolution."[38]

The Republicans countered the opposition to conscription, confisca-tion, and emancipation by arguing that these were war measures. War demanded extreme actions and opposition to such measures was, in reality, sympathy with the rebellion. When the nation verged on dissolu-tion, it was absurd not to make an all-out effort to end the war. "Let our enemies suffer," cried one Republican newspaper, "confiscate their pro-perty, and free their slaves."[39] "Can there be a doubt," asked the *Chicago Tribune*, "which must go down when it is slavery against the Union?"[40]

Although the Democrats were divided and disorganized after the defeat of the constitution, they managed to take advantage of the dissatisfaction with the war. Out of the necessity of keeping the party from splitting into war and peace factions, the Democrats conducted the campaign solely on the issue of the Republicans' failures. The State convention was poorly attended with 39 counties failing to send delegates. Most of the delegates were peace Democrats, but they wisely refrained from making pronouncements that could be construed as support for the South. In one Congressional convention, the Democrats even refused to make a platform; the chairman declared that a platform would only divide, not unite, the party.

> I do not urge, or ask this convention to make any platform. I think that we have platforms enough. Let the candidate, whom we nominate, run upon his own platform. If we make a platform today, we may be called upon to make another one next week. The exigencies of revolution and fanaticism may bury a platform we may make today. The exigencies of revolution are breaking to our view new issues every day. Let us nominate a man that can be elected without a platform.[41]

The Democratic campaign varied wildly across the State. The only common theme was that the Republicans had not settled the nation's troubles and that everything they passed in Congress aggravated the war still further. The Emancipation Proclamation, the Democrats argued, "is calculated to do much mischief in prolonging the war and rendering more uncompromising the people of the two sections toward each other." The Republicans were "determined to pass such laws as will forever preclude the hope of restoring the least degree" of unity in the nation.[42]

The Democrats were successful. Their candidates for State Treasurer, Superintendent of Public Instruction, and Congressman-at-Large won easily. Eight of the 13 Congressmen and a majority of the Illinois Legislature elected were Democrats. The party had reversed the 11,000 Republican majority in 1860 by carrying the 1862 elections with a 16,000 vote plurality. But despite this turnabout, there were few significant changes in the voting patterns.

The Southerners, Illinois-born, and Irish solidly supported the Democrats, and the party captured an additional 5 percent of the "other" U.S.-born. More importantly, the Democracy significantly increased its support among the Germans from 30 to 42 percent (see Table 27.)[43] This shift resulted in a strong liturgical correlation for the Democrats for the first time since the realignment. The liturgicals correlated with the Democracy at .24 in 1862, whereas in 1860, the correlation had been an insignificant -.08.

Table 27. Percentages Comparing Democratic Vote, 1860 and 1862

	1860 President	1862 State
Yankee	0	0
Southern	100	100
Illinois	100	100
Other	33	37
German	30	42
English	0	0
Irish	100	100
Scandinavian	0	0
Canadian	28	0
French	0	0

The Republican coalition, however, had not been damaged as much as the elections seemed to indicate. The party did lose some German and liturgical support and a fraction of the "other"-born, but on the other hand, the Republicans managed to capture the Canadians who had voted for Douglas in 1860. Certainly dissatisfaction with the progress of war hurt the Republicans, but because the regression showed few shifts among the voters, the electoral reverses for the party must be largely attributed to the inability of the soldiers in the field to vote.

The drain of the soldier vote was reflected in the turnout rates for 1862. There were almost 100,000 fewer voters in 1862 than there had been in 1860.[44] Overall, only 53.8 percent of those eligible voted in 1862 as compared to 77.3 percent in 1860. That the Republican defeat in 1862 was not caused by a massive shift of voters is demonstrated by the very strong .99 correlation between the 1860 and 1862 Republican coalitions.

Despite the fact that the coalition had not in reality been damaged, the Republicans had their backs to the wall when the Illinois Legislature assembled in January, 1863. Every bit of strength in the party had to be marshalled to prevent the Democrats from controlling the State. No factionalism could be tolerated. First, the Democrats elected William A. Richardson to fill the remainder of Douglas' unexpired term in the Senate, replacing the Republican appointee, Orville H. Browning. They then stripped the Republicans of all patronage connected with the Legislature. A more serious attack upon the Republicans, however, was the passage of resolutions by the House condemning the war and demanding an immediate armistice. Although these resolutions failed to pass the Senate because the Republicans prevented a quorum, the Legislature did authorize the sending of delegates to Louisville, Kentucky, for a peace convention. The Democrats also threatened the war effort by challenging Yates' authority to raise troops and by again calling into question the Governor's war expenditures. The Democrats also moved to disrupt the Republican party by passing a new reapportionment bill.

The Illinois Republicans were driven to desperate measures to keep the war going and the party's control of the Governor's mansion intact. An uncompromising prosecution of the war and an equally vigorous, if not unconstitutional, attack upon the Democratic party at home became the twin goals of the Republican party. Early in 1863, Yates successfully removed the threat of the Democratic controlled Legislature by ordering that body prorogued. The Democrats cried that Yates' action was a nefarious scheme to destroy the State Constitution, but the Governor had legal basis for his unprecedented action. An obscure Illinois law stated that if both houses of the Legislature failed to agree upon a date of adjournment, the Governor could prorogue the Legislature. The Democrats, deprived of a political forum in which to rally the party, were thrown into confusion. Before they had a chance to recover, the Republicans moved to crush their opposition.

The Republicans relentlessly attacked the Democrats with charges that all who opposed the party opposed the war and hence were guilty of treason. The Republicans emphasized the divided loyalties of Egypt as proof of the Democracy's plans to divide the Union. The *Belleville Advocate* reported, as an example of true Democratic sympathies, a speech delivered by former Governor John Reynolds, in which he stated that "the revolution in the South is the greatest demonstration of human greatness and grandeur that was ever performed on the globe."[45] The Democratic party was characterized as "a pack of Judases plotting to betray their country for the thirty pieces of silver or rather its equivalent, the triumph of democracy at elections."[46] The issue was simple: vote Republican and save the Union, or vote copperhead and support the rebellion.

With Union or rebellion firmly entrenched in the Republican mind as the only alternatives, the party moved in 1863 and 1864 to stamp out all signs of treason, which meant the Democratic party. As a result of President Lincoln's suspension of the writ of habeas corpus in 1862, the Republicans had new police powers to use in support of their mission. Between June and October, 1863, there were over 200 arrests in Illinois for treason, and an additional 800 for desertion. Among those arrested were a State Judge, a Legislator, a State Senator, and the Congressman-at-Large—all Democrats. The editors of the *Paris Democratic Standard* and the Jerseyville *Democratic Union* were arrested, and the *Chicago Times* and the *Jonesboro Gazette* were suppressed. Other Democratic newspapers, like the German-owned *Peoria Demokrat*, were denied the use of the mails. Although these actions provoked outrage among the voters, the Republicans pointed to ample evidence of Democratic treason. In March, 1863, a riot erupted in Charleston, Illinois, in which a number of Union men were killed. A company of troops from Egypt deserted and joined the Confederacy. The Knights of the Golden Circle, a secret band of Southern sympathizers, operated in Illinois aiding draft resisters and deserters. Finally, a conspiracy was uncovered whereby a number of Confederates operating out of Canada planned to attack the prisoner of war camp in Chicago with the aid of copperheads and release all the Confederate prisoners.[47]

Since the secession winter, the Republican party had been linked with the Union. If the Confederacy were successful, the Republicans would be lost as a political force. Every compromise and every question about the conduct of the war was as much a threat to the future of the party as a defeat on the battlefield. Faced first with the compromise proposals during secession, and then with the proposed constitution in 1862, and finally with the Democratic Legislature in 1863, the Illinois Republicans were forced to make changes in the party to insure a united effort.

The earliest change was the complete subjugation of personalities. Personal feuds and individual power bases had to be avoided if the Republicans were to remain united. During the dangerous days of the war, the slightest disruption or variance in purpose could break the party's hold on the State. Consequently, the Wentworth-Judd feud ended abruptly. "Long John" threatened the party again in 1862 when he bolted the county convention, but his defection was hardly felt by the Republicans.[48] The Davis-Trumbull feud also ceased with the outbreak of the war. Although the two men never reconciled their differences, their battle was kept private.[49]

Not only were the feuds between personalities ended, the Republican party also prevented the attempts of individuals to build up personal loyalties. Richard Yates, for example, tried to create a following through the use of patronage. As Governor, he appointed his friend, Orville H. Browning, to the Senate after Douglas' death, and he secured army commissions for friends like John Pope, Stephen Hurlbut, and Benjamin Prentiss. Yates even made alliance with John McClernand by helping him get a commission. Yates succeeded in becoming very popular, but he was never able to carve out a base of support independent of the party.

With the decline of importance of personalities, the Republican organization was able to expand and to completely dominate the party. The tendency shown by the Republicans in the 1850s to build a strong party structure now had free rein. One result was that patronage was used exclusively to aid the party rather than individual politicians.[50] County committees became standard features and the private clubs were expanded into permanent components of the party. The Union Leagues replaced the Wide-Awakes and they became a vital means of maintaining party discipline and of providing a body of workers for elections.

The Republican party came to resemble an army. The party was divided into units, each with a specific function and duty to perform. The chain of command was clear. The Union Leagues were like shock troops, always on the front line and leading the charge during the campaign. The elections were like battles. Discipline, loyalty, and personal sacrifice were required. In the Presidential campaign of 1864, the strengths of the Republican party organization were clearly visible.

The Democrats clearly understood the Republicans' dependence upon the success of the war. They continued to press the theme of the 1862 campaign that the conflict was a Republican war. "So we go," one Democratic newspaper stated; "the war for the Union is first perverted into a war for abolition, and now it is a war for the Republican succession."[51] They argued that the war was a stalemate and that the confiscation acts and the Emancipation Proclamation prolonged the conflict and made it almost impossible to resolve. Other war measures, like the National Banking system, the taxation program, the increased tariffs, and the printing of greenbacks, represented the real design of the Republicans to promote a monied aristocracy.[52] The Democrats looked for salvation to General George B. McClellan, whom they nominated as their Presidential candidate. The Illinois party was enthusiastically behind McClelland even though he was a war Democrat nominated on a peace platform. The *Register* prophesied that "instead of anarchy we see order; instead of oppression, safety and protection; in place of despotism, the restraints of law and constitution ... instead of war, peace."[53]

The Republican issue was simple. "The victories won and the territory reclaimed by us during the last three years," declared the Republicans, "have cost too much in the blood of our brave brothers and in money spent, to be now surrendered at the behest of the peace factionists [*sic*] who control the democracy of the country."[54] The Republicans prepared themselves for another campaign just as the Union armies girded themselves for the final onslaught. The *Tribune* called for the northern districts of Illinois to stand ready. "The time draws near when these steadfast legions will be called again to come forth to battle for the cause."[55] All down the line, the Republicans made final adjustments. One man wrote that he "hoped all *real unselfish* Union men, will go in for the *cause alone*, forgetting *personal* friends &

consultations."[56] Another Republican wrote that the party was strong enough to purge questionable personalities.

> We are opposed to any movement that will lead to the nomination of an untrue man. Being engaged [to the party] (as we have seen and experienced) is not always a guarantee of a man's future political cause. We are now strong enough to warrant an avoidance of experiments. We must have a candidate who is free from doubt and question.[57]

The Republican cause so overshadowed personalities in 1864 that the party was able to put aside even the strongest opposition to particular candidates. The renomination of Lincoln was the outstanding example. There was growing opposition to Lincoln within the party and Illinois was no exception. Trumbull wrote that "there is a distrust and fear that he is too undecided and inefficient to put down the rebellion."[58] Although many Republicans feared that Lincoln would lose the election, the party avoided the mistake of changing candidates on the eve of the election. Yates counselled Horace Greeley and others that "the substitution of another man at this late day would be disastrous."[59] A splinter group that had nominated John C. Fremont for President soon melted away when it became apparent that the Republican party could not be seriously divided by personalities.

The Republican party was formidable in 1864. The peace platform of the Democrats looked foolish as the election drew near, and even McClellan repudiated it. The Union armies closed in quickly upon the remnants of the South, making the Republican identification with the Union invincible. Lincoln, the party and the Union triumphed in 1864.

The voting results in 1864 reveal how badly the Democrats had miscalculated and how well the Republicans had been able to fuse patriotism with party loyalty. Lincoln carried Illinois by a 30,000 majority. Despite secession, war and revolutionary developments such as confiscation and emancipation, the basis of the Republican coalition remained intact. The Democracy, however, was splintered by these same events (see Table 28). For the first time since 1854, the Southerners did not vote solidly Democratic. Apparently the peace platform in 1864 was too much even for the Southerners, as 32 percent voted for Lincoln. In addition to this loss, the Democrats also failed to keep the support of many Germans who had voted for the party in 1862. The German vote dropped from 42 to 37 percent. The only bright spot for the Democrats was the continued increase among the "other" U.S.-born who voted 45 percent Democratic, an increase of 8 points over 1862.[60] The shifts in the voting pattern of ethnic groups again increased Democratic support among the liturgicals, which correlated at a significant .39. The sharp religious division and the major changes among the voters, however, would prove to be a temporary deviation rather than a realignment.

Table 28. Percentages Comparing Voter Results, 1860-1864

	1860 Presidential		1862 State		1864 Presidential	
	Republican	Democrat	Republican	Democrat	Republican	Democrat
Yankee	100	0	100	0	100	0
Southern	0	100	0	100	32	67
Illinois	0	100	0	100	0	100
Other	66	33	62	37	54	45
German	68	30	57	42	42	37
English	100	0	100	0	100	0
Irish	0	100	0	100	0	100
Scandi- navian	100	0	100	0	100	0
Canadian	63	28	100	0	100	0
French	100	0	100	0	100	0

Within five months after the election, the war ended. But the Republicans were still in a precarious position. The Union had been preserved and slavery destroyed, yet the thorny question of settling the peace remained unanswered. Although the party was no longer engaged in a life-and-death struggle, the Republicans lacked guarantees for the future. During the Reconstruction period, the constant pressure on the Republicans forced the party to solidify the transformations in its organization begun during the war.

The assassination of Lincoln, the Schurz report, which outlined the plight of the freedmen and the lack of loyalty in the South, and the political defection of President Andrew Johnson, all proved to the Republicans that the irrepressible conflict was not yet at an end. The restoration of the South under such circumstances would not only negate the results of the war, but also jeopardize the domination of the Republican party in the North. The Republicans were still a sectional party, and the South could easily join with Northern Democrats and once again control the federal government. Koerner realized the meaning of an unreconciled South restored to power when he wrote that "the long duration of the war, the entire abolition of slavery, the alienation of the Southern people have produced . . . new and unforseen [*sic*] results, requiring changes. We must have some guarantees for the future."[61]

The Reconstruction of the South was the means the Republicans devised for establishing some assurances for the future. The South would be kept out of the Union until loyal State governments were formed, and the rebels excluded from power. According to the *Tribune*, the Republicans had no choice but to deny the South political rights in order not to "endanger the Union, now won by our blood, or the overthrow of slavery, necessary to Union itself."

> Before we tie the hands of those who have saved the Union and restore authority to those who have sought to destroy it, before (in plain terms) we allow the latter to come into the halls of Congress and outvote the former, or to combine with Northern traitors upon such measures as they would be likely to combine upon, we will be well assured that the experiment is safe.[62]

Exclusion of the Southern States was only part of the Republican guarantee for the future. Negro suffrage was the other means by which the party hoped to maintain control of the nation. Since the whites could not be trusted, the security and the peace of the South depended upon emancipated blacks.[63] One Republican newspaper stated that its position "is most decidedly in favor of negro equality. It is, moreover, in favor of negro superiority over rebels."[64]

Implementing the Reconstruction program was no easy task. The South resisted, but since its representatives were excluded from Congress there was little it could do. Northern Democrats provided a more serious threat. They attacked Reconstruction as unconstitutional and revolutionary. The Democrats reserved special invectives, however, for the Republican stand in regard to the Negro. The Democrats charged that the people had been duped by the abolitionists, and that the war for the Union had been perverted into a war for abolition. The *Joliet Signal* wrote that the Thirteenth Amendment was the consummation of a multitude of fanatical abolition schemes. The abolitionists, after "seas of blood and scenes of woe and ruin, [have] been able to foist their darling scheme of negro emancipation upon the country," stated the *Signal*.[65] The Democrats clearly understood that the Republicans had no love for the freedmen. They accurately charged that the Republicans advocated emancipation and Negro suffrage "to maintain party supremacy, and because they hate the people of the South."[66]

The threat posed by the Democrats and the intransigence of the South kept the Republicans under constant pressure. The greatest threat to Reconstruction, however, came unexpectedly from within the party itself. President Johnson had inaugurated a Reconstruction plan acceptable to the Republicans. At the end of 1865, however, it was apparent that the President's plan had failed. All the Southern States passed through Johnson's program, but many did not repudiate the Confederate debt and did not declare secession illegal. The South had also returned to Washington many of its rebel leaders. Johnson, nevertheless, declared his restoration plan completed.[67] The Republicans were shocked. All of their guarantees for the future had been circumvented and the South restored to power. The situation was made far more dangerous to the party by the apparent defection of their own President.

After the assassination of Lincoln, the Republicans had embraced Johnson as a new Savior. Many Republicans, in fact, were relieved that Lincoln was now gone from the political scene. There had been too much talk by Lincoln of leniency. The *Tribune* jubilantly declared that "Johnson's little finger will prove thicker than were Abraham Lincoln's loins. While he whipped them gently with cords, his successor will scourge them with a whip of scorpions."[68]

By the end of 1865, however, the Republicans began to realize that Johnson's "whip of scorpions" was in reality made of silk. Disenchantment with the new President quickly turned into hatred in 1866. Johnson had been handing out pardons to former Confederates in a wholesale manner. Then in February, 1866, the President vetoed Lyman Trumbull's Freedmen's Bureau Bill. The party reacted immediately. Johnson had failed to maintain party regularity. The *Tribune* was flabbergasted.

> Since the closing scenes of the war and the sad horror of the assassination no event has created such profound sensation as the formal act by which the President has severed himself from the loyal party and united with its enemies North and South, before the Union is yet restored or the war fully ended.[69]

If any doubts remained about President Johnson's intentions, they were removed by his veto of the Civil Rights Act in March. "No political act of President Johnson has done so much to reveal his real character and define his true relations to the momentous questions now seeking solution," wrote the *Rockford Register*, "as have been done by this veto. . . ." The spirit of the veto, the paper declared, was the spirit of the slave power. Johnson had gone over completely to the rebels and the copperheads. "And nothing," the *Register* concluded, "has been done to show so thoroughly the utter worthlessness of Andrew Johnson as a representative of the great party which elected him, or of those wise and just principles upon which alone our country can be redeemed from the evil consequences of the rebellion. . . ."[70]

Johnson, under attack from what he believed to be "radicals," sought to purge the party of this element. In Illinois, he won Republican support from A.J. Kuykendall, Congressman from Egypt, Thomas J.

Turner, Chairman of the Central Committee, and Orville H. Browning, who was appointed Secretary of the Interior. Browning was put in charge of patronage in Illinois as the President tried to wield that powerful tool to drive out the radicals. There is no evidence to show, however, that either Browning or Johnson succeeded in purging the party. The problem for Johnson was that the vast majority of Republicans opposed him, not just a loud radical faction. The most that the President accomplished in Illinois was to annoy the party. Unfriendly newspapers, for example, lost federal printing contracts, but the important office-holders kept their jobs.

Unable to capture the Republican machinery, Johnson moved to create his own party. In July, a national convention was held at Philadelphia open to all conservative men opposed to the radicals.[71] The National Union party, however, flopped before it was launched. A hodgepodge of copperheads and former Confederates were prominent in the convention, giving it the odor of treason.

Once Johnson had decided to create his own party, it became certain that the Democrats would rally to his aid. Since the end of the war, the Democracy in Illinois had been on the verge of a complete breakdown. Opposition to the war had been a disastrous mistake that fragmented the party. In hopes of restoring some sense of unity and of regaining electoral respectability, the Democrats again began to emphasize Jacksonian doctrines. The party called for the elimination of the greenbacks, the banks, the tariff, and monopolies.[72] The *Belleville Democrat* declared that "we are brought back to the old issue – that the Democracy is again called upon to wage the political warfare which it so long and successfully carried on against the old Whig party, upon the tariff question."[73]

In their desperation, the Democrats also attempted to resurrect the specter of Know-Nothingism. One paper charged that the Republicans were "Know-Nothing, Anti-Catholic, Abolition, negro-equality malignants" designing to deprive the white immigrant of citizenship while elevating the black.[74] These jeremiads, however, sounded empty in 1866.

Salvation for the Democracy came with the defection of President Johnson. The Illinois party quickly embraced the Johnson supporters and the Democrats were rewarded by the President with patronage. The Democrats portrayed Johnson as a true Jacksonian, but the campaign in 1866 revolved more on the cult of personality than the issues of either Jacksonianism or Reconstruction.[75]

In Illinois, the chief topic of the Democratic campaign was John A. Logan, former Democrat turned radical Republican. Logan, running for Congressman-at-Large, had a questionable past that made him particularly susceptible to personal attack. As a Democrat, Logan had broken with Douglas in 1861 over support of the war, and he apparently considered joining the Confederacy before making a complete about-face and becoming a Republican. The Democrats charged that Logan had sought to raise a rebel force in Egypt and that he had delivered numerous treasonable speeches. It was, they said, only after the patriotic Democrats of Southern Illinois refused to follow him that Logan decided to become a Republican.[76]

Faced with the threat from the South and the defection of Johnson, the Republicans needed every bit of strength they could muster to maintain their hold on the government. To meet the threat in 1866, they emphasized two points: the victory of the war must not be jeopardized and the party must resist factionalism. Richard Yates captured in a speech the entire thrust of the Republican campaign in Illinois.

> I love my country, and believe that the salvation of the country depends upon the Republican Union party. I did not wish to see the fruits of victory won from the foe, lost by divisions in our ranks. . . . It was not until I saw that he [Johnson] was turning the warm, bosom friends of Mr. Lincoln out of his cabinet, and out of offices, everywhere, and that he was taking vile traitors, and copperheads to his bosom, that I resolved to oppose him.[77]

The Republican message was clear and simple. The party had saved the Union and now it must save the peace. President Johnson had gone over to the enemy and the party must stand firm. The voters in Illinois responded, giving the Republicans a tremendous majority of 56,000 votes. The Republicans captured all the State offices, a majority of the Legislature, and 11 out of 14 Congressional seats, including that of John A. Logan. Nearly every Yankee, Scandinavian, Canadian, Frenchman, and Englishman voted Republican. Although the Southerners returned to the Democracy, the Republicans were compensated by a major increase in the German vote from 62 to 85 percent, and in the "other"-born vote from 54 to 67 percent.[78] The Democrats, relying upon the strength of personalities, were able to carry only the Southerners and Illinois-born voters. The Republican vote was so strong that every economic and religious indicator except Baptist membership was associated with the party (see Table 29).[79]

Supported by a majority of the voters nationally as well as in Illinois, the Republicans proceeded to carry out their Reconstruction program. The South was denied readmission into Congress and the Johnson State governments were ignored. The Republicans passed the First Reconstruction Act in March, 1867, and began to establish the guarantees that the party needed against the return of a powerful unreconciled South.[80]

Table 29. Regression: 1866 Republican State Vote

	Multiple R	R Square	RSQ Change	Simple R	B	Beta
Percent Southern	.73	.54	.54	-.73	-3.41	-1.52
Pietists	.75	.56	.02	.03	-0.28	-0.01
Percent German	.77	.60	.03	.30	-0.37	-0.33
Acre Value	.79	.63	.02	.32	0.59	0.76
Percent French	.81	.65	.02	.14	0.36	0.17
Liturgical	.83	.69	.03	.30	-13.95	-0.87
Percent Scandinavian	.84	.71	.01	.31	3.91	0.92
Farm Size	.86	.75	.03	.13	0.14	0.29
Percent Illinois	.87	.75	.005	-.63	0.60	0.28
Percent Yankee	.87	.76	.004	.26	-2.80	-1.07
Percent English	.87	.77	.009	.28	1.21	0.36
(constant)					29.10	

While the Republicans moved on the national scene to reconstruct the South, the party in Illinois protected its power by completing the transformations in its organization. During Reconstruction, the party pursued still further its tendency to adopt a military style of organization. Through a complex and disciplined party structure, the Republicans made themselves better able to resist defections by leading politicians like President Johnson, and to prevent factionalism over side issues. The strength of the organization enabled the Republicans to carry out their Reconstruction program, and remove the uncertainties of elections. The organization could easily turn out the voters, and the politicians knew that the coalition would remain firm.

The key to the success of the Republican party was the high degree of voter loyalty it maintained. The party constantly reminded its adherents of the perilous situation in the nation and of their duty to their country and the party. The *Tribune*, for example, warned its readers that "all for which we have fought and toiled and bled through four years is liable to be sacrificed by any weakness or division in our ranks." "We trust," the paper continued, "[that] no true Republican will recommend any abandonment or disorganization of the Republican party . . . for any temporary or subordinate pretext."[81] Even in campaigns for minor offices, the party did not slack in its intensity. The *State Journal* sounded a typical rallying cry for the Springfield municipal elections.

If it is the duty of the soldier in the field to stand by his Government, it is no less the duty of the citizen at the polls to do the same thing. It is the

duty of the man who approaches the polls today, to vote to sustain those
principles for which our brave soldiers have been fighting and suffering at
Richmond. . . . Let Springfield respond to the Union triumph at
Richmond, with a Union triumph at the polls.[82]

Besides the constant chiding of the newspapers, the Republicans
had other devices for maintaining a high degree of voter loyalty in the
party. They skillfully used the Union Leagues and the Grand Army of
the Republic to create enthusiasm and to rally the voters. Especially
during Reconstruction, the Republicans relied upon the GAR. Formed
immediately after the war, the GAR had the charm of a secret lodge
with passwords, ceremonies, and rites. Almost every Union veteran
belonged, and it became a sort of mutual insurance company for army
officers. Although politics was originally excluded from its activities, old
generals like John A. Logan and Richard Oglesby gradually turned the
GAR into a political arm of the Republican party. The force of the
organization in politics was felt immediately. Whole lodges marched in
order to the polls and cast their ballots for the Republican party just as if
they were marching into battle. No old soldier failed in his duty. By
participating in Republican rallies, parades, and meetings, the GAR
served as a constant reminder that the party had saved the Union.[83]

Voter loyalty allowed the Republicans to formalize a highly
disciplined and organized party structure. They had already made
committees standard features of the party, and now they were able to
expand a little-used procedure to insure regularity and discipline. In the
Second Party System, primary elections had been rare, but by 1865 the
Republicans adopted this organizational tactic throughout the entire
State. The method was simple and the benefits tremendous. Republican
voters would cast ballots for previously announced candidates for office
before they elected delegates to nominating conventions. After the votes
for the candidates were counted and the winners declared, the voters
would then elect the convention delegates who were instructed to vote as
a unit for the ticket chosen by the people. Splits in the party growing
out of disputes and fraud which had characterized some of the earlier
party conventions were now effectively checked by the primary elections.
Personalities could not exist inside the party, and now they had no
legitimate excuse for bolting.[84]

Voter loyalty and the new structural techniques gave the
Republican party the strength to resist side issues as well as personalities.
According to the *Tribune*, "the Republican organization has attained a
prestige, power and momentum by virtue of its past history and brilliant
record, which cannot be assailed or resisted on any temporary, local or
side issues."[85] Defections in the party, whether by a faction concerned

with a side issue or by a personality, were dealt with in the same manner. As in the army, desertion was treason and the culprit was forever branded. Again, the *Tribune* sounded the warning to all Republicans.

> Any attempt to bolt is an attempt by a minority to rule the majority and ought to fail. They are wrong politically, because all bolting movements naturally form coalitions with the common enemy and permanently injure the unity, harmony and organization of the Republican party. Finally, they are inexpedient, because members of the party who cannot rule it by acting in and through it, cannot hope to rule it by passing wholly beyond its pale.[86]

The strength of the Republicans in dealing with those who broke party ranks is well illustrated by the case of President Johnson. The Republicans made an example of him and all of those who sided with him, cutting them off completely from the party in 1866. Then, in March, 1867, the Republican-controlled Congress passed the Tenure-of-Office Act which was designed to prevent Johnson from using his patronage. This act eventually provided the excuse to impeach the President, the ultimate punishment for desertion. The most honest Republicans admitted that impeachment was a political attack, but all agreed that Johnson had to be chastised for his defection.[87]

Although the attempt to remove Johnson from office failed, it was a successful warning to all those who dared to think of bolting the party. Lyman Trumbull knew that after he voted for acquittal in Johnson's trial, he had no political future with the Republicans. The Champaign *Union and Gazette* sounded the typical Republican reaction to Trumbull's actions.

> A kiss was the sign by which Judas betrayed his Lord and Master. A vote was the sign by which Trumbull betrayed his party. A love of money prompted the Jew to the commission of his act of betrayal, but what prompted the politician to his act of betrayal? Was it love of money too? We should dislike to think so. Was it a desire to break up the party and organize a new one in which he might be one of the Prime Ministers? We fear it was.[88]

The fate of Trumbull was sealed. The Republicans were in such a position of strength that they could expel without hesitation their own President and one of the founders of the party in Illinois.

The Republicans also now had the power to resist the rise of side issues. One particular problem facing the Illinois Republicans was the currency question. Nationally, the party was committed to paying off the war debt in hard money. In Illinois, as in many other States, there was a shortage of currency. The Democrats endorsed the inviting "Ohio idea," which proposed that the debt be paid off in greenbacks. The Democrats also demanded that bonds sold to raise money for the war be taxed. The Democrats were not bothered by this reversal of Jacksonian doctrines on currency, since inflated money was in great demand. Although many Republicans were tempted by the "Ohio Idea," the party held firm and refused to allow bond holders to be paid in anything other than gold and silver. No party man dared to break ranks.

The tariff was another problem facing the Illinois Republicans. As on the currency question, the western States were pitted against the East. Since states like Illinois benefited from low tariffs, some Illinois Republicans were prominent advocates of free trade. Nevertheless, when the national party adopted a strong tariff plank, the Illinois Republicans acquiesced.[89]

A third side issue during Reconstruction that threatened the unity of the Republican party was prohibition. In the mid-1860s, the temperance crusaders began a resurgence of activity, forgetting their earlier resolution to stay aloof from politics. The Illinois Republicans reacted immediately, denying to all prohibitionists a place in the party and adamantly refusing to allow temperance planks in the State platform. The Republicans understood perfectly that temperance would divide the party. The *Tribune* declared that the prohibitionists had "no right to expect that the Republican party will imperil the success of its principles to carry out their visionary ideas."[90]

The ease with which temperance, the tariff, and the currency question were brushed aside by the Republicans stemmed from the strength of the party organization. The ability to resist these side issues, however, also depended on the belief of a majority of the voters in the righteousness of the Republican cause. War and Reconstruction were living issues which dominated the political scene. These other questions would be handled in due time. John A. Logan captured in a speech the prevailing feeling of the Republican voters that the party that had saved the Union would also solve the lesser questions.

> They [the people] have faith in the Republican party. They judge it by what it has done, and hence they know full well what it will do. They know that the Republican party is in fact the only party of peace and prosperity. It was that party which led the hosts of the Union to the haven of peace through the red ordeal of war. Those questions which now embarrass us are but the *debris* of war. We have cared for the wounded, we have buried the dead. . . . To give stability to the currency, to equalize taxation, to harmonize States, and to insure prosperity, is still another and probably quite as difficult a portion of that same labor. But the party which did the one is unquestionably equal to the other.[91]

In 1866, the Democrats, in sharp contrast to the Republicans, were poorly organized. The party desperately searched for a means to unify its supporters. The tariff and currency questions were obvious issues for the Democrats to latch upon and the Illinois party cautiously adopted a stand in favor of a low tariff and the "Ohio idea." The party, however, was too divided to exploit these issues. A weak organization and personal quarrels prevented the Democrats from uniting upon any kind of principle.

In July 1867, the *Cairo Daily Democrat* complained that the Republicans were already organized for the fall municipal elections while the Democrats had not even begun to prepare. "It is true," the paper wrote, "the election is not, in one sense, very important, but the Radicals know that it is important, for party purposes, to keep their organization in a high state of discipline so that its full power may be brought out in the momentous political battle to be fought in 1868."[92] Unlike the Republicans, the Democrats still allowed their organization to collapse after elections. Every fall, committees, conventions, workers, and speakers had to be re-organized. Even as late as 1869, the Democrats still refused to maintain permanent organizations. In a petition to the National Central Committee some Democrats from New York expressed their frustration with the party's lassitude in preparing for elections.

> The undersigned would urge upon the Democracy the importance of preparing now for the next struggle with its enemies. Such preparation is too commonly postponed until the eve of elections. But we must begin now to plant the seed if we would reap the harvest of future victories.[93]

Interestingly, the men who sent this circular never mentioned the creation of a permanent organization, only early preparation for elections!

The Democrats in Illinois were also plagued by personal quarrels. The Party's old warhorses, McClernand and Richardson, had been replaced by new men, and there was conflict between the old and the new guard of the party. The Illinois Democrats were also sectionally divided. Cyrus H. McCormick, owner of the *Chicago Times* and wealthy industrialist, for example, constantly battled with the downstate politicians for control of the party. Such personal quarrels ran without check even on the county level, since the party lacked an effective means of disciplining members. The *Carthage Republican* complained that the problem with the Democrats in Hancock county "lies solely in the degree of importance which democrats attach to mere individual insubordination and imprudence. If every democrat will only consider that when one democrat attacks another publically [sic] or privately he has a personal ambition to serve."[94]

The differences between the Democrats and the Republicans were never more evident than in the election of 1868. The Illinois Democrats were divided by their own platform on the issues of the tariff and the currency. Petty quarrels between the downstate and the Chicago politicians and between the new and the old leaders aggravated the party divisions. The party was once again forced to rely upon popular individuals to save the election. Illinois Democrats pinned their hopes upon George H. Pendleton, author of the "Ohio Idea," as a presidential candidate, but they were forced to settle for Horatio Seymour of New York. Seymour was not well known in Illinois and created little enthusiasm in the state party.

In contrast, the Republicans quickly marshalled their forces for the election of 1868. General Ulysses S. Grant was practically the unanimous choice of the Republican National Convention in Chicago. The Republicans declared the contest to be another battle in the long struggle for freedom. "The battle for freedom and the Union of these States is not yet fought out," declared one paper, and "the issues on which we met the rebels and their nothern allies, in the contest of 1864, are the issues to-day."[95] The tariff, currency, and prohibition questions were unimportant, according to the Republicans, compared with the real issues at stake. "The party which voted for slavery before the war, fought for slavery during the war, which believes in slavery after the war, is making its death struggle today," warned the *Tribune*. "Vote down the Reconstruction laws, and by the same act you restore the rebel governments which your soldiers disbanded and put to flight."[96] Richard Yates declared even more emphatically that the struggle in 1868 was but a continuation of war. "We are here to fight the same battle which our brave boys in blue fought," Yates stated. The election "is the same fight now, between patriotism and treason."[97]

The Republican campaign rhetoric hit the mark, as Grant and the entire ticket rolled up another great victory in Illinois. The Democrats were so badly beaten, John Palmer wrote, that "no political party in the modern history of the country has suffered such a defeat as the Democracy has. It will upon its present basis go out of existence."[98]

The Republican party maintained the 50,000 vote plurality that it had in 1866, and there were no major shifts within the electorate. Although the party attracted many more voters, the 1868 Republican coalition was composed of essentially the same groups that had voted for Lincoln in 1860 (see Table 30). The Southerners, the Illinois-born, and the Irish remained Democratic, but a majority of every other ethnic group voted Republican.[99] Illinois was still geographically divided between Egypt and the rest of the State, and the presence of Southerners

Table 30. Percentages Comparing Republican Vote

	1860 President	1868 President
Yankee	100	100
Southern	0	0
Illinois	0	0
Other	66	69
German	68	80
English	100	100
Irish	0	0
Scandinavian	100	100
Canadian	63	100
French	100	100

Table 31. 1868 Republican Geographical Comparison

Northern Townships

	Multiple R	R Square	RSQ Change	Simple R	B	Beta
Percent Irish	.49	.24	.24	-.49	-1.91	-1.43
Farm Size	.63	.39	.15	.39	0.17	0.59
Percent Other	.67	.45	.05	.08	-1.04	-1.55
Percent Illinois	.73	.52	.06	.26	3.29	1.00
Percent Yankee	.78	.61	.09	.03	-2.67	-1.67
Percent German	.82	.67	.05	.03	-1.15	-1.87
Baptist	.92	.84	.17	.15	12.82	0.68
Percent Southern	.96	.93	.08	-.41	-5.65	-0.50
Liturgical	.98	.96	.02	.05	-2.02	-0.19
Pietist	.98	.97	.01	.34	-4.69	-0.41
Percent Scandinavian	.99	.98	.009	-.19	0.72	0.29
Percent Canadian	.99	.99	.009	.13	-0.72	-0.21
Acre Value	.99	.99	.0009	.04	0.49	0.11
Percent French	.99	.99	.0003	.17	-0.10	-0.09
(constant)					145.75	

Northern and Central Townships

	Multiple R	R Square	RSQ Change	Simple R	B	Beta
Percent Southern	.74	.54	.54	-.74	-2.07	-1.11
Pietists	.79	.63	.08	.17	3.94	0.27
Farm Size	.82	.67	.04	.36	-0.12	-0.29
Percent German	.85	.73	.05	.20	0.44	0.48
Percent French	.87	.77	.03	.21	1.21	0.71
Percent Canada	.88	.78	.01	.34	1.89	0.39

	Multiple R	R Square	RSQ Change	Simple R	B	Beta
Liturgical	.89	.80	.02	.39	-9.23	-0.69
Percent Other	.90	.82	.01	.03	-0.06	-0.07
Baptist	.90	.82	.003	-.20	-4.96	-0.25
Value Produced	.90	.82	.002	.008	0.12	3.69
Capital Investment	.91	.84	.01	.01	-0.12	-3.98
Percent Scandinavian	.92	.85	.009	.09	2.83	0.78
Percent English	.93	.87	.01	.29	1.35	0.48
Percent Illinois	.94	.89	.01	-.62	0.98	0.55
Acre Value	.95	.91	.02	.19	-0.07	-0.11
Percent Yankee	.95	.91	.004	.29	-1.49	-0.68
Farm Value	.96	.92	.007	.40	0.004	0.72
Percent Irish	.96	.92	.001	.05	-0.95	-0.52
(constant)					53.10	

continued to be the overriding influence on the voting patterns (see Table 31).[100] The Germans, for example, were more likely to vote Republican if they lived in Egypt than in northern Illinois. In the northern townships, the Germans correlated with the Republican vote at only .03, but when southern Illinois was included in the calculation, the correlation dramatically rose to a .27. This pattern in the voting was true for other ethnic groups as well. The presence of the Southerners also affected the religious character of the coalitions. In northern Illinois, the Republicans correlated with the liturgicals at an insignificant .05 and with the pietists at a strong .39. Again when Egypt was included, the correlations significantly changed. For the State total, pietism dropped to a mere .17 correlation with Republicanism, but the liturgical correlation increased to an impressive .39.

The remarkable feature of the Republican coalition was that it remained strong throughout the cataclysmic events of the 1860s. Secession, Civil War, emancipation, and the assassination of one President and the defection of another, circumstances that nearly destroyed the nation, only seemed to make the Republicans stronger. Principles and an efficient organization sustained the party, but the vital factor for the survival of the Republicans through the revolutionary decade was party loyalty. For Republican voters, the war and Reconstruction made patriotism synonymous with party loyalty. With the voters directly linked to the party, loyalty was now the cement that held the structure together.

The changes in the Republican party over the decade brought a change in the attitude and manner of the politicians. The early career of Shelby Cullom symbolized the new character of the party leaders. Cullom, Speaker of the Illinois House in 1860, had Congressional ambitions. In 1862, he let it be known that he was a candidate. Leonard Swett, however, also desired to run for Congress from the same district. Since Swett was an old party workhorse, Cullom deferred and prepared to run in 1864. He then found that James C. Conkling, a close friend of Lincoln, wanted the 1864 nomination. Instead of threatening the party by a direct confrontation, Cullom quietly managed affairs in order to strengthen his position. He did so by running for the State Senate in 1862 even though the district was hopelessly Democratic. Cullom recalled that he decided to sacrifice himself in the election "to keep in touch with the voters . . . [and] in order to keep Conkling from getting such a hold on the district as to strengthen him for the contest two years afterwards."[101] Cullom's strategy worked perfectly. He was defeated for the State Senate, but in 1864, he easily defeated Conkling in a primary election and was elected to Congress in the general election. Cullom's planning and working within the party was the new style of politics while Conkling's reliance upon personal friends had become anachronistic.

The change in the structure, leadership, and style of the Republican party after the war proved to be uncomfortable for many of the old politicians. Tension rose in the party and finally exploded in 1872. The exodus of the "Liberal Republicans" was the final adjustment before the Third Party System became firmly entrenched in the political scene.

The Final Adjustment

The election of Grant in 1868 brought a political calm to the nation and Illinois. One Republican paper wrote, "it was predicted that, if Gen. Grant was elected President, the whole country would settle down, recognize the situation, and peace, order and quiet everywhere prevail."[1] There were some stirrings about the tariff and temperance questions, but the Republicans easily brushed aside these issues. The elections of 1870 confirmed the belief that "peace, order and quiet" everywhere prevailed. The Republicans swept the Congressional and State elections with no alterations in the voting patterns.[2]

The political calm stemmed in part from the strength of the Republican party. It had what seemed to be an insurmountable majority. Holding the coalition, politicians, and principles together was an impressive, almost military, organization which virtually guaranteed the continued success of the Republicans for years to come.

Paradoxically, the very factors sustaining the party also became a source of tension. Beneath the calm of 1870, there was a growing dissatisfaction within the Republican party that eventually culminated in the open revolt of the Liberal Republican movement. The transformation of the party into a tightly controlled organization during the previous decade had dislocated many Republicans who were clinging to the old style of politics. The war had changed the Republican party into an army, and that army was quickly becoming a machine by the end of Reconstruction. It had a life of its own, grinding ahead without regard to individuals. By 1870 it took a new breed of men to operate the party. Politicians had become managers and mechanics whose duty it was to keep the party machinery well lubricated and in repair. The old flair in politics had been replaced by the dull routine of marching out the voters on election day. There was no room for unpredictable behavior or independent action. Many of the old politicians, whose careers had begun in the Second Party System, could not understand the new style of politics. Like the Know-Nothings in 1855, they could not adjust to a changing system. The party, they felt, had become a god, and it seemed that principle had given way to the worshipping of patronage and spoils. The Liberal Republican movement was the response of these old personalities to the new party system. Their revolt signaled the final adjustment before politics was completely transformed into the Third Party System.

Historians have only vaguely recognized that the Liberal revolt was an adjustment in the party system.[3] Most have viewed it as resulting from other sources of discontent. Reconstruction, especially, has been considered the prime factor causing the Liberal revolt.[4] Impeachment, talk of confiscation, the inability of the freedmen to control the Southern State governments, and the corruption growing out of the excesses of the federal government in handling Reconstruction were all viewed as contributing to the Liberals' discontent. Although there has been some debate over the importance of states' rights and economic reform as issues, the main emphasis has remained upon Reconstruction.[5] While it is true that all of these points of dissatisfaction were addressed at one time or another by the Liberals of Illinois, it is significant that there was never an articulated statement combining all of these grievances into clearly defined principles. In fact, the Liberals varied widely in their reasons for bolting the party. Their only unifying characteristic was a deep sense of frustration over the changes in the Republican party.

The list of Republicans in Illinois who joined the Liberal revolt reads like a Who's Who of the party. Lyman Trumbull, U.S. Senator; John M. Palmer, Governor; Newton Batemen, Superintendent of Public Instruction; and Edward Rummel, Secretary of State, all embraced the movement. In addition to these men who held crucial posts in Illinois, a number of former office holders also joined the movement: Gustave Koerner, Francis A. Hoffman, and William Bross, all ex-Lieutenant Governors; Jesse K. Dubois and O.H. Miner, ex-State Auditors; O.M. Hatch, former Secretary of State; Washington Bushnell, ex-Attorney General; William Butler, former Treasurer; S.W. Moulton, ex-Congressman-at-Large; and John Wentworth and Leonard Swett, former Congressmen. Along with David Davis, these men had been the founders of the Republican party in Illinois. Each had known Lincoln personally, and each had made great sacrifices in the battle against slavery in the early days of the party. Now all of them were leaving the party in protest.

Their discontent covered a wide range of issues. David Davis was outraged by the attempt to impeach President Johnson. For Davis, Reconstruction had become a vindictive policy that was destroying the moral character of the nation. Davis complained that there was "no hope except in the disintegration of the dominant party."[6]   Others also expressed the feeling that the Republicans had abandoned their principles. Joseph Brown, mayor of St. Louis, wrote that "the old issues are lived out . . ." and that "as the two parties stand today there is nothing between them."[7]

Other Liberals were not as concerned with Reconstruction as they were with other problems. Horace White of the *Tribune*, for example, was dissatisfied with the tariff. With the tariff rising since the war, White, a free trader, argued that the Republicans must turn their attention to economic reform. He believed not that the Republicans had abandoned their principles in Reconstruction, but that the party must focus its attention on new problems. "For 10 years the Republican party has been wholly engrossed with the slavery and rebellion questions," the *Tribune* declared. "But these are happily and permanently disposed of." The work of Reconstruction was completed, and the party must now turn to the "reform of our monstrous system of tariff taxation."[8]   A number of Liberals echoed White's call for economic reforms. One man suggested that the tariff had become the new principle of the party, while Governor Palmer believed that the Republicans had become too "whiggish."[9]

Other Liberals were less concerned with economic reform or the indignities of Reconstruction. Their dissatisfaction stemmed from the erosion of states' rights and the centralization of power in Washington. Palmer complained that the Republicans, through the federal government, had usurped the power of the states, and he argued that the proper balance in government must be restored.[10]   One man wrote to O.M. Hatch stating his fear that a new form of despotism, in the guise of the Republican party, was destroying the nation.

> Many years ago you and I were ranged under the same banner battling against the usurpations of the Slave power.   That ferosious [sic] power having been crushed out I find myself acting with those who are resisting the efforts of the party in power to a centralization of all the powers of the Government in the Central Government or administration at Washington. This power if successfuly [sic] carried out will be as deadlie [sic] a blow to liberty and free institutions as would have been the triumph of the Slave power.[11]

Significantly, the Liberals never debated among themselves what had gone wrong in the nation. All were generally dissatisfied with Reconstruction, but while some argued that the party had abandoned its principles, others suggested that it was time to leave the war and Reconstruction behind and move on to new questions. The hodgepodge of concerns over states' rights, the tariff, and Reconstruction was too varying and unrelated to provoke a unified response from the Liberals. Their discontent lay deeper than those issues. What unified the Liberals and pushed them into action was a sense of frustration with the changes that were occurring in the party system.

Each of the men who became Liberals had been an important politician, and in the tradition of the Second Party System, had been used to the personal control of politics. Now all of them were at the end of their careers. Trumbull had broken party ranks over the impeachment of President Johnson, and in 1868, he did not participate in the campaign. By 1870, the Senator was advocating the heresy of unconditional readmission of the Southern States.[12] The Republicans made it clear that Trumbull would pay the price of his independence by not being returned to the Senate in 1872. John M. Palmer, elected Governor in 1868, also defied the party. Believing that the Republicans had become too Whiggish, Governor Palmer vetoed a number of bills passed by the Republican Legislature to promote the interests of corporations. The action that sealed his fate with the party, however, was Palmer's insistence that states' rights must be preserved. The issue came to a head after the Chicago fire in 1871, when the Governor became embroiled in a controversy with President Grant over the use of federal troops.[13] Like Trumbull, Palmer had exercised too much independence and the Republicans decided to check his influence.

Most of the other Liberals in Illinois were already out of office by 1870. Having been pushed aside in the 1860s by the new party managers, these Republicans lingered on the fringes of the party, hoping to regain their lost influence and prestige. Although none of these other Liberals were as flamboyant as John Wentworth, "Long John's" situation was typical. Wentworth had been a powerful leader in Chicago since the 1840s, but by 1862 he was forced into retirement by the Republican party. He was elected again to Congress in 1864 because of a series of accidental circumstances but forced to retire once more at the end of the term.[14] Hoping to recapture his former position, "Long John" ran for Congress in 1870 as an independent, but he lost the election. Clearly, he had no future in politics. The Liberal revolt gave Wentworth new life and an opportunity to regain lost power. The same opportunity existed for other Republicans who had lost their influence, such as Dubois, Hatch, Swett, and Koerner.

Frustrated by their loss of position in the party, the Liberals focused their attack upon the Republican organization. One new facet of the party that they singled out for criticism was party discipline. No political party had ever enforced discipline as severely as the Republicans did during Reconstruction. To the old politicians, this discipline was a form of tyranny. Lyman Trumbull, feeling the pressure of party regularity, complained that "one of the greatest evils of our time is party despotism & intolerance. . . . Most of the corruptions in government are made possible through party tryanny. Members of the Senate are daily coerced into voting contrary to their convictions through party pressure."[15]

The Liberals also railed against the manner in which the Republicans handled nominations. Nominations no longer went to the best qualified men but only to political hacks; they were bestowed as rewards for party loyalty and service. Koerner believed that "since the war most all important offices . . . had been given to military men . . . without regard to qualifications for civil offices."[16] The *Tribune* expressed the prevalent Liberal concern that good men could not be nominated because patronage workers controlled the conventions. The newspaper was very vocal in condeming the "unfair means resorted to by Federal office-holders to control nominations."

> It is alleged that Collectors and Assessors of Internal Revenue, and their subordinates, with Post-masters and special agents of all kinds holding their offices upon the nomination of their Representative, have conspired to pack county conventions, and, by bribery and corruption, and the use of their official patronage, and threats of official vengeance [*sic*], have forced, or tried to force, the nomination of the men to whom they owe their own offices.[17]

Koerner's complaint about military men and the *Tribune's* accusations about office-holders expressed the Liberals' frustration over the fact that new men controlled the party. During the party's transformation, a new breed of politician had risen to prominence, replacing the old personalities. One man wrote that "to me there has seemed during the past three years to emenate [*sic*] from the White House a most wicked and systematic attempt to degrade and destroy the influence of nearly all our old anti-slavery leaders."[18] Although there was no effort to destroy the old anti-slavery men, a change in party leadership had occurred. Even the Democratic *Register* noticed that at one Republican convention, none of the State's original Republicans were in attendance. "In the lobies [*sic*] of the Legislature, hotels, bar rooms, etc.," stated the newspaper, "are to be found an entirely new set of politicians."[19]

To the Liberals, these men were patronage workers, office-holders, and wire-pullers. Referring to the new politicians as "Barnacles" because they had attached themselves to the ship of state and fed off it, the

Liberals believed they could be nothing other than corrupt. Trumbull wrote that "the National Administration seems to me to be men of late to a great extent in the interest of selfish & unscrupulous men, who, in the name of party, manage to keep themselves in power."[20] One man summed up all the Liberal frustration by stating that "organization, patronage, and party discipline had taken place of zeal for a cause."[21]

When the Liberal movement was launched by the Missouri Republicans, the Illinois old guard responded enthusiastically. The Illinois Liberals agreed to meet in a mass convention in Cincinnati in April, 1872. Initially, they had no intention of making nominations at Cincinnati. As Koerner explained, "the general idea was to organize the Liberal party, recommend State conventions to assemble that should appoint regular delegates to a national convention, to be held after the administration Republicans had held theirs." The hope was that "the regulars would be terrified, and not nominate Grant, but some distinguished man of reformatory tendencies . . . [whom] the Liberals might then endorse."[22]

As the Liberals prepared for the convention, their maneuverings reflected frustration with the new party system and inability to adjust to the new style of politics. The political devices they resorted to were the old techniques of mass meetings and open conventions. Personalities had full reign, and in the end, the old rivalries nearly destroyed the movement.

Illinois Liberals began to hold mass meetings and conventions to elect delegates to Cincinnati. Quickly, however, these preliminary activities were turned into a contest between Palmer, Davis, and Trumbull for control of the Illinois delegation. It soon became apparent that nominations would be made at Cincinnati, as candidates across the country began organizing delegates. It was equally clear that since the convention was to be an open one, the man who sent the most supporters would control the delegates.

The contest between the Liberals in Illinois developed along familiar lines. "Long John" Wentworth, Jesse W. Fell, and Leonard Swett supported David Davis for President against their old antagonists, the *Tribune* clique, which went for Trumbull. John Palmer, the other candidate, was soon pushed aside, where he remained glumly watching the proceedings. Like a page out of the 1850s, the battle between the Trumbull and Davis forces was based upon the strength of personal appeals.

The Davis candidacy received an unexpected boost in February when a convention of laboring men nominated him for President. This convention adopted a platform opposed to the National Banking system and land grants to railroads, and in favor of paper money, a revenue tariff only, the abolition of Chinese labor, an eight-hour work day, and government control of the railroad and telegraph rates. Although Davis, an old Whig, was against every one of the measures the platform favored, he accepted the nomination since it strengthened his political position.[23]

The Democrats, who were in a quandary about how to react to the Liberal movement, were impressed with Davis' nomination by the labor convention. The *Chicago Times* wrote that "since the first nomination of Abraham Lincoln for president of the United States, no political occurrence has created so profound a public sensation as the nomination of David Davis by the labor convention in Columbus."[24] Many Democrats were slowly coming to believe that the party should back whomever the Cincinnati convention might nominate, and they began cautiously to support Davis' candidacy.

The growing Democratic support for Davis, however, opened an opportunity for Trumbull to stop the Davis movement. Trumbull wrote that "democrats are injuring Davis by committing themselves to him in advance. The Liberal republicans must first name the candidate, and not have him dictated by the Democrats."[25] Horace White of the *Tribune* became so concerned with the growing Democratic support for Davis that he threatened to abandon the movement.

> We could support Cincinnati as a Republican movement not embarrassed [*sic*] by Democratic complications or endorsements. We could not support it if it had a democratic 'send off.' The fact that Judge Davis was a candidate before the Dem. convention in N.Y. four years ago and has held the same attitude ever since . . . would prevent us from exercising any considerable influence with our own readers in his behalf. And of course it would be useless for us to join in a movement where we could not exercise such influence.[26]

The battle between Trumbull and Davis for control of the Illinois delegation to Cincinnati quickly became bitter. Horace White was fearful that all the independent activities in Illinois in support of the Liberal movement were in reality Davis movements.[27] Consequently, the Trumbull supporters moved to capture the regular Republican organization. Trumbull based much of his hope for controlling the party upon the growing dislike between President Grant and John A. Logan.[28] White made a special trip to Springfield to work with the Legislators and to convince Palmer to support Trumbull, but he failed to get support from either the regular Republicans or Palmer. Trumbull's forces then began to organize special meetings to elect delegates to the Cincinnati convention.

The Davis supporters understood perfectly the maneuverings of Trumbull and White. Jesse Fell wrote to Davis about White's actions in Springfield, and he warned the Judge that White had no other goal in mind than to promote Trumbull. "I think there is nothing more certain than that White is expecting Trumbull to be nominated," concluded Fell, and "that all he says and does has direct influence to that object." "If I were giving to 'guess,'" Fell continued, "I'd say if they [the *Tribune*] get their choice [for the nomination] the Tribune will be *all right*—if *not, not.*"[29]

As the Trumbull movement gained momentum, the Davis people became incensed with what they believed to be political trickery on the part of the *Tribune* clique. Wentworth wrote that "the friends of T[rumbull] should cease to embarrass the opposition to Grant by their intrigues in our state." Wentworth, however, was less worried about the Liberal cause than he was about Davis' candidacy for he concluded that "it is time we had a clear field."[30]

The Davis people were not above political tricks of their own. Leonard Swett and Jesse Fell, concerned over the growing support for Trumbull, and all of the special meetings his forces were organizing to elect delegates, planned to counter by sending as many people as they could to Cincinnati.

> There is a strong Trumbull feeling at Springfield, Alton & Belleville—I suppose fifty people will go from Springfield to Cincinnati in his interest, and if we don't look out, after all we will be overslaughed [*sic*] by numbers.
>
> It must be arranged that a train with a low rate of fare, if not entirely free should start from Bloomington with a view of taking a large delegation. . . . These counties [surrounding Bloomington] are unanimously for Davis, and we must get the bulk of our delegation from them.[31]

In the end, Davis sent several hundred men to Cincinnati as delegates, far more than Trumbull. Because of the total confusion at Cincinnati resulting from the haphazard arrangements for the meeting, the convention decided that the only resolution to the Illinois problem was to split the delegation evenly.[32]

When the Cincinnati convention convened in April, it appeared that Davis had the momentum, but the Trumbull backers effectively checked Davis' nomination. Meeting secretly, Horace White, Samuel Bowles, editor of the Springfield, Massachusetts *Republican*, Henry Watterson of the Louisville *Courier-Journal*, and Murat Halstead of the Cincinnati *Commercial* agreed to prevent Davis from getting the nomination.[33] Wentworth was furious. "Trumbull can kill Davis but can not get it [the nomination] himself," "Long John" wrote. "For once cannot Trumbull be magnanimous & call off his relatives . . . ?"[34] When it became apparent that Davis could not win the nomination, Wentworth resolved to beat Trumbull.

The choices of the convention were narrowed down to Charles Francis Adams and Horace Greeley. To most observers it looked as if Adams, a close friend of Trumbull, had the most support. Wentworth, however, in his determination to punish Trumbull, kept the Illinois delegation divided, thus preventing a victory for Adams. Many assumed that Trumbull would have been Adams' running mate, but Wentworth's actions blocked any chance for the nomination. Horace Greeley finally won and the Cincinnati convention almost dissolved in confusion.[35]

Koerner and Trumbull left the convention thoroughly disgusted. Koerner believed that Greeley's nomination was a death blow to the whole movement.[36] Thomas A. Hendricks, Democratic leader of Indiana, agreed. "My opinion now," explained Hendricks in a letter to Davis, "is that the movement is a failure . . . I do not know what I will advocate. The position is exceedingly embarrassing. . . . Now all is broken up & confused."[37] Almost immediately, a scheme developed to force Greeley to decline the nomination and to hold a new convention. Led by Carl Schurz, the movement gained wide support, including Koerner's. The plan eventually failed, however, because many Liberals felt that it might destroy the cause.[38]

The widespread dissatisfaction with Greeley stemmed from the fact that the Cincinnati convention was entirely a contest between personalities. The convention had been called to launch a reform movement, but the principles as stated by the platform emphasized only one thing—victory over Grant. The platform was a restatement of the platitudes of the original Missouri call: universal amnesty, local self-government, equality before the law, civil service reform, return to specie payment, and opposition to land grants to railroads. The only point of the platform that potentially had any substance was the tariff. But because the Liberals were divided between protection and free trade, this issue lost its real meaning by being compromised. The platform simply took a non-committal stand proposing that the tariff should be referred to the people.[39] The only aspect of the platform that was not innocuous was the listing of abuses committed by Grant. "Anybody to beat Grant" was the prime concern and, consequently, the disappointment over the nomination of Greeley was far more intense than it would have been if the Liberals had been united on principle. The unimportance of the platform could not have been emphasized more: Greeley, an uncompromising protectionist, had been nominated to run on a mild free trade platform.[40]

The irony of a reform movement to purify politics of corruption whose members resorted to intrigue and back room deals was not lost on the participants. The Davis people blamed Trumbull for the Judge's defeat. Special invectives were saved for Horace White and his infamous meeting with the other editors to choose a candidate. Many of the Davis people, including the Judge himself, were so embittered that they refused to participate in the campaign. The *Tribune* also noted that the Cincinnati convention had been marred with political intrigue, but it blamed the Davis men for soiling the purity of the movement. In a thinly-veiled attack upon the Judge, the *Tribune* complained that "the packing of a convention by delegates picked up and shipped at a candidate's expense is not promising of Reform; it gives no indication of improvement over the system of packing conventions through office-holders."[41]

The rancor of the battle between Davis and Trumbull persisted long after the convention. When Davis and his supporters abandoned the Liberal movement, they left the State ticket to the Trumbull men. Trumbull's supporters themselves, however, fell into quarrels as they jockeyed for position on the State ticket. Horace White wrote to Trumbull that "all our friends think that you will have to run for Governor with Koerner for Lieut. Gov. . . . If we carry the State your future will be what ever you most desire."[42] Many others agreed that Trumbull should run for Governor, but Governor Palmer and Koerner also had their supporters.[43] Typifying the maneuverings to find a place on the State ticket, Jesse Dubois wrote to Trumbull offering his support and suggesting that he himself "should desire the Treasurers Office for two reasons. The pay is fully equal to any of the others and labor almost nothing."[44]

Few Liberals were satisfied with the direction in which the movement had developed. The Cincinnati convention had nominated the wrong man, the platform was weak, and the movement was seriously divided by personal feuds. Trying to find some basis for optimism, Horace White wrote that "we came here to break up two old rotten political parties. We have not done everything that we wanted to, but I think we have done *that*."[45] The effect of the Cincinnati convention, however, was not to destroy both parties, but to disrupt only one—the Democrats. "It is plain that the Cint Convention insteading [*sic*] of dividing the Republican party," wrote David Davis, "has split the Democratic party in twain."[46]

The Democrats might not have had difficulty in supporting Davis for President, but Horace Greeley was a different question. When the unexpected news of Greeley's nomination reached Illinois, the party was thrown into confusion. The Democrats had been on the brink of oblivion since 1864, and now they were faced with the ultimate question of their survival. To remain aloof from the Liberal movement could only mean, at best, prolonging their minority status, and, at worst, it might spell the destruction of the party. Joining the movement, however, was hardly an attractive alternative. Fusion with the Liberals could destroy the party more quickly than remaining independent. On the other hand, if Greeley were elected with Democratic support, the party might be revived.

With these choices facing them, the Democrats began a protracted debate, which threatened to divide the party. As early as November 1871, the Illinois Democrats began to struggle with the question of appropriate action. The Chicago *Times* endorsed the idea of "relaxing party discipline" and joining together the "better men" of the existing parties, either temporarily or permanently, into a new organization. The *Register* took up the *Times'* proposal, stating that "in such an extremity, whatever of party pride or prejudice stand in the way of public deliverance, should be freely and promptly sacrificed upon the sacred altar of country and morality."[47]

Much of the party recoiled from the idea of abandoning the Democracy and labeled the fusion proposal the "passive policy." This group of Democrats insisted that the only course to follow was to maintain a distinct organization and remain aloof from the division within the Republican party. "Active principle," they argued, was the only means of keeping the party alive.

Pressure from this group was so great that the *Times* and the *Register* quickly modified their original proposal. The *Register* maintained that the duty of the Democracy was to "assist and encourage, by every means in their power" the efforts of the Liberals. But the *Register* began to retreat from its earlier position advocating the abandonment of the party. In supporting the Liberals, the paper maintained, "the democracy retract nothing and explain nothing. . . . The party is not to be disbanded, not disorganized, not weakened in energy or purpose." The only way to beat Grant, however, was a union of the opposition, and therefore the Democrats must cooperate in such a union.[48]

Cyrus McCormick, owner of the *Times* and Chairman of the Illinois Democratic party, in an effort to achieve unity, called for a Democratic newspaper convention to meet in January to discuss general strategy. Some 27 editors assembled in Peoria and under the direction of McCormick endorsed the "passive policy." The editors declared that, although the Democrats must maintain their distinct party organization, they should accept the Cincinnati nominations.[49]

The "active principle" men were denied the use of the major newspapers in Illinois, but their continued protests were still heard by the Democratic leaders. Apparently, the faction was large and vocal enough to stall McCormick's strategy, for in March, the official word was that the party would settle the issue in convention.[50] The assembling of the Liberals in April at Cincinnati acted as a deterrent to the finalizing of Democratic strategy. The fact that all Democratic efforts to encourage the Liberals were rebuffed, especially by the Trumbull men, cast further doubt upon the "passive policy."

The nomination of Greeley at Cincinnati was a blow to the "passive policy" Democrats, but they bravely praised the choice. The *Register* began printing excerpts from other Illinois newspapers that endorsed Greeley.[51] McCormick and the *Times*, however, backed off and declared that Greeley was "repugnant to the good sense of every honorable man."[52] The Chicago *News* also rejected the Liberal ticket and declared that the party would be better defeated than dishonored.[53]

The Democrats were now more divided than ever. The Carlinville *Enquirer* accused the Chicago *Times* of being bought by Grant and asserted that the sooner "the democratic party is rid of such political villains the better."[54] The *Times*, in response, began to attack the supporters of the "passive policy" as a gang of "political prostitutes." Special invectives were reserved for old John A. McClernand, the leader of the "passive" wing, who was accused of having been dismissed from the army for incompetence.[55]

Another editors' convention was called in May to try to patch the divisions in the party. The meeting, however, was far from successful. The 25 editors who attended endorsed the "passive policy," but since the "active principle" men had not joined the proceedings, the resolutions were empty.[56] The final struggle between the factions took place at the state convention.

In June, the Democratic state convention convened in Springfield. The "passive" wing had complete control of the delegates, which made the outcome a foregone conclusion despite the warnings from the *Times*. The Illinois Liberal convention met on the same day in the same city. Each convention appointed a committee of conference to discuss terms of fusion, including a slate of candidates. Once the work of the conference committee was finished, the Liberals marched to the Opera House, the location of the Democratic convention, and led by Governor Palmer, entered the meeting to the cheers of the Democracy.[57] A joint meeting proceeded to endorse Gustave Koerner for Governor, as neither Trumbull nor Palmer wanted to run; a Democrat, Charles Black, for Lieutenant Governor; and a combination of Liberals and Democrats for the other offices, including Edward Rummel, Newton Bateman, and Charles Lanphier. Finally, the Democrats elected their delegates to the national convention with instructions to vote for Greeley.

When the national Democratic convention convened at Baltimore, it nominated Greeley and Brown, and the fusion was complete. Although the vast majority of the party swallowed the Greeley ticket, not all Democrats were reconciled to the Liberal alliance. A small, but vocal, number bolted and supported Charles O'Connor for President; and, in Illinois, these "active principle" men held their own convention.

Since the nomination of McClellan in 1864, the party had been politically bankrupt. Through the Reconstruction years the Democrats desperately searched for a new organizing principle, first by trying to reactivate Jacksonian doctrines, and then by revamping Douglas' stand of 1860. The result was that the party was fragmented more than before. The only solution to its predicament was to latch onto personalities, adopting President Johnson and then popular military heroes. The reliance upon personalities somewhat compensated for the party's difficulty in finding principles, but also perpetuated its unstable position. The acceptance of Horace Greeley, an old Whig and Republican, was the ultimate sacrifice in the party's search for a means of survival. James W. Singleton understood perfectly what had happened and he exposed the Democrats' problems in a fiery speech before the Illinois "active principle" convention.

> [W]e were transferred from principle to policy, and from one policy to another, as extreme as heat and cold, in the vain hope that something would turn up. . . . We were led from pillar to post by one captain and then another, until in the weakness of demoralization our emaciated members, the living skeleton of what was once the invincible party . . . was [sic] made to perform a sort of mystic dance upon the outer edge of a Republican platform. . . . At the end of this disgraceful carnival we were called upon to make still greater sacrifices than we had yet done. Nearly two millions of Democrats were required to foreswear their principles and surrender unconditionally to 25,000 disappointed and sore-headed Republicans. . . . [The Democrats have] issued a call for political miscegenation to those who believe that the great disideratum [sic] for political organization is a big party rather than a sound one, and that size can only be obtained by cross-breeding.[58]

Although Singleton understood the problems of the Democracy, he could offer no acceptable alternative to the Liberal fusion. Support of Greeley was a gamble, but standing pat was certain defeat.

The organization and the style of the campaign conducted by the Liberal-Democratic coalition reflected the character of both groups. The

Liberals, unable to adjust to the new Republican party, and the Democrats, still without a permanent organization except for the State Central Committee, relied upon the old campaign techniques of the 1850s. The result was that personalities were once again called upon to carry the campaign.

The common bond between the Liberals and the Democrats was opposition to Grant, and that became the sole issue of their campaign in 1872. Greeley was honest and Grant was corrupt. Grantism came to stand for all the abuses in the nation. "*Pure* zeal must be opposed to the zeal of the Army of office-holders—Postmasters, Assessors and the like," wrote McCormick. "They are an interested party: we are not—having nothing but the good of the Country at heart." The charge was that Grant had turned the government into personal property and ruled by whim, not by law. The Republican party existed only to keep him in office.[59]

"Grantism" proved to be a weak issue. By basing the campaign upon personalities, the Liberal-Democratic campaign made itself vulnerable. It appeared to many that the Greeley men were simply soreheads who desired government offices for themselves. C. E. Lippincott, a Republican who was tempted by the Liberal movement, resolved to remain loyal because the Greeley candidacy was nothing more than "a coalition of men of every possible political creed and character, held together by the single tie of a universal wish to get into the offices of the government."[60]

The weakness of the issue could not be overcome by a strong campaign as the Liberals and Democrats were plagued by ineffectual organization. The attempt to start the campaign early in July met with a number of difficulties. The National Democratic Committee sent directives to the State Committees immediately after the Baltimore convention, instructing them in the procedures to be adopted in the campaign. The National Committee directed that the State party should support the fusion ticket, but maintain its distinct organization. The other proposals by the Committee revealed how weak the Democratic organization was in 1872. Reminiscent of the Second Party System, the Democrats still directed individuals to assume responsibility for the party in local areas and to draw up lists of voters so that documents could be mailed to them.[61]

The Liberals and Democrats in Illinois, however, had a difficult time coordinating their efforts. The Liberals appointed a Central Committee, which began to call meetings and direct the campaign, paying only slight attention to the regular Democratic organization. The Democrats protested and a rift opened between the two camps.

Complicating the matter was a quarrel between personalities. Isaac Fuller, a Democrat, accepted the Liberal Committee's authority in hopes of becoming the State's leading Democrat. Meanwhile, Daniel Cameron, editor of the Chicago *News*, tried to use the Liberal Central Committee to force the removal of an old enemy from the regular Democratic Central Committee.[62] The conflict was not resolved until late August when a Greeley and Brown Campaign Committee was organized with Cyrus McCormick, Chairman of the Democratic Central Committee, appointed to head the new organization.

Because of the wrangling between personalities and the confusion over procedures, the campaign remained uncoordinated until September. McCormick finally issued a circular directing the organization of the State. The circular once again, reviving the political techniques of earlier decades, called upon individual politicians to organize every precinct and ward with committees. Ironically, the circular conceded that the Republicans had a "perfect organization" to aid them and urged this as a reason for Liberal-Democratic industry.[63] Even as late as October, the Greeley newspapers were still chiding their supporters to organize the counties and townships for the election.[64]

The Liberals and the Democrats belatedly tried to organize the State. Using mass meetings addressed by flamboyant politicians, the Liberals hoped to rally the voters at the polls. Astute observers realized that such methods could not take the place of an effective organization. One Liberal wrote to Trumbull that "we are loosing [*sic*], not gaining ground. . . . There is a manifest change in popular feeling going on. The tide is not so clearly with us as it has. Something must be done soon to regain our lost prestige." The answer, according to the writer, was "organization, more complete, thorough & compact than we now have."[65]

It was too late, however, to recapture the ground lost because of an ineffective organization. All the Liberals and the Democrats could hope for was that distinguished personalities could influence enough voters. John G. Thompson, Chairman of the Ohio Democratic Committee, advised Trumbull that success depended upon converting Republicans. "This can be accomplished most readily and effectively," wrote Thompson, "by distinguished gentlemen lately in their confidence and who can convince them of the purity of their motive in withdrawing from that party."[66] Although Trumbull, Palmer, and Koerner campaigned in Illinois, their efforts seemed to help little. The outlook was so depressing by the middle of October that two Democrats writing to Cyrus McCormick suggested that the Democratic party force Greeley to withdraw and nominate a new man for President.[67]

The Republicans, in contrast to the Liberals and the Democrats, were united and well prepared for the election. Even though the founders of the Illinois party and most of the leading officers in the State government, including the Governor, had bolted the party, the Republicans were unhurt and the party organization was unaffected. President Grant wrote to his old friend, Elihu Washburne, that the Liberal revolt "has apparently harmonized the party by getting out of it the 'sore-heads' and knaves who had all the trouble because they could not controll [sic]."[68]

The Republicans were able to withstand such a large-scale defection of politicians because of their party structure. By 1872, the organization had many permanent, uniform features. The State Central Committee had become a set structural device as early as the 1850s, and now each county had standing committees. The permanent structure was maintained even at the precinct level in many areas, especially in the cities. Disputes were quickly settled by primary elections, and in election years, it was easy for the Republicans to nominate their candidates and to get the campaign started. Aiding the party were a number of semi-official clubs, the most important being the Grand Army of the Republic, which could arrange for rallies and get voters to the polls. A more crucial aspect of the party, however, was the army of workers. The Republicans fielded an impressive number of loyal workers who canvassed voters, handled the daily details, and rallied the voters on election day.

Patronage was one of the key factors that kept the party rolling and the workers in the field. According to the Liberals and Democrats, virtually every Republican newspaper editor or publisher held an important patronage post. The editor of the Springfield *Journal*, for example, was the Sangamon County Internal Revenue Assessor.[69] Every member of the Republican State Committee held a patronage post as either a collector, assessor, or post master.[70] By awarding offices to loyal party men, the Republicans commanded a large body of men whose only employment was through patronage.

The real cement for the Republicans, however, was party loyalty, without which patronage would have meant little. The Civil War had firmly identified the Republicans as the party of the Union, and Reconstruction reinforced that image. For many, the war was not yet over. The Fifteenth Amendment had not been ratified until 1870, and only then were Mississippi, Texas, and Georgia finally readmitted to the Union. That was not the end of sectional conflict, however; constant violence in the South kept Reconstruction and the war alive as issues. The Ku Klux Klan reached its zenith in 1871, spreading terror through the South. The violence plus the "redemption" of Tennessee, North Carolina, and Georgia by 1871 convinced many Northerners that the South was unrepentant. This apprehension led to the passage of the First Enforcement Act in 1870, and the Second and Third Enforcement Acts a year later. One Liberal, writing to Trumbull, recognized the importance of Reconstruction in the coming election. Noting the general dissatisfaction with President Grant, the man expressed the belief that the people would vote against the administration *"provided* they were satisfied that the extreme men of the South were not to be included into power. . . . *If* anything defeats Mr. Greeley's election, it will be this *apprehension."*[71]

The loyalty of the voters to the Republican party was reinforced by the constant turmoil in the South. Many perceived the struggle in 1872 as no different from that in 1868 or 1864. Richard Yates, in a letter not meant for public consumption, expressed the sincere fear felt by most Republicans of a Liberal-Democratic victory.

> I would oppose the Cincinnati nominations because they comtemplate coalition with the Democratic party, North and *South* and if elected would I believe be controlled by that party . . . and the success of the party is the success of theories which led to the war. . . . I say that considering the unsettled condition of the South, I believe the success of the democratic party through Greeley & Brown would lead to oppression, anarchy and finally war or *peaceable* disunion.[72]

Yates, who had no special fondness for Grant, expressed a desire that the party find another candidate. Loyalty to the party, however, proved stronger than personal predilections and the renomination of Grant did not lessen his party spirit. Disappointment over nominations was hardly a valid reason for bolting the party. Again, Yates expressed the prevailing sentiments among Republicans.

> You know that I have had many offices for all of them I had the nomination of my own party in convention and those who could not beat me were required to submit to the disappointment of defeat and to support me. After such men as Greeley, Trumbull, Palmer, Brown etc. have claimed and enjoyed the benefits of such a usuage [*sic*] it is not in my view honorable for them to bolt the party because they forsee the nomination of a candidate who is not their choice.[73]

The Republican party in Illinois was as well organized and as efficiently run as at any other time in its history. Oiled by loyalty and patronage, the party machinery seemed to move inexorably ahead. The party was so well regulated and disciplined that its parts could be replaced without disrupting its effectiveness. The defection of a Senator, the Governor, and many of the State officers only meant that new men had to be placed in these vacancies. No major overhauls were needed to repair the party. Richard Oglesby, Edward Rutz, and C. E. Lippincott were slated to fill the places left by Palmer, Rummel, and Bateman.

With an assurance that comes only with unequivocal strength, Illinois Republicans met in convention late in May. They efficiently nominated a new State ticket and drew up a platform with precision. After making resolutions of gratitude to those who had saved the Union and praising the record of the party, the Republicans endorsed the tariff, welcomed the immigrant, and demanded strict adherence to the Fifteenth Amendment. They also wisely resisted the urging of prohibition advocates and condemned, as unconstitutional, legislation for the cure of intemperance.[74] After the convention adjourned, the Republicans confidently opened the campaign with deadly efficiency.

The Liberals and the Democrats, without any mobilizing principles, attacked the Republicans in a piecemeal fashion. The Liberals continued to flail at corruption and patronage, while the Democrats tried to stir the voters by attacking a range of issues. Some centered their appeals on the need to restore states' rights and others talked about the need for reconciliation with the South. The *Register* even attempted to arouse the voters by taking a strong temperance stand and by accusing the Republicans of violating the Sabbath.[75] By the fall, the uncoordinated Liberal and Democratic campaign began to fizzle, as it became difficult even to find speakers for their rallies.

The Republicans won a resounding victory. Grant and the entire state ticket swept Illinois. Thirteen out of 19 Congressmen elected were Republicans, and the Legislature was returned with a safe Republican victory. Many historians have argued that the Liberal revolt was an "escape hatch" allowing those Democrats who had joined the Republicans in 1860 to return to the old party.[76] In Illinois, however, this was not the case. The Liberal revolt had no permanent effect upon the Republican coalition and it contributed little to the Democratic party.

As had been the basic pattern since 1860, Illinois was sectionally divided with the Southerners and the Illinois-born voting Democratic. Grant maintained the solid support of the Yankees, English and Canadians, along with 62 percent of the "other"-born and 84 percent of the Germans. The only Republican losses in 1872 were a drop of 17 percent of the Scandinavians and 69 percent of the French, but these percentages represented only a small number of actual voters (see Table 32).[77]

Table 32. Percentages Comparing Republican Vote, 1860-1872

	1860	1864	1868	1872
Yankee	100	100	100	100
Southern	0	32	0	0
Illinois	0	0	0	0
Other	66	54	69	62
German	68	62	80	84
English	100	100	100	100
Irish	0	0	0	0
Scandinavian	100	100	100	83
Canadian	73	100	100	100
French	100	100	100	30

The voter shifts were so slight in the 1872 election that the religious pattern of the coalitions remained virtually unchanged. Overall, the Republicans continued to be positively correlated with both the pietists and the liturgicals. Again, however, the sectional divisions in Illinois had an important effect upon the religious character of the Republican coalition. The liturgicals, for example, correlated at an insignificant .07 with the Republican vote in the northern townships. The inclusion of Egypt in the calculation, however, dramatically increased the liturgical correlation with the Republican party to .32, indicating that the presence of the Southerners was still the dominant influence in the voting pattern.

The Republican coalition had been untouched by the Liberal revolt. The Republican victory in 1872 had been so complete that the Liberal party ceased to exist.[78] David Davis vindictively wrote: "Was there ever such a political defeat!" With a great deal of satisfaction, Davis wondered "how Horace White and Judge Trumbull and their particular followers feel at their future prospects."[79] The outlook for the Liberals was certainly bleak, and the revolt appeared to be nothing more than an aberration. The Liberals had failed to achieve their goals and they had not provided an "escape hatch" for former Democrats to return to the party. The consequences of their actions, nevertheless, had a profound effect upon the party system.

For one thing, the Liberals were completely expelled from the Republican party. An observer, writing years later, noted that "political parties have no gratitude and political sins are hardly ever condoned. A revolt from a party, like that of the Liberals in 1872, is suicidal unless successful."[80] After the election, only Trumbull retained a major office, but as soon as the Legislature assembled, it removed the old politician from his Senate seat. The Liberals were so stripped of offices, patronage, and influence that, for the Republicans, it was as if those men had never existed. In the campaigns to come, the past contributions of Trumbull, Davis, and Palmer to the party were never mentioned.

For the Liberals, the results of the election had only one meaning. Their political careers, molded in the turbulent days of the Second Party System, now were at an end. Some of these men, such as Rummel, Bateman, Hatch, and Dubois, remained life-long Republicans, although they were denied the offices of the party. John Wentworth, the most flamboyant of the Liberals, made one last effort to gain the good graces of the party in 1880. Ironically, "Long John" chose to support Grant for a third term as the means to rejoin the party. After one final bitter campaign in Cook County, Wentworth was sent as a delegate to the national convention. The defeat of Grant, however, spelled the end for "Long John" and he retired forever from public office.[81]

Other Liberals, like Horace White and David Davis, refused to ask the party for forgiveness and remained independent. Both men retained great influence in Illinois, but not within the party. White, through the *Tribune*, endorsed every Republican platform and ticket after 1872, but he no longer participated in party policy making. Davis sat serenely on the Supreme Court until 1876, when he accepted a seat in the Senate as a compromise candidate. After that, however, his career ended.[82]

The Liberals who hoped to salvage something out of the disaster joined the Democratic party. Led by Trumbull, Palmer, and Koerner, these men fared no better than the other Liberals. Koerner's influence faded quickly once it became obvious that he could not even carry any German voters with him. Palmer proved to be too troublesome to the Democrats, as the old Governor stuck steadfastly to a Jacksonian monetary policy at a time when the party was pushing for an inflated currency. He finally ended his career by running for President in 1896 as a Gold Democrat with Simon Bolivar Buckner, whose only claim to fame was as a Confederate General who surrendered Fort Donelson to Grant. Trumbull too was unsuccessful in saving his career. Because of his popularity, he was used for a while by the Democrats, who nominated him for Senator and Governor, but he never really had much influence in the party. Trumbull eventually became a Populist, and he was seriously considered as a Presidential candidate by the People's Party in 1892. He died, however, before the movement gained any real strength.[83]

The Republicans emerged from the election of 1872 stronger and more unified than ever before. The party was now completely transformed, with a character much different from the political parties of the 1850s. The party was so strong that not only could it resist personalities, but it also could survive without principles. It remained only for the Democrats to reconstruct their party before the Third Party System took final shape.

The Third Party System

Between 1872 and 1876, the Democrats finally adopted the new party techniques that had been developed by the Republicans over the previous decade. Led by a new generation of politicians, the Democratic party established permanent and uniform structures. The characteristics of the Third Party System became clearly visible, with both parties now greater than the sum of their individual leaders. No politician had an existence independent of the party. The parties, in fact, became so powerful that they could survive even the loss of principles.

By 1874, it was evident that the principles surrounding the slavery issue were fading. Slavery was dead, the war concluded, the rebellion crushed and Reconstruction was rapidly losing its vitality as a political question. As the principles became less significant, side issues, especially economic ones, began to grow in importance, threatening the voter coalitions established by the slavery realignment. Instead of splintering and dissolving into factions, or reverting to politics by personalities, as had happened in the Second Party System, the parties remained strong. The party organizations provided the means of keeping the voter coalitions unified. But what made the organizations so effective was the party loyalty established during the war and Reconstruction. Voter loyalty was the real cement holding the parties together, and this was the most distinguishing feature of the Third Party System. Voter loyalty made the political parties into institutions, greater than personalities and even principles.

Since the death of Stephen Douglas in 1861, the Democratic party in Illinois had been demoralized. During the war, the party split into peace and war factions, and that basic division persisted until the end of the decade. The party could not even achieve unity in opposition to the Republican Reconstruction policy. Their position that the Reconstruction Acts violated the Constitution only perpetuated their image as copperheads, which in turn aggravated the tensions between the party's peace and war factions. As long as the sectional issues persisted, the Democratic party remained hopelessly divided.

The impossiblity of uniting on principle forced the Democrats to search for other means to maintain the party. First, they attempted to resurrect Jacksonian issues in order to restore unity. Failing in that, the Democrats then avoided identification with any particular principle and attached themselves to personalities like President Johnson. Finally, the party latched onto transient causes and fused with all kinds of groups in hopes of success. Each of these ploys temporarily staved off dissolution, but none of them could bring stability to the party.

In the 1870s, the Democrats were finally able to achieve some unity. The party studiously avoided internal divisions by ignoring the war and refusing to make specific judgments on Reconstruction. Instead, they focused their attention upon the corruption of the Republicans and the general excesses associated with Reconstruction. Simply, opposition to the abuse of government by the Republicans allowed the Democrats to avoid internal squabbles. The careful avoidance of sectional issues cleared the path for the reorganization of the party. Central to this rebuilding was the adoption of the party techniques developed by the Republicans over the last decade. The new organization brought unity to the Democrats for the first time since Douglas' death.

The building of the new party organization was a gradual process. The State Central Committee had become responsible for directing the party after Douglas' death, but because of the deep divisions, party members had virtually ignored the Committee's efforts. Under the energetic leadership of Cyrus H. McCormick, however, the Central Committee expanded its authority and took a firmer hand in directing the party. By 1868 it was clearly recognized as the head of the party. Two years later, in nearly every county it had organized a committee responsible for the local conventions and the campaign. The Democrats also finally adopted the primary system. After the first few areas used this nominating device in 1869, the system quickly gained wide acceptance.[1] The primary system brought immediate benefits: debilitating quarrels between personalities subsided and conventions became much more orderly and unifying than in previous days.

The Democrats also formalized their political clubs. The old method of organizing clubs in support of a specific candidate gave way to establishing permanent associations. In Chicago, for example, there were the "Jeffersonians" and the "Cosmopolitans." Each had a charter outlining its specific duties and functions, and each was a continuing organization. The "Jeffersonians" operated among the richer Democrats and were concerned with policy making, while the "Cosmopolitans" did the more mundane work of rallying the voters.[2] By making the clubs permanent, the Democrats finally had a reliable body of party workers.

In their efforts to build a new party organization along the lines established by the Republicans, the Democrats were substantially aided in the 1870s by the rise of new politicians.[3] The political leaders of Douglas' generation clung to power long after his death. McClernand, Richardson, and Lanphier still had great influence in 1868, although their power had been on the decline since the war. As time took its toll among the older generation, however, new men rose to power. These men reached political maturity free from the shadows of Andrew Jackson and Stephen Douglas. They had no experience in the Second Party System and in the realignment over slavery. Consequently, this generation did not carry a burden of old principles and party techniques. Their rise to power was aided by the new organization and their loyalty was to the party, not to men or to principles.

Although the Democrats lagged behind the Republicans in the depth and efficiency with which they employed new party techniques, they benefited from the resulting changes. The new Democratic organization inspired confidence and enthusiasm. By 1874, the effects of the organization began to be felt in the vigor with which each campaign was carried on.[4] For the first time Illinois was thoroughly organized, even though some problems persisted, such as the lapse in the activity of some county committees after elections. By 1880, the *Missouri Republican* noted that "the vastly improved condition of the Democracy there [in Illinois] as compared with any previous presidential year since 1856 is seen and recognized by all. . . . There is efficient organization in every county and nearly every precinct, directed by exceptionally excellent organization at headquarters."[5]

By 1874, both the Republicans and the Democrats had the distinct structural features that characterized the Third Party System. Although committees, political clubs, and conventions had been developed in the Second Party System, the effectiveness of those party techniques had been hampered by the domination of politics by personalities. The most outstanding structural feature of the Third Party System was that the party organization was made permanent, coordinated, and specialized, while individual politicians were completely subjugated to the organization. Discipline, regularity, and loyalty became the reality of politics rather than the goal, as was the case in the Jacksonian parties.[6] The parties resembled armies and the style of political campaigning reflected that resemblance.[7] Politics between 1874 and 1876 illustrate the new political behavior, but also a more important development. The new structures of the parties were able to sustain the Republicans and the Democrats even after their principles had become irrelevant.

During the first Grant administration, it was apparent in Illinois that the principles of the Republican party were losing their vitality. Factionalism and the nuisance of side issues began to plague the Republicans. In 1869, factionalism in the party on the local level was a particular problem. Dissatisfied Republicans in Will County, for example, joined in a "people's movement" with Democrats to oust the Court House party of old Republicans.[8]   The Cook county "citizens' movement," however, was by far the most celebrated of the local revolts. Discontented Republicans, led by the *Tribune*, joined with Democrats to depose the party grafters.[9] They charged the Republicans in control of Chicago, whom they characterized as "Barnacles" and "Ring politicians," with corruption, subversion of the public interest, and general maladministration. The *Tribune* made it clear, however, that it remained loyal to the party in State and national affairs. The fact that local concerns were growing in importance indicated a general weakening of the party ranks. Since the party had been formed in 1856, local quarrels and factions had always been set aside by the importance of national questions. Now that Reconstruction was fading in significance, quarrels erupted more frequently over city and county matters. The Democrats gleefully pointed to these incidents as proof that "the radical party is falling to pieces of its own rottenness."[10]

There were other signs of a growing Republican factionalism. Temperance once again gathered political strength in Illinois. In 1870, prohibitionists began to talk of creating a new party and to prepare for nominating tickets for all offices down to the local level.[11] Republicans were understandably concerned; that issue had threatened to divide the party since 1855. Some of the State's leading Republicans actively pursued temperance as a poiltical question, thereby reopening old wounds in the party. Although most party men sought to avoid the temperance issue because they realized it would divide the party, it could not be so easily brushed aside as it had been in the past.

An equally serious threat to the Illinois Republicans was the tariff issue. The *Tribune* declared that "the work of reconstruction being completed, the next thing in order is a thorough revision and reform of our monstrous system of tariff taxation."[12]   Many of the leading Republicans supported the *Tribune's* stand for free trade, maintaining that the tariff was promoting monopolies and strangling the working class. Other Republicans, however, argued just as forcefully that the tariff was a necessity. The *Illinois State Journal* declared that free trade "would not only be the death of all American manufactures . . . but *it would take directly from the pockets of the people the* $180,000,000 *of revenue to supply that now derived from customs.*"[13]

The divisions in the Republican party over the tariff, prohibition, and the spoils of office were becoming more pronounced by 1870. Trumbull wrote that "the war pressure is pretty much taken off & there is now no great principle to hold it [the Republican party] together."[14] Trumbull was partially correct. The war pressure was off and the anti-slavery principles were losing their vitality, but there was much more holding the party together. Loyalty, built up by the party over the decade, and the party machinery, sustained the Republicans.

While the weakening of the war and Reconstruction issues hurt the Republicans, it helped the Democracy considerably. The fading of these questions allowed the Democrats to avoid their own internal divisions, and more importantly, it meant that the party could unite in general opposition to the Republicans without being charged with treason. The Democracy could now be sustained by its new organization, even though no principles were defined for the party. Once the Democrats found some semblance of unity, they were no less threatened than were the Republicans by the rise of side issues. Questions about the tariff and the currency fiercely divided the Democrats. In the 1871 State Convention, for example, the party was badly split by these issues.[15] The persistence of economic questions in the 1870s shows the gradual decline in the importance of the sectional issues, but at the same time it reveals the strength of the Third Party System in preventing a new realignment based upon economic principles.

Economic questions were a complex problem growing out of the Civil War. In order to raise vast sums of money in a short time to carry on the war, Congress had enacted four measures. The first, which provided for new taxes in the form of tariffs, consisted of the Morrill Tariff Acts of 1861, 1862 and 1864. These acts brought in new revenue, but not enough to finance the war. As a second method of securing funds, Congress authorized the Treasury Department to borrow money by selling bonds. Another means of raising revenue was embodied in the National Banking Act which reorganized the banks into a system of "national banks." These banks, chartered by the government, sold bonds and relieved the currency shortage by issuing "national bank notes" in lieu of hard money. Finally, Congress raised money by printing "greenbacks" without gold or silver backing.[16]

After the war, Congress was faced with an immense fiscal problem. Greenbacks and national bank notes had become the monetary medium. Everyone expected, and the government had promised, that the paper money would be converted into gold. The problem, however, was that inflation put gold at a premium and the paper money was discounted. The Treasury could hardly resume specie payments until the paper money and gold were equalized in value.

The resolution to the problem was to remove the paper money from circulation, and in 1866, the Treasury Department began a policy of contraction. By 1868, however, the plan was scrapped because the economy slid into a depression and because of the overwhelming burden of the national debt. Because of the debt, the government was forced to buy its own bonds back to preserve the national credit. Consequently, while trying to collect enough gold to resume specie payment, the government was drained of gold by the debt.

The national debt was a problem not only because of its immense size, but also because of the heavy interest rates. Some politicians suggested that the problem could be solved by paying the bonds in greenbacks.[17] To most, however, such a plan smacked of repudiation. The solution decided upon was to renegotiate the debt at lower rates of interest. The cost of extending the payment period on the bonds at a lower interest rate would be an increase in the size of the total debt. Although this plan imposed a heavy burden upon the taxpayers, it did solve the crisis at hand.

In July 1870, Congress passed the "Public Credit Act," which refunded the national debt. The immediate problem was relieved, but the monetary system remained disordered. Paper and gold had to be brought into par before resumption could begin. This could not be realized, however, until a favorable balance of trade ended the drain of gold to foreign markets. Fortunately, trade was good in the 1870s. The government felt confident enough that in January, 1875, the Specie Resumption Act was passed, and in 1879 resumption began.

The questions surrounding the debt, the currency, and resumption opened a number of new issues. One question concerned the banks. The National Banking Act had destroyed independent banks, and since there were no forms of currency other than national bank notes and greenbacks, areas with few banks had little currency. Consequently, in such areas, including Illinois, there were strong advocates in both parties for free banking as a solution to the currency shortage. Another issue growing out of the fiscal crisis was that of inflated versus hard currency. Resumption was not universally favored since gold was scarce. The western regions in particular were increasingly opposed to the resumption of specie payments because of their short supply of money.[18] Finally, the high taxation needed to pay off the debt and to redeem the greenbacks made the tariffs the focus of much discontent. All of these issues divided the electorate into new patterns that threatened to destroy the Republican and Democratic coalitions.

These economic questions began to surface in the political arena in 1870. The first real sign that the monetary problem was affecting the parties was evident in the Liberal revolt. Even though Liberals were divided over the economic questions, their numbers included many of the most outspoken critics of the government's fiscal plans. Nevertheless, the issues of tariffs and currency failed to make a real impact in the 1872 campaign as Reconstruction prevailed as the dominant issue. Soon, however, Democrats began flirting with the new questions. In the post mortems for the elections in 1872, the leading party newspapers blamed the "railroads, capitalists, banks, express companies, telegraphs and negroes" for their defeat.[19]

In 1873, independent movements sprang up across Illinois in response to the depression of that year. Newly formed Farmer Associations gathered strength and organized independent tickets for the local elections. Typically, these movements called "upon men of all former political parties to join . . . to bring about the needed reform . . ." The reforms demanded were more honesty in government, an end to monopolies, lower taxes, and an equal taxation system.[20] By the fall, these local Farmer Associations had loosely organized themselves into the Anti-Monopoly party.

As the Democrats watched the growth of the Farmers' Movement, they were once again tempted by fusion. Almost immediately, the party began to aid the Farmers and many Democrats became so deeply involved that the Republicans labeled the associations the "new Democratic party." One Republican paper observed that at a local meeting "the men who composed the convention were, with perhaps a half dozen exceptions, old Democratic politicians and last year's liberals."[21]

By 1874, the Democrats were again on the verge of abandoning the party and fusing with the new movement. The remnants of the Liberal movement were overjoyed at the prospect and urged the Democrats to dissolve their party and clear the way for a new opposition organization.[22] The Democrats, however, slowly realized the mistake of another fusion. Thomas Hendricks of Indiana, one of the party's national leaders, came to Illinois in February, 1874, to rally the Democracy. He convinced the party leaders that their interests lay in maintaining a distinct organization.[23] Democrats from Egypt were particularly responsive to Hendricks' appeals, since the Democratic strongholds in that part of the State would only be hurt by an abandonment of the party organization.

Elsewhere in the State, Cyrus McCormick and many other leading Democrats also recognized the logic of Hendricks' appeal. They understood that temporary success might result from fusion, but in the long run, the Democracy would be weakened. Fusion was one more step toward the complete abandonment of the party. Consequently, McCormick issued on behalf of the Central Committe a directive calling for a convention and proposing a platform, which simply affirmed Democratic adherence to the policies of a revenue tariff, resumption, and free commerce.[24] Most Democrats fell into line. The *Carlinville Enquirer* stated that the politicians who pandered to popular prejudices by advocating inflation had no reason to complain. "If they do not believe in a speedy return to specie basis, free commerce, individual liberty, etc.," declared the paper, "then the call don't [sic] mean them, and they can stay at home."[25] A German newspaper, the *Freie Presse,* stated that "while we may hold somewhat different views as to the financial plank of the committee's suggestion . . . it is a sketch for just such a platform as every honest, intelligent democrat could desire."[26]

The Democrats had learned the lesson of 1872 well. In fusing with the Liberal Republicans, they had abandoned the party label and tried to create a new organization. The resulting confusion in the campaign and the lack of enthusiasm among the voters had proved to the Democrats the necessity of maintaining a distinct organization. Fusion had only weakened the Democracy by destroying the bonds of the voter to the party. Maintaining a distinct organization meant more unity, enthusiasm, and loyalty in the party.

Although in January, 1874, the *Register* openly supported the Farmers' Associations, by May, the paper was calling for a Democratic State Convention.[27] Other Democratic newspapers took up the call. The *Jonesboro Gazette,* the *Lincoln Herald,* and the *Chester Clarion* all called for straight-out Democratic tickets.[28] One Republican newspaper, commenting on its Democratic counterpart, stated that the *"Peoria National Democrat* weakens on the Farmers' movement. It thinks that the only issue the farmers will make is with the monopolists, and that there are other more important questions which the people will not overlook in the coming campaign."[29]

The resolution by Democratic leaders to maintain a distinct organization met with a certain amount of resistance from within the party. One Republican paper, after noting that the Democratic politicians were determined "that the glorious old party organization must and shall be preserved at all hazards," went on to state that "except in a few counties where Democratic majorities are large, [most party men] are turning 'independent' and declaring for the 'Independent' movement."[30] The Democrats who favored fusion argued that maintaining the old party only helped the Republicans by preventing a combination of all opposition groups.[31]

As the Democrats debated among themselves about fusion, the Farmers' Movement and other independent groups coalesced into the Anti-Monopoly party. In June, the Illinois Anti-Monopolists met in a convention to nominate candidates and to write a platform. Although the questions of taxation, the national debt, and specie payment had given rise to the independent movements, the Anti-Monopolists proved incapable of handling those economic issues. Questions about resumption, inflation, and repudiation divided their convention. The Anti-Monopolists found that they could unite only on a platform that called for reduced taxes, revenue tariffs only, civil service reform, and opposition to the national banks.[32]

The Democrats quickly realized that if the Anti-Monopolists were divided by the fiscal issues, then fusion would be foolish; it would only cause division in their own party on those same questions. Resolving to maintain their own organization, the Democrats met in convention in August and nominated party men to run for the State offices. Only S.M. Etter, a Democrat who had been nominated for Superintendent of Public Instruction by the Anti-Monopolists, was slated for the same post by the Democratic convention.

Although the Democrats escaped the danger of fusion, they still faced the problem of preventing their own party from dividing on the economic issues. Carefully avoiding the tough questions, the Illinois Democratic platform in 1874 was no more specific on economic issues than that of the Anti-Monopolists. In fact, many of the planks were the same. The Democrats called for a revenue tariff and declared themselves against monopolies. The main difference between the two platforms was that the Democrats explicitly stated their support for early resumption of specie payments.[33]

By maintaining a separate party organization, and by making only general references to the nation's economic problems, the Democrats discovered that they were now competing with the Anti-Monopolists for the same voters. The existence of the Anti-Monopoly party, consequently, became a threat to the Democrats. The *Register* declared that "to form a new party now is impossible, there is no room for it, there are no live principles for it, there are no people who want to join it, and there are no leaders. . . ." Ignoring the striking similarity between the Democratic and Anti-Monopoly platforms, the *Register* stated that the "principles proposed for the new party are . . . indefinite and vague. . . ." "How a third great national homogeneous party is to be formed upon the issues of the present day," concluded the *Register*, "we confess we are unable to discover."[34]

Although the Republicans were much less bothered by the rise of the Anti-Monopolists, the same economic questions seriously divided their party. Like the Democrats, the Republicans were unwilling and unable to commit themselves to a specific stand. The *Bloomington Pantagraph* reported that "there *is* such a very material division of opinion, among the Republicans of Illinois especially, that the passage of a furious inflation resolution . . . will simply split the Republican party of Illinois into two equal parts. . . ." "The simple truth is," the paper concluded, "that there is a very great and widespread difference of opinion among the Republicans of Illinois on the currency question."[35] The Republicans understood the divisiveness of the issue and made all possible efforts to avoid it. The *Register*, commenting upon the division among the Republicans, warned "all Republicans, on either side of the question, not to come here on June 17 [for the State Convention], expecting to carry any endorsement of anything." The paper predicted that "efforts of all who want to maintain the integrity of the party will be directed toward a compromise resolution which shall commit nobody to anything."[36]

The Republicans prevented division on the economic questions by carefully compromising the issues. The platform called for an early resumption of specie payment but expressed opposition to retiring Treasury notes. The only concession to the monetary problem was a plank recommending free banking.[37] Essentially, the Republicans emphasized the importance of maintaining confidence in the party. The main thrust of the platform was the statement that "the republican organization is amply sufficient in the future, as it has been in the past, to meet and settle all the questions which may arise. . . ." The party had solved slavery, secession, war, and Reconstruction and it was capable of handling any future problem. "Stand by the old party flag" was the Republican call, and everything would be resolved.[38]

Besides the economic questions, the Republicans were forced to contend with the issue of prohibition. Temperance had re-emerged as a political question in Illinois in the late 1860s and many leading Republicans had taken up the crusade. Typical of the temperance spirit within the party, one Republican delivered a sermon upon the evils of liquor, charging that Chicago had become a new Babylon.

> Beer is our Mayor, whiskey is our Chief of Police, and so far as our Christian civilization is concerned, good men have no rights which these Babylonians feel bound to respect. The Atheism of the old world and the devils of the under world are in league . . . to drug and govern and plunder the city. They have voted God's Sabbath out of its place of distinction; . . . They have cast out honor and character and native citizenship as useless rubbish; their police protect infamous occupations and infamous men, but give our Godly women over to the mob. . . .[39]

By 1874 it was apparent to the Republican leadership that the temperance issue had to be controlled or the party would lose substantial liturgical support, especially among the Germans. The State Convention adopted a resolution opposing prohibition, but worded it vaguely enough not to completely alienate the temperance men. According to the *Tribune*, however, the resolution was so vague, that it would "offend the temperance people without satisfying the Germans."[40]

The election in 1874 was the first collision between the Third Party System and these new issues, and the Third Party System received a heavy blow. The war and Reconstruction seemed to be dead issues. The Republicans barely won the Treasurer's office over the Anti-Monopolist and Democratic candidates, while S. M. Etter, the fusion candidate, defeated the Republican for Superintendent of Public Instruction, the first time a Republican had lost a State office since 1862. The Republicans only elected 7 out of 14 Congressmen and captured a bare plurality, not a majority, of the Legislature. The disclosure of corruption in the Grant administration, including the Crédit Mobilier scandal and the "whiskey ring," hurt the Republicans.[41] But the most telling blow was the panic of 1873. It appeared that economic issues had overridden the slavery realignment.

Table 33. Percentage Comparisons, 1874

	Republican	Democrat	Anti-Monopoly
Yankee	100	0	12
Southern	0	91	23
Illinois	0	79	31
Other	63	37	0
German	56	45	0
English	100	0	41
Irish	0	100	0
Scandinavian	76	51	0
Canadian	100	0	0
French	40	7	51

The cracks in the Third Party System were evident in the voter coalitions. An analysis of the vote in 1874 shows the effect of the new issues upon the old voting patterns (see Table 33).[42] In past elections, the Republicans had normally been supported by nearly all the Yankees, English, Scandinavians, Canadians, and French, along with a large majority of the Germans and "other" U.S.-born. In 1874, however, the Republicans lost approximately 28 percent of the Germans who had voted for Grant in 1872, and more importantly a significant proportion of the Yankees and the English.[43] The defection of these voters from the Republican party made the coalition far more homogeneous religiously and economically. For the first time, the Republicans seemed to have attracted the richer farmers in the State regardless of geographic location. In 1874, the Republicans correlated with high farm values at a strong .47, whereas in 1860, the richer farmers voted Republican only in the northern counties. The Republicans also received more pietistic support in 1874 than ever before. The party correlated at .21 with pietism as compared to only a .02 correlation in 1860.

The Democrats were also hurt by the economic issues. Some 23 percent of the Southerners, 31 percent of the Illinois-born, and all of the French who had joined the Liberal revolt in 1872 dropped out of the party, voting for the Anti-Monopolists. The Democracy, however, did gain a significant number of Scandinavian and German supporters in 1874 as compared with the 1872 elections.[44] These ethnic shifts also resulted in economic and religious changes in the party. The Democratic vote showed a strong negative correlation with high farm value. Democrats in 1874 more than ever were heterogeneous in religious composition, as shown by the negative association with both pietism and liturgicalism. The Democrats also lost their solid Baptist support, which correlated at an insignificant -.005 with the overall Democratic vote.

The Anti-Monopolists captured most of the discontented voters. Close to 12 percent of the Yankees, 23 percent of the Southerners, 31 percent of the Illinois-born, and 51 percent of the French voted the independent ticket.[45] Significantly, with the exception of the 1864 aberration, this was the first time the Yankees and the Southerners had been united in the same coalition since the slavery realignment.

The independents were firmly based among the Baptists, showing a correlation of .16. Pietism had almost no correlation, while the liturgicals negatively correlated with the vote at -.16. Economically, the Anti-Monopolists were not exclusively poor farmers. Regions with high-ranked farm values gave 15 percent of their votes to the independents while low-ranked regions produced a 21 percent Anti-Monopoly vote. The net effect was a mild correlation at .11 with rich farming areas.[46] Clearly, the Anti-Monopoly movement could not be considered a class revolt by poor farmers. In fact, most of the poor farmers remained in the Democratic camp.

The voter pattern in 1874 reveals the strength and the weakness of the Third Party System. The Democratic and Republican coalitions that had formed around the slavery issue were damaged by the cross-cutting economic questions. Although segments of certain ethnic groups, formerly divided by the sectional issues, were now united by common economic problems, the tariff, currency and monopoly questions were not yet strong enough to cause a realignment. There was no class division in the electorate; the majority of the poor farmers remained in the Democracy, which did not have a signficantly different economic position from the Republicans. Considering the impact of the depression in 1873, both parties showed remarkable success in straddling the economic issues. Both the Democrats and the Republicans owed this success to the strength of voter loyalty, which permitted the party machinery to dominate politics and to control the new issues.

Despite the efforts of the Democrats and the Republicans to control the economic questions, those issues continued to plague politics. The resulting tension between the new issues and the old principles persisted until the realignment of 1896. Unlike the Second Party System, however, the Third Party System was able to contain the cross-cutting issues. Party structure held the Democratic and the Republican coalitions together without the assistance of relevant principles. The resilience and strength of the Third Party System was evident in the 1876 elections.

In September, 1876, Lyman Trumbull delivered a speech in Chicago in which he pinpointed the state of politics.

> The Republican party of to-day is not composed of the same material, nor are its purposes and aims the same as the Republican party of 10 or 20 years ago; that it is not the inheritor of the grand old principles which gave the party its fame, nor of anything belonging to it save its name; that it has degenerated and become venal and corrupt, and that there is no reason why any independent man should now support or oppose it simply because it is called Republican. I have endeavored to show you that the Democratic party of to-day is not composed of the same material and does not have the same purposes and aims as the Democratic party of 15 or 20 years ago; that it has inherited the name without any of the pro-slavery views which distinguished the party at that day, and that there is no reason why any independent man should support or oppose it, simply because it is called Democratic.[47]

Trumbull was partially right in his appraisal of the political parties. The Republicans did still cling to anti-slavery principles even though those principles had become irrelevant, and Trumbull was correct in saying that the Democrats no longer represented pro-slavery principles. He was wrong in believing that the composition of the parties had changed. It appeared to Trumbull that the parties had changed because the old principles were no longer viable, but the Republican and the Democratic coalitions were still essentially the same groups that had composed the parties since the war. Trumbull's complaint that the voters should not vote for a party because it was called Republican or Democrat was directly to the point. Most voters did respond to party labels. Loyalty sustained the parties in 1876, not principles. And that loyalty was maintained by tightly disciplined party structures.

With the fading of principles based on the sectional questions, it was certain that new issues would plague the elections. Economic questions in particular became prominent after 1874. The Anti-Monopolists and the Farmers' Associations continued to agitate for financial reforms. In January, 1876, independents in Illinois held a convention at Bloomington and announced a new platform, wider in scope than the 1874 proposals. It called for a repeal of the Resumption Act, withdrawal of National Bank notes, the issuance of paper currency directly by the government, and bonds to be paid in greenbacks only.[48] By April, the independents organized into the Greenback movement and began preparations for the Presidential contest in the fall.[49]

The Illinois Democrats attempted to remove the danger a third party posed to their resurgence by swallowing the Greenbackers. The Democrats began to carry out their strategy in 1875. Once the Legislature convened, they attempted to strike a bargain with the Anti-Monopolist members of the Assembly in order to control the proceedings.[50] The plan failed, however, because the independents realized that the Democrats had no intention of supporting their economic reform programs. Nevertheless, the Democrats continued to aid the Anti-Monopolists and to hatch schemes for luring them into the party.[51]

The problem with the Democratic strategy was that, in order to attract the independents, who were now calling themselves Greenbackers, the Democrats might be forced to take a stand upon the divisive economic questions. In order to avoid such a commitment, the Democrats moved in opposite directions at the same time. By attacking high taxes and monopolies, but ignoring the tough issues concerning the currency, the Illinois Democrats induced many of the Greenbackers to join the party. Meanwhile, they endorsed Samuel J. Tilden and a hard-money platform at the national convention in St. Louis.[52]

This strategy showed results in 1876, when the Democratic and Greenback conventions fused, agreeing upon a slate of candidates and a platform.[53] The platform, however, bore the Democratic influence. It was a solid retreat from the independents' declarations at Bloomington in January. The Democrats accepted only statements against the tariff, taxes, monopolies, and national bank notes, and these declarations were diluted to the point of becoming platitudes. The more important questions of resumption and bonds were carefully avoided.[54]

Even though the Democrats had swallowed the Greenbackers for the State contest, they refused any cooperation with the independents in the Presidential campaign. The Democrats, consequently, carried on two distinct campaigns in 1876. At the State level, they attacked the Republican ticket as the "Kid Glove Candidates." The party presented an image of itself as battling for the producing class against the rich who claimed the privilege of ruling by "divine right."[55] The Presidential campaign, however, avoided all fiscal questions and concentrated merely upon the corruption of the Republican party.[56] In both campaigns the Democrats were successful in avoiding new divisions and in capturing discontented voters without sacrificing any of their traditional support. For the first time since the end of the war, the Democrats posed a threat to the Republican party in Illinois.

The Republicans had less of a problem than did the Democrats in dealing with the economic issues and the third party movement. The party machinery easily kept the Republicans in line. The State convention drew up a platform that focused on Reconstruction, declaring that the unionists in the South needed government protection and that the three Reconstruction Amendments required strict enforcement. The only mention of economic issues was a statement of confidence in the Administration's ability to solve whatever problems existed.[57]

The campaign waged by the Republicans has been commonly referred to as waving the "Bloody Shirt." The attempt to revive old principles, however, was not new to politics. The Democrats had tried the same tactic as late as the 1860s by recalling the glory of Andrew Jackson. The Republicans were endeavoring to reinforce loyalty to the party by reminding the voters of the war and Reconstruction. The "Bloody Shirt" also was important to distract attention from divisive new issues by emphasizing the original principles of the party.

Typical of "Bloody Shirt" rhetoric was an editorial in the *Tribune* attacking the Democratic doctrine of non-interference and State sovereignty.

> Love for the Union is no greater in the South today than it was fourteen years ago. The spirit of rebellion is as rampant as ever. Proclaim the principle that the Southern people may do what they like; put them where, holding the balance of power, they shall control the destinies of this nation; let them have a ten years' lease of power, and he would be a bold man who would venture to predict that, at the end of that time, we should not be called upon to witness another rebellion, bloodier and more protracted, and perhaps more successful than the first.[58]

Governor John J. Beveridge, in a speech in Chicago, echoed these same sentiments. He declared that "it is not reconstruction, nor the currency, nor the tariff, nor taxation, nor the issue of 'corruption or honest

Government,' which constitutes the 'great issue' of the day, but that it is 'whether the Government shall remain in the hands of the men who fought for and preserved it, or whether it shall pass into the hands of the people who fought to destroy it.'"[59]

With both the Democrats and the Republicans studiously avoiding the economic issues and with slavery principles fading in relevance, success in 1876 depended entirely upon party loyalty. The *Tribune* noted that "at no time within the last half-century has it been so evident on the eve of a presidential election as now that the success of parties must depend essentially upon the public confidence."[60] Victory in the elections, consequently, required a maximum effort on the part of the parties to rally the voters. The *Tribune* observed that "a new school of tactics has been inaugerated [sic] and most successfully cultivated for the capture of the office. The cardinal doctrine of the new school is: By sociability we conquer."[61]

The intense efforts of the parties made the campaign the most exciting since 1860. The Republican clubs were out in full in their military garb, holding meetings at every crossroads. Wigwams were erected across the State to signify the glory of Lincoln. Besides the Grand Army of the Republic and the Union Leagues, there were Hayes and Wheeler clubs, Swedish Republican, German Republican, and even Colored Republican clubs working for the party. The Democrats countered with Tilden clubs and organized large barbecues and social meetings. Despite the fact that the economic issues were kept at a minimum, debates during the campaign were long and bitter. The Democrats attacked corruption, extravagance in government, and patronage. "Tilden and Reform" was their slogan. The Republicans preached retrenchment and the "Bloody Shirt." Brass bands, torchlight processions, and great mass rallies were the order of the day. Political oratory reached new heights. According to the *Tribune*, there never was before a "more gorgeous galaxy of similes, metaphors, and hyperboles."[62]

The Greenbackers were swamped by all of this campaign activity which blunted the sharpness of the economic issues. Furthermore, the Greenbackers lacked the organization and skill of the Republicans and Democrats to make an energetic canvass of the voters. Reminiscing about the campaign of 1876, one independent from New York expressed the frustration of the third party when he wrote that, "looking at the platforms of the two parties, except as so far as each praises itself and expressed distrust and dislike of the other, there was really but little to choose." "At the present," he continued, "there is but little difference in the avowed principles of the two parties. Whatever differences there are, and whatever preferences people have for one party over the other, arise mainly from disbelief in the sincerity of those who control one or the other of these parties."[63] The problem was that the parties no longer represented principles. Fealty to party had been substituted for fealty to principle. As the Know-Nothings and the Liberal Republicans had done, this independent speaker attacked change in the political parties, and in so doing, he correctly recognized the transformations that had occurred in the party system.

The election in 1876 demonstrated the complete irrelevance of the principles related to sectionalism. At the same time, however, the election also showed the strength of the Third Party System in maintaining voter coalitions in the face of powerful cross-cutting issues. The most significant change in 1876 was that the overriding influence of the Southerners upon the voting pattern in Illinois was broken. For the first time since the slavery realignment, the Democratic and Republican coalitions had a distinctive religious and economic character.

Table 34. Correlation Coefficients of
Party Strength with Ranked Farm Value

Republican	Farm Value
1860	.21
1864	.16
1868	.40
1872	.26
1876	.51
Democrat	
1860	-.23
1864	-.19
1868	-.40
1872	-.25
1876	-.49

The outstanding proof that party principles had been overshadowed by other issues was in the behavior of the voters as economic groups (see Table 34). While there had always been a slight economic difference between the Democratic and Republican voters, this division had been moderated by the presence of the Southerners. In 1856, for example, the Republican vote correlated with large farms in northern Illinois at a very strong .93, but in Egypt, this relationship was almost reversed. Farm size and the Republican vote at that time correlated at -.29, indicating that the Southerners voted Democratic regardless of their economic status. A geographical breakdown of the Republican vote in 1876, however, showed no substantial difference between Egypt and northern Illinois in the behavior of economic groups. The Republican vote correlated at a strong .51 with high farm value while the Democratic vote correlated at an equally impressive -.49. These correlations, which were significantly stronger than at any other time since the realignment, signified that the sectional divisions in Illinois had been considerably weakened and that the slavery principles were all but dead.

The irrelevance of the slavery principles was also reflected in the religious character of the coalitions in 1876. Pietism and liturgicalism had never been clearly identified with the Republican and the Democratic voter coalitions in Illinois, but in 1876 there was a sharp religious division in the electorate (see Table 35). Previous Republican correlations with pietists, for example, had been weak, and at times insignificant. In 1876, however, pietists correlated with the Hayes vote at an impressive .45. Although not as dramatic, there was also a shift in the liturgical vote, which for the first time, had a positive correlation to the Democracy. The increasing political significance of religion was reflected in a speech delivered by Richard Yates in the Senate. The old Governor stated: "I have rather favored the idea that, though religion and politics were separate to a certain extent, there was yet a sort of personal connection between true piety and true republicanism."[64]

Table 35. Correlation Coefficients of Party Strength with Religion

| | | Republican | | | |
	1860	1864	1868	1872	1876
Pietist	-.05	.20	.17	.22	.45
Liturgical	.008	.11	.39	.26	.06
Baptist	-.27	-.28	-.20	-.09	-.35

| | | Democrat | | | |
	1860	1864	1868	1872	1876
Pietist	.05	-.20	-.17	-.16	-.54
Liturgical	-.02	-.11	-.39	.34	.13
Baptist	.23	.26	.20	.08	.22

Although religion played a larger role in politics in 1876 than previously, unlike economic status it failed to override completely the basic voting pattern established by the slavery realignment. Despite significant shifts, pietistic Southerners still voted Democratic and liturgicals in Egypt remained Republican. The Hayes vote, for example, correlated at a very strong .77 with pietists in northern Illinois, but in the central townships, the correlation dropped to .50, and in Egypt, there was no correlation between Republican voters and pietists. The effect of the Southerners upon the religious composition of the voter coalitions also was reflected in the behavior of the Baptists. The Republicans correlated with the Baptists in northern Illinois at .34, but once Egypt was included in the equation, the correlation was reversed to -.35. The increase in pietistic support for the Republicans and in liturgical support for the Democracy was consequently limited to northern Illinois, which was uncomplicated by the presence of Southerners.

While economic and religious changes in the electorate signified the irrelevance of slavery principles in 1876, the election also demonstrated the strength of the Third Party System. Despite significant changes among the voters, the Republicans and the Democrats successfully held their coalitions together (see Table 36). The voter shifts of 1872 and 1874 proved to be deviations; in 1876 most of the voters began to return to the patterns established by the slavery realignment. Virtually all the Yankees, for example, returned to the Republican party, as did all but 18 percent of the Scandinavians and 24 percent of the French. The only group not to resume the old pattern was the Germans. Although the Germans continued to vote Republican in Egypt and Democratic in northern Illinois, the Democrats carried around 44 percent of the group overall, which was consistent with their 1874 percentage and a significant increase since 1872. Ethnically, then, the 1876 Democratic and Republican coalitions were virtually no different from what they had been in 1860. Nearly all of the Yankees, English, Canadians, a majority of the Scandinavians and French, and a consistent 64 percent of the "other" U.S.-born voted Republican. The Democratic coalition was again composed mainly of Southerners, Illinois-born, Irish, and the Germans in northern Illinois.[65]

The stability of the Democratic and Republican coalitions is evident in the vote for Peter Cooper, Greenback candidate for President. The Greenbackers were able to carry only some 18 percent of the Southerners, 13 percent of the Illinois-born, and 6 percent of the "other" U.S.-born.[66] Every other group voted either for Hayes or Tilden. The fact that the Greenbackers captured fewer votes than the Anti-Monopolists in 1874 can be partly attributed to the nature of the election in 1876. In a Presidential contest, voters are less willing to "waste" their vote on a third party candidate. This was especially true in 1876, since the Republican and Democratic machinery was geared toward enforcing voter regularity. The strength of the party structures, as well as the efforts of the two major parties to avoid the economic issues, prevented any chance of success for the Greenbackers.

Table 36. Percentage Comparisons of Party Strength

	Republican					
	1860	1864	1868	1872	1874	1876
Yankee	100	100	100	100	100	100
Southern	0	32	0	0	0	0
Illinois	0	0	0	0	0	0
Other	66	54	69	62	63	64
German	68	62	80	84	56	59
English	100	100	100	100	100	100
Irish	0	0	0	0	0	0
Scandinavian	100	100	100	83	76	90
Canadian	63	100	100	100	100	100
French	100	100	100	30	40	77

	Democrat						Anti-Monopoly/Greenback	
	1860	1864	1868	1872	1874	1876	1874	1876
Yankee	0	0	0	0	0	0	12	0
Southern	100	67	100	100	91	100	23	18
Illinois	100	100	100	100	79	92	31	13
Other	33	45	30	37	37	26	0	6
German	30	37	19	16	45	44	0	0
English	0	0	0	0	0	0	41	0
Irish	100	100	100	100	100	100	0	0
Scandinavian	0	0	0	17	51	18	0	0
Canadian	28	0	0	0	0	0	0	0
French	0	0	0	69	7	24	51	0

The election of 1876 marked the point in the Third Party System where its rationale, the principles causing the realignment, began to lose vitality. Yet, instead of the voter coalitions disintegrating and the parties reverting to personal factions, as had happened to the Jacksonian parties, the Democrats and the Republicans remained unified and strong. Unlike the Second Party System, which began to collapse immediately after its principles lost relevance, the Third Party System persisted for another two decades. The difference was party organization. While the Whigs and the Democrats had committees, clubs, and conventions, the structure was uneven and ad hoc, and therefore easily manipulated by personalities. In the Third Party System, the parties avoided the same fate by creating tightly structured organizations.

The Republicans had been forced to make organizational changes in order to survive the war and Reconstruction. The Democrats belatedly adopted the same strategy in the 1870s because it was the only way the party could effectively challenge the Republican domination of Illinois. Committees, clubs, and conventions became uniform and permanent. A clear hierarchy was established between units so that the party could not be carved into political fiefdoms. But the real key to the success of the parties in withstanding the loss of principles and the emergence of powerful new issues was voter loyalty. The war and Reconstruction had fused the voter directly to the party by making the purpose of the party the purpose of the nation. The party became as much of an institution in the country as the Congress or the Presidency. Voter loyalty was the real strength which allowed the party organization to dominate politics. The result was that the party came to have a life of its own, and could resist the designs of any individual and the impact of any issue. In the Second Party System, the Illinois Democracy had no existence apart from Stephen Douglas. But, in the 1870s, no politician or issue could exist independently of the parties.

Conclusion

Writing about the effects of the Civil War, Allan Nevins stated that one of the most important results "was the conversion of an unorganized nation into an organized nation, with an irresistible impetus toward greater and greater organization."[1] Nothing reflects this change in America as much as the transformation of the party system.

An examination of the dynamics of the party system clearly identifies the depth of the political change caused by the Civil War and Reconstruction. Both the Second and Third Party Systems were strong as long as the principles that gave the parties their rationale remained energetic. At the point the principles began to lose relevance, however, the differences between the two systems became distinct. The Second Party System began to crumble immediately as the Whigs and the Democrats were unable to maintain their voter coalitions in the face of cross-cutting side issues. The Third Party System, however, continued to flourish long after the principles surrounding the slavery realignment had lost their vitality. The essential difference was that the war and Reconstruction had given a new meaning to political parties. The parties of the Third Party System had a life of their own, even without principles or personalities.

The principles around which the Jacksonian parties were organized had lost their relevance to politics by 1850. The tariff, internal improvements and the Bank were dead issues. The Second Party System began to disintegrate immediately. The party structures of the Whigs and the Democrats were incapable of sustaining unity. The parties were helpless as the voter coalitions eroded under the pressure of uncontrolled side issues. Voter loyalty had never really been cemented to the party itself. Individual politicians had always been the intermediary between the voters and the party. The parties lost their vitality once the principles had faded, and because of ineffective party structures, there was nothing left for the voter but personalities. Personalities became the organizing feature of the Whigs and the Democrats in the 1850s.

The Second Party System was on its deathbed by 1854. The coalescing of the slavery issue as a result of the Kansas and Nebraska Act put a quick end to the Jacksonian parties. The old coalitions were shattered as voters moved into new configurations. New principles and new voter combinations gave birth to new political parties. Although the new party system differed from the Jacksonian parties in terms of rationale and composition, it initially duplicated the character and style of the Second Party System. There were few structural innovations and the individual politician continued to play a large role in the new parties. The war and Reconstruction, however, forged a distinctive character for the Third Party System.

Between 1860 and 1868, the nation struggled with the fundamental question of survival. Out of this cataclysmic decade were born the special features of the Third Party System that permanently changed the shape of American politics. The war and Reconstruction made the political parties national institutions. The two-party system had become institutionalized in the Age of Jackson, but it was the Civil War that grafted the political party permanently into the life of the nation. Despite future voter realignments and party systems, the Republican and the Democratic parties would remain. The war had given them a durability and sanctity that comes only with institutionalization. The political party had become as permanent as the Congress or the Presidency. There would no longer be a succession of weak party systems collapsing quickly with the fading of principles, nor would success and durability be dependent upon dynamic personalities.

The War and Reconstruction institutionalized the political party by making it a vehicle for patriotism. The Civil War was a struggle for control of the nation, and the particular principles of the Democrats and the Republicans stood as different expressions of how the federal government and the nation should be preserved. With the future course of the nation dependent upon the success of a particular party, voter loyalty became a declaration of patriotism. The interchangeability of patriotism and party loyalty transformed the political party from merely a political collection of men into a national institution preserving the stability of the nation.

Initially, the triumph of the North in 1865 meant the successful transformation of the Republican party into a national institution and the near destruction of the Democracy. For the Republicans, victory for the South, in any form, meant defeat for the nation and the party. Under this pressure, the Republicans made important structural changes in the party. They developed a party structure featuring uniformity and efficiency in order to avoid internal divisions and disputes that would jeopardize the party and hence the war. Under the force of party discipline, personalities lost the independence that had been available to them in the Second Party System.

Victory in the war and Reconstruction guaranteed the existence of the Republican party. The Democrats, however, were nearly ruined by the same events. The successful identification of the Republican party with the Union meant that Democratic opposition was treason. The Democrats' notion of the Union became seditious, and consequently, their patriotism was seen as treachery. The war splintered the party and Reconstruction perpetuated the internal divisions. It was not until the 1870s that the Democrats were able to recover. The fading of slavery principles allowed the party to unify in opposition to the Republicans without the stigma of treason. Under energetic new leadership, the Democrats began to rebuild, adopting the structural devices developed by the Republicans to sustain voter loyalty.

In the election of 1876, the qualities of the Third Party System were clearly identifiable in both parties. Slavery principles had become completely irrelevant, yet the voter coalitions remained intact. The inevitable surfacing of new issues, which had plagued the parties since 1874, was kept well under control, but unlike the parties of the Second Party System after their principles became irrelevant, the Democrats and the Republicans remained strong.

In the Second Party System, fealty to the party was transferred to personalities after the principles lost relevance. The public battles between dynamic politicians like Lincoln and Hardin, Wentworth and Judd, and Douglas and Breese confirmed the status of the political party as a temporary assemblage of men. It is significant that in the Second Party System, the Democrats were always the party of Jackson, while in the Third Party System, the Republicans referred to themselves as the Grand Old Party. The GOP promoted the image of an institution to which a voter gave permanent loyalty. In the Third Party System, personalities would come and go, but there was nothing transient about the party.

Party loyalty became so entrenched in the minds of the voters that it was considered a natural manifestation of patriotism long after the end of the Civil War. In the 1870s, a man in Ohio captured the meaning of party loyalty when he stated:

> In the Ohio of those days it was natural to be a Republican; it was more than that; it was inevitable that one should be a Republican; it was not a matter of intellectual choice, it was a process of biological selection. The Republican party was not a faction, not a group, not a wing, it was an institution like those Emerson speaks of in his essay on Politics, rooted like

oak-trees in the center around which men group themselves as best they can. It was a fundamental and self-evident thing, like life, and liberty, and the pursuit of happiness, or like the flag, or the federal judiciary. It was elemental, like gravity, the sun, the stars, the ocean. It was merely a synonym for patriotism, another name for the nation. One became in Urbana and in Ohio for many years, a Republican just as the Eskimo dons fur clothes. It was inconceivable that any self-respecting person should be a Democrat. There were, perhaps, Democrats in Lighttown; but then there were rebels in Alabama, and in the Ku-Klux-Klan, about which we read in the evening, in the Cincinnati Gazette.[2]

The political party was an institution as fundamental as gravity and it was the same for a Democrat in Egypt as it was for a Republican in Ohio.

The effect of voter loyalty upon the party system was reflected in the behavior of the voters between 1850 and 1876. By examining voter turnout levels, it is evident that the Third Party System was more successful than the Jacksonian parties, not only in maintaining a higher level of voter participation, but also in retaining voter consistency. In 1850, when the Whigs and the Democrats had no viable principles, the voter turnout was only 35.7 percent (see Table 37).[3] When the Democrats and the Republicans were faced with the same problem in 1874, however, voter turnout remained at a consistently high 52.4 percent. The ability of the Third Party System to maintain a high level of voter participation was also reflected in the Presidential elections. In 1852, Scott and Pierce attracted to the polls 62.5 percent of the voters, while in 1876, when Hayes and Tilden battled for the Presidency without relevant party principles, voter turnout reached 72.5 percent.

Table 37. Voter Turnout: 1850-1876

Election	Eligible Voters	Actual Voting	Percent Voting
1850	201,161	71,947	35.7
1852	248,787	155,497	62.5
1854	296,413	133,869	45.1
1856	344,039	238,981	69.4
1858	391,665	252,110	64.3
1860	439,293	339,693	77.3
1862	476,462	256,778	53.8
1864	513,631	348,226	67.7
1866	550,800	350,106	63.5
1868	587,969	449,436	76.4
1870	625,139	316,496	50.6
1872	662,308	429,940	64.9
1874	699,478	366,773	52.4
1876	736,648	554,066	75.2

The ability of the Third Party System to maintain a consistently high voter turnout level is more dramatically illustrated by the correlations between turnout rates for succeeding elections (see Table 38).[4] In both the off-year and the Presidential elections, the Third Party System attracted significantly more voters. Between 1840 and 1844, for example, the number of Democrats and Whigs who voted in both elections correlated at only .42. The Republicans and the Democrats, however, were far more successful. The number of voters who went to the polls in 1868 and 1872 correlated at .87, indicating that even with viable party principles, the Third Party System was able to consistently mobilize more voters.

Table 38. Correlation Coefficients Measuring County Level Turnout Rates

Presidential	Pearson's r	Off-Year Elections	Pearson's r
1840-1844	.42	1844-1846	.51
1844-1848	.40	1846-1850	.14
1848-1852	.55	1850-1854	.55
1852-1856	.76	1854-1858	.34
1856-1860	.78	1858-1862	.37
1860-1864	.68	1862-1866	.54
1864-1868	.44	1866-1870	.73
1868-1872	.87		

The Third Party System was more successful than the Jacksonian parties in retaining voter cohesiveness. Once party principles had become irrelevant, the Whigs and the Democrats had difficulty in carrying their coalitions from one election to another (see Table 39). In 1850 and 1852, the Whig voters correlated at only .14 between the two elections. Between 1874 and 1876, however, the Republican voters continued to correlate at a strong .75. Just as the Republicans and the Democrats were successful in maintaining the coalitions over time, they were also better able to maintain voter cohesiveness within each election (see Table 40). The Whig voters for Treasurer and Congress in 1850, for example, correlated at only .15, while in 1852, the correlation between Whig Presidential and gubernatorial voters was .52. Republican voters, on the other hand, correlated at .83 in 1874 between the Treasurer and the Congressional contests and at a .95 in 1876 between the Presidential and gubernatorial elections.

The remarkable consistency in voter behavior in the Third Party System confirmed the Republican and Democratic parties as political institutions. Like institutions, the parties were sustained by highly organized structures. The common description of the Democrats and the Republicans in the 1870s was that the parties were machines. It was an apt label, for like machines, the parts of the political parties meshed together to perform a single function. No unit could exist independently,

Table 39. Correlation Coefficients Measuring Political Party Cohesion

	Whig	Democrat
1850-1852	.14	.11
1852-1854	.64	.71
	Republican	Democrat
1856-1858	.88	.91
1858-1860	.91	.92
1860-1862	.99	.88
1862-1864	.92	.83
1866-1868	.90	.90
1868-1870	.93	.93
1870-1872	.78	.77
1872-1874	.66	.38
1874-1876	.75	.62

Table 40. Correlation Coefficients Measuring Intra-Party Cohesion

	Whig	Democrat
1850	.15	.17
1852	.52	.33
1854	.05	.70
	Republican	Democrat
1856	.97	.98
1858	.99	.99
1860	.99	.99
1862	.99	.99
1864	.99	.99
1866	.99	.99
1868	.99	.99
1870	.97	.97
1872	.97	.97
1874	.83	.46
1876	.95	.91

and the efficiency of the party depended upon regular performance by each part. At the top of the political hierarchy, coordinating the units, was the State Central Committee. It determined policy and started the party moving for each campaign. Directly below the Central Committee were the county committees. These committees carried out the campaign directives and coordinated the town and precinct organizations. The chief duty of the county committee was to organize the campaign at the local level, arranging for speakers and rallies, raising funds, and turning out the voters. To perform many of these duties, the county committee organized large bodies of workers into clubs. Except for the Grand Army of the Republic, the clubs worked for the local party even though they were loosely grouped into a State organization. The special feature of this party structure was not that the devices were new, but that the structure performed its duty regularly and efficiently.

Nothing reveals the machine-like character of the parties as much as the nominating process. The State and county committees started the process by calling for conventions and arranging primary election dates. Once primaries were set, candidates worked among the party voters organizing support and workers. The primaries elected delegates pledged to particular men, making the conventions a formality. County conventions then elected delegates to the district convention and to the State convention. Unlike the Second Party System, conventions were orderly and representative. Self-appointed delegates, delegates-at-large, and open conventions were unheard of in the 1870s. With the primaries as the basis of the conventions, the nominating process was legitimatized by direct voter involvement. The regular and uniform nominating process minimized factionalism and party splits.

The intensity of party loyalty, sustained by sophisticated party machinery, changed the style of politics. Electioneering in the Second Party System had been a colorful kaleidoscope of brawling rallies, conventions, and stump speeches. Each election was different and had its own particular flavor depending upon the candidate. The campaigns were cluttered, confused, and unrestrained. In the Third Party System, however, the parties, not personalities, engaged the voters. The primary system brought the voter directly into the party. Since loyalty was the cement of the party, the role of the politician was to foster the voters' identification with the party. Richard Yates noted the change in political style when he observed that the politician no longer "stood" for a program, but instead sought favor with the public.[5]

Even though the parties were directly involved in the campaigns, electioneering in the 1870s lacked the flair of the earlier days. Rallies, barbecues, parades, and stump speaking were still the order of the day, but these activities were carefully orchestrated. There was little spontaneity in the Third Party System and no uncertainty. All understood that the bonds of the voter to the party were so strong that electioneering to convince men to change parties was wasted energy. Each campaign was geared to the single purpose of turning out the faithful. Parades, rallies, and speeches were enthusiastic, but in a sense, routine. Candidates would change, but election after election, the campaign was the same.

The changes in the party system resulted in a new type of politician. Men were needed who could manage the various agencies of the party. A politician had to be willing to temporarily sacrifice his ambition for the sake of party regularity. Matthew Hale of New York correctly observed the changes in the politicians when he complained about the Third Party System.

> It has become impossible for men who cannot control the organization – or, as it is commonly termed, 'run the machine' – to have any influence. . . . Under the prevailing party machinery the primaries in cities are absolutely controlled by a few political 'workers'. These primaries elect delegates to the district or the county conventions; district or county conventions to the State conventions; and the State convention selects delegates to the national convention. It is evident, therefore, that the men who control the primaries practically control the nomination for presidents. . . . This country is under the despotism of party, and is governed . . . by the managers of the machine. . . . living by politics – men of no principle.[6]

"Men of no principle" was the epitaph ascribed by Hale to the politicians of the Third Party System, but a better inscription would be "managers of the machine." Gone from politics was the flamboyance that characterized the early politicians. In the Third Party System, there was no one comparable to "Long John" Wentworth, who changed parties at least four times, or to the whimsical Usher Linder, a Jackson admirer who voted for Clay and later worked for Douglas before becoming a Republican. And certainly there was no politician in the 1870s like the "Little Giant." Stephen Douglas was the epitome of the Second Party System politician. He made his own issues, directed his own campaign, used patronage for his own benefit, and controlled the party through the force of his personality.

The politician of the Third Party System was a manager. Charisma was meaningless without the ability to work the party machinery. It was no accident that there was no one like Wentworth or Douglas. Success depended upon patience, discipline, loyalty, and sacrifice. The party machinery could not be circumvented. Consequently, it required a man who could work within the party structure, not a politician bent on dominating the structure.

Perhaps more than any other politician, Shelby Cullom represented the Third Party System. He managed his career carefully and patiently.

In the 1860s, he sacrificed his Congressional aspirations in order to tighten his grip upon the local Republican organization. Once in control, he easily carried the primary election for the nomination to Congress, against a man who relied entirely upon personal influence.[7] In 1875, Cullom desired the Governor's seat, but again he carefully bided his time. Knowing that a number of Republicans would seek the nomination, Cullom quietly laid the groundwork within the party. He again accepted a lesser office in order to stay in the public's attention while he rounded up support for the gubernatorial nomination. "I determined to become a candidate for Governor," Cullom candidly wrote, and "to be successful, it seemed to be important that I should go back into the Legislature, which I did."[8] Cullom was elected Governor in 1876. From that time on, he was elected either Governor or Senator well into the 20th century. Cullom lacked the notoriety and the charisma of the Second Party System politicians, but he was more successful than Wentworth, and, in many ways, Douglas. Just as Douglas characterized the Second Party System with its personal control of politics, its flamboyance and its unsystematic, yet energetic, activities, Cullom represented the Third Party System. Cullom, like the parties in the 1870s, was methodical, disciplined, durable, and successful.

Appendix

Methodology

The validity of any quantitative study depends upon sampling, the choice of variables, and the use of proper statistical routines. For historians, these problems are immense. Election analysis, in particular, poses difficulties in sampling, gathering data, and until recently, statistical manipulation. The use of aggregate data requires special care. Sampling must reflect the population, and not ecological voting units; the variables need to account for a variety of factors that affect elections; and the statistical technique must yield the proper information.

Sampling is the key to any methodology. For this study, the technique used was random sampling without replacement. Since the time frame in this work covers the years from 1850 to 1876, a period of very rapid growth in Illinois' population, three separate samples of townships were drawn in order to reflect accurately the population changes in the State. Each sample was based on the federal census, with the midpoint of the decade as the division between the samples. Consequently, the first sample, drawn from the 1850 census, was used to analyze elections until 1855, while the second sample, from the 1860 census, covered the elections from 1856 to 1865, and the third sample, based on the 1870 census, included the elections between 1866 and 1876.

The sampling of any kind of population presents certain problems. For 19th century election analysis, which must rely upon aggregate data, care must be taken to insure that the sample is of the voters and not of counties and townships. Another problem, this one specific to Illinois, is that the State did not have uniform governmental divisions. Many of the northern counties had township organizations, which are of manageable sizes for election analysis, but central and southern Illinois had no governmental units below the county level except for cities and towns.

In order to solve these problems, a weighting scheme was used. Townships and counties without township organization were assigned consecutive numbers based upon the voting population, i.e., the number of adult white males. In the 1850 sample, one number was given for every 500 voters. For example, Beverly Township, Adams County, had a population of 459 and was assigned the number one, and Burton Township, Adams County, with a population of 647, which also had a weight of one, was given the number two. This weighting scheme was carried on alphabetically to Williamson County, which had a voting population of 3,668, and, therefore, a weight of seven, giving it the numbers 883 to 889. Counties with a large population, then, received many more numbers than smaller counties or townships, and therefore, had more of a chance of being sampled. By assigning weights in this manner, each group of 500 voters had an equal chance of selection and the sample was guaranteed to be a random selection of the population and not of voting units.

The weighting process was repeated for the other samples. Because Illinois' population expanded so rapidly, however, the 1860 sample was weighted by one number for every 1,000 voters, while for the 1870 sample, the weight was one number for every 2,500 voters. Each sample was drawn separately by using a table of random numbers. The result was that for the 1850 sample, 86 cases were drawn; for the 1860 sample, 76 townships and counties were selected; and for the 1870 sample, 69 townships were drawn.[1] A larger number of cases was purposely taken for 1850 and 1860 because of fragmentary election data, which reduced the number of cases to be analyzed in any given election. Because of the lack of data, the final sample sizes were: 55 for 1850, 60 for 1860, and 65 for 1870.

In order to test the validity of the samples, the election returns were compiled and checked against the actual results for the state as a whole (see Table 41). In most cases, the margin of error was less than 5 percent. For the 1850 sample, the Presidential election of 1852 was typical, showing a very accurate Democratic vote of 51.5 percent whereas the actual vote was 51.8 percent. The 1850 sample Whig vote, however, was overestimated at 45.2 percent when, in reality, the Whig vote was only 41.7 percent. This margin of error was reflected in the Free Soil vote, which the sample underestimated, showing a 3 percent vote when it was actually 6 percent. The 1870 sample contained the highest margin of error of the three samples. In the 1866 election, for example, there was a 7.5 percent error in predicting the Republican vote. But the size of this error was due to the large number of missing cases rather than the unreliability of the sample. Far more typical of the dependability of the 1870 sample was the 1876 election, in which the margin of error was less than one percent. With the exception of the 1866 and 1868 elections, then, the sample proved to be quite reliable and easily within the reasonable margin of error of 5 percent.

Table 41. Measurement of Sampling Error

	Cases	Missing Values	Percent Whig / Republican			Percent Democrat			Percent Other		
			Sample	Actual	Error	Sample	Actual	Error	Sample	Actual	Error
1850 State	55	25	12.4	17.0	-4.6	86.3	80.0	6.3	0.	2.5	-2.5
1852 Presidential	55	25	40.0	41.7	-1.7	55.2	51.8	3.4	4.7	6.4	-1.7
1854 State	55	25	41.3	41.8	-0.5	54.5	52.4	2.1	4.0	5.7	-1.7
1854 State	55	25	46.9	48.9	-2.0	52.8	51.0	1.8			
1856 Presidential	60	24	44.8	40.2	4.6	41.2	44.0	-3.8	13.6	15.6	-2.0
1856 State	60	24	47.0	46.9	0.1	44.3	44.9	-0.6	8.7	8.0	0.7
1858 State	60	4	51.3	49.7	1.6	47.7	48.2	-0.5	0.9	2.0	-1.1
1860 Presidential	60	6	52.7	50.6	2.1	46.1	47.1	-1.0	0.7	1.4	-0.7
1860 State	60	6	51.6	51.3	0.3	47.5	47.4	0.1	0.4	0.7	-0.3
1862 State	60	26	44.2	46.7	-2.5	55.7	53.2	2.5	0.8	1.0	-0.2
1864 Presidential	60	21	54.0	54.4	-0.4	45.9	45.5	0.4			
1864 State	60	21	54.1	54.7	-0.6	45.8	45.2	0.6			
1866 State	65	27	65.4	57.9	7.5	34.4	42.0	-7.6			
1868 Presidential	65	27	61.6	55.6	6.0	38.3	44.3	-6.0			
1868 State	65	27	61.3	55.5	5.8	38.7	44.4	-5.7			
1870 State	65	9	57.8	53.3	4.5	42.0	45.5	-3.5			
1872 Presidential	65	18	57.4	56.2	1.2	0.2	0.8	-0.6	42.2	43.0	-0.8
1872 State	65	18	56.2	54.4	1.8	0.2	0.4	-0.2	43.4	45.0	-1.6
1874 State	65	20	42.8	44.4	-1.6	44.7	34.9	9.8	12.3	20.6	-8.3
1876 Presidential	65	17	51.3	50.2	1.1	45.3	46.6	-1.3	3.2	3.1	0.1
1876 State	65	17	51.4	50.5	0.9	47.7	49.3	-1.6	0.8	0.06	0.74

Note: The "Percent Whig" column heading applies to the first four rows (1850–1854); beginning with 1856 Presidential the column is labeled "Percent Republican." The repeated sub-labels "Percent Democrat" and "Percent Other" appear in the lower portion of the table.

The variables used in each sample were designed to reflect the ethnic, religious, and economic composition of the voters in Illinois. As a check on the validity of the variables used, in all cases, at least 75 percent of the variance in the election results was explained and usually over 90 percent was explained. Variance is explained statistically when, for example, the reason one township is Republican and another area is mostly Democratic is shown to depend on the presence or absence of certain variables. The high percentage of explained variance verifies that the religious, ethnic, and economic variables used in this study were highly reliable in describing the Illinois voting pattern.

Determining the ethnic composition of each sampled township and county was straightforward. The population manuscripts of the federal census provided the place of birth of every resident. Residents born in the New England States were classified as Yankees; those born in the States that formed the Confederacy, including the border States of Missouri and Kentucky, were called Southerners; and all born in the remaining States, including New York, Pennyslvania, New Jersey, Delaware, Maryland, Ohio, and Indiana were categorized as "Other" U.S.-born. The "Other" U.S.-born variable defies ethnic characterization since it included second generation foreign-born, Yankees, and Southerners, but because the census did not record the place of birth of parents, finer ethnic divisions could not be determined. Finally, within the native-born, a category for the Illinois-born was established. Predominantly, this group consisted of second generation Southerners since Southerners had been the first settlers of the state and generally only their children would have been of voting age by 1850.

The ethnic divisions of the foreign-born represented the major groups immigrating into the United States and Illinois. Again, only the first generation could be determined, but because the immigrant population of Illinois was very small before 1850, the effect of second-generation immigrants on the elections was insignificant. All born in the various German states were simply classified together, and those born in Sweden and Denmark were called Scandinavians. The English, Irish, and French-born provided no classification difficulties. The Canadians, however, presented a slight problem. The census did not distinguish between French and English Canadians, and consequently, the two groups had to be categorized together. Undoubtedly, the animosities between these groups partially explains the erratic voting behavior of the Canadians. There were also a few immigrants in Illinois from Poland and Russia, but their number was far too small to be represented in the sample (see Table 42).[2]

Table 42. Ethnic Breakdown for Illinois

	1850		1860		1870	
	N	%	N	%	N	%
Yankee	10,646	1.3	66,093	3.9	71,066	2.9
Southern	163,941	20.2	167,044	9.9	194,549	7.9
Illinois	343,618	42.4	706,925	42.0	1,181,106	48.3
Other	184,478	22.7	426,868	25.4	511,048	20.9
German	38,160	4.7	130,804	7.7	203,750	8.3
English	23,861	2.9	52,285	3.1	72,745	2.9
Irish	27,786	3.4	87,573	5.2	120,162	4.9
Scandinavian	3,631	0.4	12,073	0.7	45,570	1.8
Canadian	10,699	1.3	20,132	1.1	32,388	1.3
French	3,396	0.4	9,493	0.5	10,908	0.4
	810,216	99.7	1,679,290	99.5	2,443,292	99.6

To determine the ethnic composition of each sampled township and county, a sufficiently large number of names had to be selected. The size of the sample of voters in each unit depended upon the degree of accuracy and the expense of drawing a larger sample. The Theory of Large Numbers states that an increase of the sample size from 250 to 1,000 reduces the margin of error from 4 to only 2 points (at a 20 percent level, i.e., 20 samples in every 100 population).[3] Because the number of cases was over 65 townships and counties for each sample, the expense of sampling over 250 voters in each unit was too great, but the margin of error in sampling under 250 names was too large. The number of names drawn, then, to determine the ethnic composition of each sample unit was 250. This meant that for many small townships, the entire population was sampled. Using 250 names per unit, from the 1850 census, 13,049 voters were sampled; from the 1860 census, 14,405 voters; and from the 1870 census, 14,781 voters.

The economic variables were determined from the non-population manuscripts of the federal census, which provided farm and industrial production data for each township and county. For the industrial variables, which were to measure the industrial development and wealth of each unit, the data for capital investment and for the value of industrial production were used. The farm variables included the size of farm, the value per acre, and the total value of the farm production. This information was provided for each individual farm and in order to be put into a manageable form, the data were converted into arithmetic averages for each county and township and then transformed into ranked data. For example, each sampled unit was ranked as either low, medium, or high in terms of farm size, acreage value, and value of farm production. No pretensions were made to use any of the economic variables to draw conclusions about individual voting behavior, but rather, these variables were used to characterize the economic condition of the townships and counties.

For this study, the religious denominations were grouped into pietist, liturgical, and Baptist. The Pietist and liturgical categories are commonly recognized by historians.[4] Although most ethno-cultural historians classify the Baptists as pietists, it was found necessary for this study to create a separate Baptist variable. One reason for having a Baptist variable is that the Baptists were only loosely organized into a denomination and the individual congregations were very autonomous.

Theologically, the Baptists were united on only a few points of doctrine and there were crucial differences between Free Will, Missionary, Southern, and Regular Baptists.[5] Because of the imprecise nature of the religious data available in Illinois and because even the Regular Baptists differed theologically from congregation to congregation, it was necessary to have a separate variable so that the pietist and liturgical categories would not be distorted.

Religion proved to be the most difficult of the variables on which to acquire significant and reliable data. Unlike other States, the federal census in Illinois provided only spotty information on the size and location of churches. An attempt was made to gather relevant church data through the minutes of church conferences and synodal meetings, but information for too many of the denominations was missing, and the data for the large denominations were unmanageable. Church information was finally gathered from county histories. Fortunately, most county histories written in the 1870s provided information on the year of organization, type, and number of churches in each community. Each sampled township and county was initially ranked on the basis of number of churches in each category as none, low, medium, or high. However, since a township could have the same number of both pietist and liturgical churches, the ranking of the religious variables proved to be misleading in the election analysis. Say, for example, that one township had 10 pietistic churches and 10 liturgical churches and a neighboring township also had 10 pietistic churches of equal size, but no liturgical churches. Both of these units would have the same ranking for pietism, but the first township would also be equally ranked for the liturgicals. In the all-pietistic township, the vote might be 100 percent Republican, producing a very strong correlation between Republicans and pietists. In the other township, however, the Republican vote might be only 50 percent becuase of the large number of liturgicals, thus producing a significantly weaker correlation between pietists and Republicans. Clearly, then, even though the size and number of pietistic churches was the same in both townships, they could not be ranked the same. In order to solve this problem, a single religious index was created whereby the numeric values assigned for the rankings were subtracted from each other. In the first township, consequently, high pietism and high liturgicalism cancel out, but in the neighboring township, the index would still be high pietism. The index, therefore, provided a more realistic variable for election analysis.

The gathering of election data was also a major difficulty. Illinois recorded election returns only for the county level. It was necessary, therefore, to search through the local newspapers to get township returns. Virtually every county in Illinois had at least one newspaper even as early as 1850. Although enough election returns were found in this manner, newspapers were not entirely reliable sources. Often, important issues were missing. Far more frustrating, however, was the discovery that a newspaper occasionally refused to publish the complete returns of an election that went against its political party. The result was that, for the elections, especially in the 1850 and 1860 samples, there are a number of missing cases.

Statistically, the object of election analysis can be either to under-stand individual voting behavior or to identify voter coalitions. In both cases, the basic statistical routine can be the same, but the distinction in objectives is important. Without a clear understanding of the purpose for which a specific statistical technique is employed, erroneous assumptions are often made about the results of the method. For example, the early ethno-cultural historians made conclusions about both individual voting behavior and the nature of entire voter coalitions from the same statistical routine.[6] They concluded that a man voted Republican because he was a pietist and, therefore, all Republicans were pietists. This involved not only the logical fallacy of circular reasoning, but also a misuse of statistics. The specific routine used for determining voter behavior must be employed in a different manner to identify the entire voter coalitions.

The purpose of this study is to identify and characterize the voter coalitions as a whole. Accordingly, the statistical routines of bivariate and multivariate analysis were employed to analyze the election returns. The specific method chosen for identifying the voter coalitions was multiple regression, a technique for drawing a straight line between different variables, which is necessary for predicting the influence of one factor upon another. The method analyzes the 18 ethnic, religious, and economic variables in this study and determines the importance of these independent variables in explaining the election returns. By knowing the effect of each of these variables upon election returns, it is then possible to identify entire voter coalitions.

According to J. Morgan Kousser, multiple regression is a superior technique for voter analysis which was ignored by the early ethno-cultural historians.[7] The advantage of this type of routine is that it does not depend upon homogeneous townships, which are at best oddities in American society. Secondly, multiple regression produces far more powerful statistics than simple correlations, which can be misleading and, consequently, the erroneous assumptions of linear patterns that are often made from strong correlations can be avoided. Thirdly, multiple regression gives the actual predicting power of each variable and its standard error of estimate. On the other hand, simple correlation coefficient, often used by the ethno-cultural historians, indicated only the strength of association between two variables. Finally, multiple regression minimizes the ecological fallacy of assuming group behavior from ecologically based data. By being a function of the standard deviation, regression can account for variance which is necessary in analyzing this type of data.[8]

Multiple regression, and specifically, a routine called step-wise regression, which ranks the independent variables by significance, was used to identify the voter coalitions of the political parties. This routine is important because it gives a complete picture of the coalitions and the relative importance of each variable in determining the composition of the political parties. Instead of simply saying that the Yankees, Germans, and pietists were Republican, it is possible, through the use of multiple regression, to show all of the Republican voters and the influence of the Yankees, Germans, and pietists in the entire coalition.

Although multiple regression can solve many methodological problems, the technique has limitations. While it can determine the power of any independent variable in predicting a dependent variable, it cannot be satisfactorily employed to determine the opposite relationship, that is, the strength of the dependent variable in the independent variable. For example, multiple regression can determine the composition of the Republican coalition and the effect of the variables, such as the German vote, in explaining the overall Republican vote, but it cannot adequately determine the equally important question of what percentage of the Germans voted Republican.

To illustrate more precisely, regression is a routine to provide the straight-line formula of $Y = a + b(X)$. The "Y" in the equation is the dependent variable, which in this case is either percentage Republican or percentage Democratic, and the "X" is the independent variable, one of the 18 ethnic, religious, or economic variables. The "a" represents the point where the regression line crosses the "Y" axis when "X" equals zero, and the "b" is the slope of the line. The "b" coefficient indicates the degree of change in "Y" for every change in "X." However, because the "b" coefficient is tied to the variance in the dependent variable, all the "b's" in multiple regression affect one another. For example, in determining percentage Republican, the independent variable "Yankee" may explain 60 percent of the variance. The "b's" for the remaining 17 variables become less powerful as the amount of variance to be explained is reduced. This relationship is crucial for determining the most powerful variables in predicting percentage Republican, but at the same time, it makes it impossible to clearly calculate, for example, what percentage of the Germans voted Republican.

Consequently, in order to determine the percentage of each ethnic group voting Republican or Democratic, a bivariate analysis was used. This technique employs the same straight line equation, but instead of the formula being $Y = a + b(X) + b_2(X)_2 \ldots + b_{18}(X_{18})$, it is simply $Y = a + b(X)$. Because only one independent variable is being analyzed, the "b" coefficient will be able to reach its maximum size, since the variance in the dependent variable will not be "soaked" up by the other independent variables. Therefore, through a bivariate analysis, the percentage of Germans voting Republican can be determined. The formula would read: percentage Republican $= 20.4 + .52(100)$, or, the Germans voted 72.4 percent Republican.

While bivariate and multivariate regression provides much useful information, any statistical analysis of aggregate data must be handled with caution. Neither of the routines employed in this study can account for covariance and for ceiling effects. Covariance exists when two or more variables are so closely associated that the effect of one cannot be clearly separated from the effect of the other. For example, the Yankees were predominantly pietistic and lived in regions with high farm values. The effect of high farm value upon the Republican vote, therefore, could be a result of the fact that the Yankees are Republican and not of economic status. Statistically, regression cannot control covariance, and consequently, the "pure" effect of, say, high farm value cannot be determined.

Multiple and bivariate regression also do not consider ceiling effects. In the data, the vote always adds up to 100 percent, as does the ethnic breakdown of the sample units. The regression routine, however, cannot account for this. Consequently, the regression line is extended far beyond reality. For example, statistically the Yankees consistently voted over 100 percent Republican, which is, of course, an impossibility.

Covariance and ceiling effects make it impossible to argue that regression presents an exact picture of voting. Nevertheless, the routine can provide a fairly accurate estimate, and despite its limitations, regression has proved to be a reliable means for interpreting aggregate data.

Methodologically, this study is very similar to the technique used by the news media today for predicting election results. The difference, of course, is that historians already know the outcome of the elections in the past. This method is very reliable in determining the components of a voter coalition, and more precisely, the strength of each political party within the ethnic groupings of the voting population.

Notes

Introduction

1. For a good survey of the literature on the sectional conflict see Edwin C. Rozwenc, ed., *The Causes of the American Civil War*, 2nd ed. (London: D.C. Heath and Company, 1972), and Thomas J. Pressly, ed., *Americans Interpret Their Civil War* (New York: The Free Press, 1962). The most complete analysis of Civil War historiography is found in David M. Potter, *The South and the Sectional Conflict* (Baton Rouge: Louisiana State University Press, 1968), pp. 34-85, 87-150, 151-76. For a review of recent trends in the historiography, see Eric Foner, "The Causes of the American Civil War: Recent Interpretations and New Directions," *Civil War History* 20 (September 1974): 197-214.

   On the Reconstruction literature, see Barnard A. Wiesberger, "The Dark and Bloody Ground of Reconstruction Historiography," *Journal of Southern History* 25 (November 1959): 427-48; Gerald N. Grob, "Reconstruction: An American Morality Play," *American History*, ed. George Billias and Gerald N. Grob (New York: The Free Press, 1971), pp. 191-231; Lawanda and John H. Cox, "Negro Suffrage and Republican Politics: The Problem of Motivation in Reconstruction Historiography," *Journal of Southern History* 33 (August 1967): 303-30; and Larry Kincaid, "Victims of Circumstance: An Interpretation of Changing Attitudes Toward Republican Policy Makers and Reconstruction," *Journal of American History* 57 (June 1970): 48-66. Finally, a good examination of the recent trends in the Civil War and Reconstruction literature is found in Richard O. Curry, "The Civil War and Reconstruction, 1861-1877: A Critical Overview of Recent Trends and Interpretations," *Civil War History* 20 (September 1974): 215-38.

2. For a good discussion of the First Party System, see William N. Chambers, *The Political Parties in a New Nation* (New York: Oxford University Press, 1963); Richard Hofstadter, *The Idea of a Party System: The Rise of Legitimate Opposition in the United States, 1780-1840* (Berkeley: University of California Press, 1969; Noble E. Cunningham, Jr., *The Jeffersonian Republicans: The Formation of Party Organization* (Chapel Hill: University of North Carolina Press, 1957); Paul Goodman, *The Democratic-Republicans of Massachusetts* (Cambridge: Harvard University Press, 1964); James M. Banner, Jr., *To the Hartford Convention: The Federalists and the Origins of Party Politics in Massachusetts* (New York: Alfred A. Knopf, 1970); Norman K. Risjord, *The Old Republicans* (New York: Columbia University Press, 1965); and Joseph Charles, *The Origins of the American Party System*, with a Foreword by Frederick Merk (Williamsburg: Institute of Early American History and Culture, 1956).

3. For a characterization of the Second Party System, see Richard P. McCormick, *The Second American Party System: Party Formation in the Jacksonian Era* (New York: W. W. Norton & Company, Inc., 1973); Robert V. Remini, *Martin Van Buren and the Making of the Democratic Party* (New York: W. W. Norton & Company, Inc., 1959); Remini, *The Election of Andrew Jackson* (New York: Harper & Row, Publishers, 1964); and Hofstadter, *The Idea of a Party System.*

4. Morton Borden, gen. ed., *Political Parties in American History*, 3 vols. (New York: G. P. Putnam's Sons, 1973), vol. 2, *Political Parties in American History, 1828-1890,* ed. Felice A. Bonadio, p. 523.

5. For a discussion of the political parties in the Gilded Age, see Alexander B. Callow, Jr., *The Tweed Ring* (New York: Oxford University Press, 1966); Seymour J. Mandelbaum, *Boss Tweed's New York* (New York: John Wiley & Sons, Inc., 1965); Ari Hoogenboom, *Outlawing the Spoils: A History of the Civil Service Reform Movement, 1865-1883* (Urbana: University of Illinois Press, 1961); John Sproat, *The Best Men: Liberal Reformers in the Gilded Age* (London: Oxford University Press, 1968); and Richard Hofstadter, *Anti-Intellectualism in American Life* (New York: Alfred A. Knopf, 1964). Two outstanding exceptions are David J. Rothman, *Politics and Power: The United States Senate, 1869-1901* (Cambridge: Harvard University Press, 1966) and Moisei Ostrogorski, *Democracy and the Organization of Political Parties* (New York: The MacMillan Company, 1902).

6. See, for example, Allan Nevins, *Ordeal of the Union* (New York: Charles Scribner's Sons, 1947), pp. 329-31 for the "natural sympathy . . . among the temperance men, slavery men, Whigs, and Northern Know-Nothings." This consensus-type approach to the voters and the parties was reaffirmed by Michael F. Holt, *Forging a Majority: The Formation of the Republican Party in Pittsburgh, 1848-1860* (New Haven: Yale University Press, 1969); and Ronald P. Formisano, *The Birth of Mass Political Parties, Michigan, 1827-1861* (Princeton: Princeton University Press, 1971). The major exceptions to this interpretation are in Eric Foner, *Free Soil, Free Labor, Free Men: The Ideology of the Republican Party before the Civil War* (New York: Oxford University Press, 1970); and Roy F. Nichols, *The Disruption of the American Democracy* (New York: The Free Press, 1948).

7. Until recently, Roy F. Nichols, *The Invention of the American Political Parties* (New York: The Macmillan Company, 1967), provided the most complete statement of a party system. According to Nichols, the American political machinery was completed in the 1850s with the institutionalization of the 2 party system. Nichols maintained that this basic pattern has never been altered, and, consequently, that it is America's only party system. While Nichols is correct in saying that America has had a 2 party system, that point of view cannot account for the important changes in politics over the last 100 years.

8. William N. Chambers and Walter Dean Burnham, eds., *The American Party System: Stages of Political Development* (New York: Oxford University Press, 1967), and James L. Sundquist, *Dynamics of the Party System* (Washington, D.C.: The Brookings Institution, 1973).

9. Chambers, "Party Development and the American Mainstream," in Chambers and Burnham, eds., *The American Party System,* pp. 289-304.

10. Sundquist, *Dynamics of the Party System.*

11. A good account of the importance of party loyalty after the decline of issues is found in Joel H. Silbey's *The Shrine of Party: Congressional Voting Behavior, 1841-1852* (Pittsburgh: University of Pittsburgh Press, 1967).

12. For examples of voter studies that make assumptions about the composition of party coalitions from an analysis of individual voting behavior, see Ronald Formisano, *The Birth of Mass Political Parties*; Paul Kleppner, *The Cross of Culture: A Social Analysis of Midwestern Politics, 1850-1900* (New York: The Free Press, 1970); and Richard Jensen, *The Winning of the Midwest: Social and Political Conflict, 1888-1896* (Chicago: The University of Chicago Press, 1971).

13. See, for example, Formisano, *The Birth of Mass Political Parties,* pp. 5-8, and Holt, *Forging A Majority,* pp. 6-8.

14. For a complete critique of antebellum voter studies, see Richard B. Latner and Peter Levine, "Perspectives on Antebellum Pietistic Politics," *Reviews in American History* 4 (March 1976): 15-24, and Eric Foner, "The Causes of the American Civil War: Recent Interpretations and New Direction," *Civil War History* 20 (September 1974): 197-214.

15. U.S. Census Office, *The Seventh Census of the United States: 1850; Embracing a Statistical View of Each of the States,* pp. xxxvi-xxxvii, 702. U.S. Census Office, *Population of the United States in 1860; Compiled from the Original Returns of the Eighth Census,* pp. v-vi, 102-4.

16. *Washington States,* 16 July 1858, quoted in Robert W. Johannsen, *Stephen A. Douglas* (New York: Oxford University Press, 1973), p. 645.

17. Joshua Giddings to George W. Julian, 25 May 1860, quoted in Don E. Fehrenbacker, *Prelude to Greatness, Lincoln in the 1850's* (Stanford: Stanford University Press, 1962), p. 5.

Chapter 1

1. Richard P. McCormick, *The Second American Party System: Party Formation in the Jacksonian Era* (New York: W. W. Norton & Co., Inc., 1966), p. 354.

2. Ibid.

3. *Ottawa Free Trader,* 28 February 1852.

4. *Illinois State Register,* 14 June 1854.

5. *Western Citizen,* 21 September 1852, Arthur C. Cole's Notes, Illinois Historical Survey, Urbana, Illinois (hereinafter cited as "Cole's Notes, IHS").

6. *Illinois State Journal,* 29 September 1856.

7. *Illinois State Register,* 15 July 1852.

8. Ibid., 2 August 1852, and *Western Citizen*, 11 May 1852, Cole's Notes, IHS.

9. *Illinois State Register*, 4, 5 April 1852.

10. *Belleville Advocate*, 28 July 1852, 4, 11, 18 August 1852, 20 October 1852.

11. *Illinois State Register*, 8 January 1852.

12. Ibid., 29 December 1857 (my italics).

13. For an example of a convention called by the voters, see the *Illinois State Register*, 26 March 1840, quoted in Robert W. Johannsen, ed., *The Letters of Stephen A. Douglas* (Urbana: University of Illinois Press, 1961), p. 81.

14. *Quincy Whig*, 12 April 1852.

15. *Illinois State Register*, 15 July 1852.

16. Ibid., 19 January 1852.

17. Ibid., 20 May 1852.

18. Stephen Douglas to Lewis W. Ross, 17 March 1838, quoted in Johannsen, ed., *Letters*, pp. 55-56.

19. "Circular from the National Democratic Committee," 5 September 1852, George S. Kimberly Collection, Chicago Historical Society, Chicago, Illinois (hereinafter cited as "CHS").

20. For a good description of political clubs, see William E. Barringer, "Campaign Technique in Illinois—1860," *Transactions of the Illinois State Historical Society* 39 (1932), pp. 203-81; and Don E. Fehrenbacher, "Illinois Political Attitudes, 1854-1861" (Ph.D. dissertation, University of Chicago, 1951). Also see the *Illinois State Journal*, 8 August 1860, and the *Quincy Whig*, 3 September 1852.

21. John M. Palmer, *Personal Recollections of John M. Palmer; The Story of an Earnest Life*, (Cincinnati: Robert Clarke Co., 1901), p. 43.

22. John M. Palmer, ed., *The Bench and Bar of Illinois, Historical and Reminiscent*, 2 vols. (Chicago: The Lewis Publishing Co., 1899), 1:2-3.

23. Usher F. Linder, *Reminiscences of the Early Bench and Bar of Illinois*, 2nd. ed. (Chicago: Chicago Legal News Co., 1879), p. 18.

24. Ibid., p. 218.

25. I.R.R. Gwinn to David Davis, 10 July 1850, David Davis Papers, CHS.

26. Stephen Douglas to Lewis W. Ross, 12 August 1837, and Stephen Douglas to Levi Woodbury, 6 October 1837, Johannsen, ed., *Letters*, pp. 39-41.

27. *Joliet Signal,* 7 February 1854.

28. Palmer, *Recollections,* p. 63.

29. Willard L. King, *Lincoln's Manager, David Davis* (Cambridge: Harvard University Press, 1960), p. 48.

30. For a good account of Douglas' efforts to pass the land grant to Illinois, see Robert W. Johannsen, *Stephen A. Douglas* (New York: Oxford University Press, 1973), pp. 120-24.

31. Stephen Douglas to Charles H. Lanphier, 30 December 1851, Charles H. Lanphier Papers, Illinois State Historical Library, Springfield, Illinois (hereinafter cited as "ISHL").

32. William H. Pickering to Joseph Gillespie, 12 September 1848, Joseph Gillespie Collection, CHS.

33. *Illinois State Register,* 15 April and 2 July 1852.

34. David Davis to William P. Walker, 17 October 1852, David Davis Papers, CHS.

35. *Quincy Whig,* 23 March 1852.

36. *Illinois State Register,* 23 April 1853 and the *Joliet Signal,* 18 January 1853.

37. On the formation of the Free Soil Party, see David M. Potter, *The Impending Crisis, 1848-1861,* Don E. Fehrenbacher, ed. (New York: Harper & Row, Publishers, 1976), pp. 90-121. For a discussion of the Free Soil Party in Illinois, see Clarence W. Alvord, gen. ed., *The Centennial History of Illinois,* 4 vols. (Springfield: The Illinois Centennial Commission, 1919), vol. 3: *The Era of the Civil War,* by Arthur C. Cole, pp. 53-75.

38. On the Compromise of 1850, see Potter, *Impending Crisis,* pp. 96-112.

39. *Quincy Whig,* 23 May 1853.

40. Ibid.

41. *Illinois State Register,* 25 November 1852.

42. Ibid., 16 November 1852.

43. For a complete discussion of the methodology, see the Appendix.

44. Homogeneous townships are misleading for voter analysis because they oversimplify the relationship between the voter and the party. Voting patterns in homogeneous townships, for example, tend to show linearity when in reality the relation is curvilinear. Also, there are too many questionable assumptions made for the public at large when extrapolating from voting in homogeneous areas. For a complete discussion, see J. Morgan Kousser, "The 'New Political History': A Methodological

Critique," *Reviews in American History* 4 (March 1976), pp. 1-14; Eric A. Hanushek, et al., "Model Specification, Use of Aggregate Data, and the Ecological Correlation Fallacy," *Political Methodology* 1 (1974), pp. 89-107.

45. Ronald P. Formisano, *The Birth of Mass Political Parties, Michigan 1827-1861* (Princeton: Princeton University Press, 1971), and Michael F. Holt, *Forging a Majority: The Formation of the Republican Party in Pittsburgh, 1848-1860* (New Haven: Yale University Press, 1969), are the outstanding examples of the ethno-cultural interpretation of voter behavior. These historians argue that ethnic and religious considerations are the most important factors in determining party preference. According to this theory, native-born revivalistic, or pietistic, voters were generally Whig while ritualists, or liturgicals, were Democratic. "Pietistic" and "liturgical" are general descriptions of different theological positions of various churches and denominations. Broadly defined, pietists are adherents of evangelical religions. Theologically, pietism was Arminian, i.e., the idea that man can be saved through direct confrontation with God. Pietistic groups were Methodists, Quakers, Congregationalists, Disciples of Christ, New School and Cumberland Presbyterians and Free Will and Missionary Baptists. Liturgicals were anti-revivalistic and stressed the historic doctrines of the church as the true and only way to salvation. Man could be saved only through the church by strict adherence to its doctrine. Liturgical groups were Catholics, Lutherans, Episcopalians, Old School Presbyterians, and strict Calvinists.

46. These percentages are calculated from a bivariate regression. The straight line formua is $Y = a + b(X)$ and the regression technique provides the values for the "a" and "b" coefficients. The constant, "a", is the intercept of the line on the axis between "Y", the dependent variable, and "X", the independent variable. The "b" coefficient is the slope of the line and it shows how much "Y" changes for every change in "X". Consequently, to determine what percentage of Southerners voted Democratic, the formula would read: percent Democratic $= 87.1 + (-.02) (100)$. The Southerners, then, voted approximately 85 percent Democratic.

In order to better judge the validity of the regression calculations, a number of statistics are printed with the coefficients. The Standard Error of Estimate (hereinafter cited as "SEE") is the average score of the residuals which are the difference between the actual and the estimated values of "Y". The SEE, therefore, is the average error of prediction. Consequently, the percent of Southerners voting Democratic falls between $a + b(X)$ and plus or minus the SEE. The simple r or Pearson's correlation is a test of association between the variables where 1.0 is a perfect association and -1.0 is an exact opposite relationship with .0 being no association. If the Southerners have only a -.02 correlation, then one can judge that even though they voted 85 percent Democratic, there are more important variables affecting the Democratic vote and that the overall association with the Southern variable is weak. Finally, the regression technique provides the r square, which is a measure of the proportion of variance in the dependent variable explained by the independent variable. In regression, variance is the dispersion of the data about the mean of the dependent variable. If the r square is high, then the independent variable is powerful in explaining the dependent variable.

The bivariate coefficients for the 1850 Democratic Treasurer vote:

	a	b	SEE	r	r^2
Yankee	82.2	.55	19.6	.20	.04
Southern	87.1	-.02	20.1	-.02	.0005
Illinois	97.1	-1.33	17.7	-.47	.22
Other	83.0	.10	20.0	.08	.006
German	87.9	-.30	19.9	-.12	.01
English	83.4	.69	19.8	.14	.02
Irish	84.0	.39	19.8	.14	.02
Scandi-navian	85.6	1.03	19.9	.14	.02
Canadian	86.1	.30	20.1	.02	.0007
French	86.7	-.93	20.0	-.04	.001

47. The bivariate coefficients for the 1850 Democratic Congressional vote:

	a	b	SEE	r	r^2
Yankee	63.2	-.10	18.5	-.04	.002
Southern	58.2	.11	18.3	.14	.02
Illinois	57.4	.60	18.0	.23	.05
Other	83.1	-.65	15.4	-.55	.31
German	58.2	.81	17.3	.34	.12
English	62.0	.06	18.5	.01	.0002
Irish	60.6	.25	18.4	.12	.01
Scandi-navian	61.7	1.04	18.3	.15	.02
Canadian	63.9	-1.83	18.2	-.17	.03
French	61.7	1.75	18.5	.07	.006

48. Bivariate coefficients for the 1852 Democratic Presidential vote:

	a	b	SEE	r	r^2
Yankee	59.6	-.57	12.2	-.33	.10
Southern	54.9	.00	12.9	.01	.0001
Illinois	54.0	.15	12.8	.08	.007
Other	66.1	-.36	11.6	-.43	.19
German	52.2	.38	11.8	.40	.16
English	56.5	-.29	12.8	-.11	.01
Irish	52.9	.31	12.5	.25	.06
Scandi-navian	54.4	.94	12.6	.21	.04
Canadian	54.7	.49	12.9	.06	.004
French	54.8	.91	12.9	.05	.003

49. Bivariate coefficients for the 1852 Democratic Congressional vote:

	a	b	SEE	r	r^2
Yankee	59.6	-.30	13.0	-.36	.01
Southern	54.9	.17	13.1	.50	.005
Illinois	54.0	.83	13.7	.32	.001

	a	b	SEE	r	r^2
Other	66.1	-.38	12.7	-.21	.005
German	52.2	.41	14.6	.48	.33
English	56.5	-.51	13.4	-.30	.004
Irish	52.9	.14	13.0	.32	.001
Scandi-					
navian	54.4	-.07	13.6	-.03	.001
Canadian	54.7	.38	13.7	.08	.002
French	54.8	-.63	14.0	-.37	.003

50. Bivariate coefficients for the 1850 Whig vote for Treasurer:

	a	b	SEE	r	r^2
Yankee	16.8	-.59	20.2	-.21	.04
Southern	11.4	.02	20.7	.03	.001
Illinois	10.1	1.40	18.1	.48	.23
Other	16.3	-.12	20.6	-.09	.009
German	10.5	.35	20.5	.13	.01
English	15.5	-.74	20.4	-.15	.02
Irish	14.8	-.41	20.4	-.15	.02
Scandi-					
navian	13.1	-1.10	20.4	-.14	.02
Canadian	12.7	-.37	20.7	-.03	.001
French	11.9	1.22	20.6	.05	.002

51. Bivariate coefficients for the 1850 Whig Congressional vote:

	a	b	SEE	r	r^2
Yankee	36.7	-.01	18.9	-.03	.01
Southern	39.5	-.08	18.8	-.13	.006
Illinois	53.9	-1.83	17.0	-.13	.03
Other	57.6	.26	17.6	.57	.33
German	44.3	-.57	18.3	-.49	.11
English	32.8	-.01	18.8	-.01	.04
Irish	21.5	-1.45	19.1	-.13	.03
Scandi-					
navian	28.5	-.35	17.9	-.20	.05
Canadian	40.3	.63	18.0	.05	.01
French	19.2	-.32	17.7	-.06	.01

52. Bivariate coefficients for the 1852 Whig Presidential and Congressional vote:

Presidential

	a	b	SEE	r	r^2
Yankee	41.9	-.23	12.0	-.14	.02
Southern	34.1	.17	11.3	.35	.12
Illinois	38.0	.27	11.9	.15	.02
Other	35.2	.16	11.8	.20	.04
German	43.1	-.39	10.9	-.44	.19

	a	b	SEE	r	r^2
English	40.8	-.15	12.1	-.06	.004
Irish	43.4	-.46	11.0	-.40	.16
Scandi-					
navian	40.8	-.88	11.8	-.21	.04
Canadian	41.2	-1.29	11.9	-.18	.03
French	40.3	-.54	12.1	-.03	.001

Congressional

	a	b	SEE	r	r^2
Yankee	32.2	.39	17.7	.16	.02
Southern	37.7	-.08	17.9	-.10	.01
Illinois	43.9	-1.10	16.0	-.45	.20
Other	19.2	.53	15.9	.46	.21
German	37.8	-.30	17.4	-.24	.06
English	32.1	.63	17.7	.18	.03
Irish	35.2	-.01	18.0	-.01	.0001
Scandi-					
navian	34.9	.19	18.0	.03	.001
Canadian	35.3	-.27	18.0	-.02	.0008
French	33.5	3.81	17.7	.17	.03

53. Bivariate coefficients for the 1851 Banking Law:

For

	a	b	SEE	r	r^2
Yankee	39.3	.77	27.6	.19	.03
Southern	49.8	-.13	28.0	-.09	.009
Illinois	59.3	-1.55	25.8	-.39	.15
Other	15.0	1.05	23.6	.54	.29
German	50.1	-.93	26.4	-.34	.11
English	45.7	-.28	28.1	-.04	.001
Irish	46.4	-.32	27.9	-.10	.01
Scandi-					
navian	45.4	-3.95	27.8	-.14	.02
Canadian	43.8	1.50	28.1	.05	.003
French	43.9	2.54	28.1	.04	.002

Against

	a	b	SEE	r	r^2
Yankee	60.4	-.76	27.5	-.19	.03
Southern	49.8	.13	27.9	.09	.009
Illinois	40.4	1.55	25.7	.39	.15
Other	84.7	-1.05	23.6	-.54	.29
German	49.6	.92	26.4	.34	.11
English	54.1	.27	28.0	.03	.001
Irish	53.5	.30	27.9	.10	.01

	a	b	SEE	r	r^2
Scandi-					
navian	54.3	3.90	27.8	.14	.02
Canadian	56.0	-1.53	28.0	-.05	.003
French	55.9	-2.67	28.0	-.05	.002

54. *Illinois State Register*, 24 April 1852.

55. *Joliet Signal*, 22 July 1851.

56. *Illinois State Register*, 27 June 1853.

57. Ibid., 1 June 1852.

58. *Boston Times*, quoted in the *Illinois State Register*, 17 January 1852.

59. *Illinois State Register*, 20 January 1850.

60. Ibid., 26 April, 6, 10, 15 May 1852.

61. Ibid., 3 June 1852.

62. Ibid., 2 and 4 June 1852.

63. See, for example, John Wood, et al., to Joseph Gillespie, 7 September 1852, Joseph Gillespie Collection, CHS.

64. *Illinois State Register*, 11 November 1852.

65. Ibid., 16 November 1852.

Chapter 2

1. John M. Palmer, *Personal Recollections of John M. Palmer; The Story of an Earnest Life* (Cincinnati: Robert Clarke Co., 1901), p. 64.

2. Usher F. Linder, *Reminiscences of the Early Bench and Bar of Illinois,* 2nd edition (Chicago: Robert Clarke Co., 1879), p. 347.

3. Stephen A. Douglas to Sidney Breese, 6 November 1846, in Robert W. Johannsen, ed., *The Letters of Stephen A. Douglas* (Urbana: University of Illinois Press, 1961), pp. 144-45. A good account of Douglas' early career and his feud with Breese is in Robert W. Johannsen, *Stephen A. Douglas* (New York: Oxford Universiy Press, 1973), pp. 187-88, 257-60.

4. Stephen A. Douglas to Hall Simms, 16 November 1846, Jos. Roberts to Stephen Douglas, 16 November 1846, in Stephen A. Douglas Papers, UC; Stephen A. Douglas to William Martin, 19 November 1846, and Stephen A. Douglas to John D. Caton, 24 November 1846, in Johannsen, *Letters*, pp. 148-50.

5. Joseph Gillespie, *Recollections of Early Illinois and Her Noted Men* (Chicago: Fergus Printing Co., 1880), pp. 48-50.

6. John A. McClernand to Stephen A. Douglas, n.d. May 1849, and S. Hayes to Stephen Douglas, 13 April 1850, Stephen A. Douglas Papers, UC.

7. *Illinois State Register*, 6 February 1851.

8. Sidney Breese to "William," 14 October 1851, Sidney Breese Collection, CHS.

9. Sidney Breese to William Brown, 22 April 1851, Sidney Breese Collection, CHS.

10. William Jayne to Lyman Trumbull, 20 January 1856, Lyman Trumbull Family Papers, ISHL.

11. *Springfield (Mass.) Republican*, 21 July 1860, quoted in Johannsen, *Stephen A. Douglas*, p. 4.

12. *Chicago American*, 14 February 1841, quoted in Johannsen, *Stephen A. Douglas*, p. 97.

13. John M. Palmer, ed., *The Bench and Bar of Illinois, Historical and Reminiscent*, 2 volumes (Chicago: The Lewis Publishing Co., 1899), 2:752,755.

14. Stephen A. Douglas to Charles H. Lanphier, 13 Feburary 1854, Charles H. Lanphier Papers, ISHL.

15. On the early career of John Wentworth, see Don E. Fehrenbacher, *Chicago Giant; A Biography of "Long John" Wentworth* (Madison: The American Historical Research Center, 1957), pp. 34-51.

16. For the agreement between Douglas and Wentworth, see Johannsen, *Stephen A. Douglas*, pp. 351, 365, 372; and Fehrenbacher, *Chicago Giant*, pp. 117-18.

17. Stephen A. Douglas to Charles H. Lanphier, 21 November 1853, Charles H. Lanphier Papers, ISHL.

18. On the early career of Lincoln, see Benjamin P. Thomas, *Abraham Lincoln* (New York: Alfred A. Knopf, 1952).

19. Abraham Lincoln, "Address to the People of Illinois," 4 March 1843, in Roy P. Basler, et al., ed., *The Collected Works of Abraham Lincoln*, 9 volumes (New Brunswick: Rutgers University Press, 1953), 1:309-18 (hereinafter cited as "CWAL").

20. Abraham Lincoln to Robert Boal, 7 January 1846, *CWAL*, 1:352-3.

21. Abraham Lincoln to B. F. James, 9 February 1846, *CWAL*, 1:465-6.

22. Gillespie, *Recollections*, pp. 37-38.

23. Theodore Calvin Pease and James G. Randall, eds., *The Diary of Orville Hickman Browning*, 2 volumes (Springfield: Illinois State Historical Library, 1925), 1:15.

24. Pease and Randall, eds., *Browning Diary*, 1:64.

25. Ibid., 1:80.

26. On the nomination of Joel A. Matteson, see Fehrenbacher, *Chicago Giant,* p. 79, and Johannsen, *Stephen A. Douglas,* p. 126.

27. Palmer, *Recollections,* p. 37.

28. Gillespie, *Recollections,* p. 19.

29. Isaac R. Diller to Stephen A. Douglas, 16 September 1850, Stephen A. Douglas Papers, UC.

30. *Joliet Signal,* 6 September 1853.

31. *Illinois State Journal,* 20 September 1860.

32. Joseph L. Hayes to John A. McClernand, 15 April 1850, John A. McClernand Papers, ISHL.

33. Abraham Lincoln to Richard Yates, 18 August 1854, *CWAL,* 2:226.

34. Stephen A. Douglas to William S. Prentice, 30 August 1841, in Johannsen, *Letters,* pp. 99-101.

35. John Knox to John A. McClernand, 16 April 1850, John A. McClernand Papers, ISHL.

36. *Illinois State Register,* 4 June 1853.

37. John A. McClernand to Stephen A. Douglas, 24 March 1853, Stephen A. Douglas Papers, UC.

38. Stephen A. Douglas to Charles Lanphier, 3 December 1852, in Johannsen, *Letters,* pp. 257-58.

39. Quoted in Fehrenbacher, *Chicago Giant,* p. 61.

40. *Aurora Beacon,* 28 September 1855, Cole's Notes, CHS.

41. Palmer, *Recollections,* p. 40.

42. Linder, *Reminiscences,* p. 240-41.

43. Ibid.

44. D. W. Lusk, *Politics and Politicians: A Succinct History of the Politics of Illinois, From 1856 to 1884* (Springfield: H. W. Rokker, Printer, 1884), pp. 106-7.

45. Richard Yates to Jesse W. Fell, 17 November 1852, Jesse W. Fell Papers, ISHL.

46. *Illinois State Register,* 23 November 1858.

47. J. Wilson Schaffer to Lyman Trumbull, 15 August 1860, Lyman Trumbull Papers, Library of Congress, Washington, D.C. (hereinafter cited as "LC").

48. Douglas to George W. Sheahan, 23 February 1857, George W. Sheahan Collection, CHS.

Chapter 3

1. Robert W. Johannsen, *Stephen A. Douglas* (New York: Oxford University Press, 1973), pp. 389-90.

2. Stephen A. Douglas to Charles H. Lanphier, 11 November 1853, Robert W. Johannsen, ed., *The Letters of Stephen A. Douglas* (Urbana: University of Illinois Press, 1961), pp. 267-68.

3. Johannsen, *Stephen A. Douglas*, pp. 390-400.

4. The prolonged debate over Douglas' motives for the Kansas-Nebraska Act is contained in Roy F. Nichols, "The Kansas-Nebraska Act: A Century of Historiography," *The Mississippi Valley Historical Review*, 43 (September, 1956), pp. 187-212. More recently, David Potter concluded that while Douglas did have the building of the Pacific Railroad through the new territory in his mind, the Senator was innocent of any sordid intentions; David M. Potter, *The Impending Crisis, 1848-1861*, ed., Don E. Fehrenbacher (New York: Harper & Row, 1976), pp. 147-171. Johannsen agrees with Potter that the railroad played a role in Douglas' motivation, but concludes that it was all part of the westward expansion program; Johannsen, *Stephen A. Douglas*, pp. 390-400.

5. See, for example, Allen Nevins, *Ordeal of the Union*, volume 2: *A House Dividing* (New York: Charles Scribner's Sons, 1947); Clarence W. Alvord, general ed., *The Centennial History of Illinois*, 4 volumes (Springfield: Illinois Centennial Commission, 1919), volume 3: *The Era of the Civil War*, by Arthur C. Cole; and Charles A. Church, *History of the Republican Party in Illinois, 1854-1912* (Rockford: Press of Wilson Brothers Co., 1912).

6. See, for example, Michael F. Holt, *Forging a Majority: The Formation of the Republican Party in Pittsburgh, 1848-1860* (New Haven: Yale University Press, 1969), Ronald P. Formisano, *The Birth of Mass Political Parties: Michigan, 1827-1861* (Princeton: Princeton University Press, 1971); and Richard Jensen, "The Religious and Occupational Roots of Party Identification: Illinois and Indiana in the 1870's", *Civil War History*, 16 (December, 1970), pp. 325-42.

7. See Formisano, *The Birth of Mass Political Parties*, p. 8, for the ethno-cultural interpretation that "religious and ethno-cultural cleavages structured the realignment . . . just as they had powerfully shaped the earlier party formations."

8. Douglas to the Editor of the Concord (N.H.) *State Capitol Reporter*, 16 February 1854, Johannsen, *Letters*, p. 284.

9. *Illinois State Register*, 24 June 1854.

10. *Rock Island and Western Illinois Times*, 13 November 1854.

11.   *Illinois State Register,* 21 October 1851.

12.   Multiple regression is used here because it is better able to handle the confusing patterns during the realignment than bivariate analysis, which was employed in Chapter 1. The percentages for the voting behavior of groups determined from the bivariate regression would be misleading for the 1854 election since there were an inordinate number of political groups competing for voters. With five separate factions, the sample is subdivided into too many units, which greatly increases the margin of error in each estimated percentage. Multiple regression is useful because it provides a ranking of the variables which explains each party's composition without having to calculate voting percentages.

13.   R. McKinley Ormsby, *A Historical of the Whig Party,* 2nd edition (Boston: Crosby, Nichols & Co., 1860), p. 372.

14.   The multiple regression table is a step-wise procedure, i.e., the independent variables are ranked in order of their predicting value. All of the variables are significant at .05 or better which means that it is possible to be 95 percent sure that this pattern is not a result of chance. The multiple r is the accumulated simple correlation of the variables which indicates the strength of association between the independent and dependent variables. R square is the explained variance. Variance is the dispersion of the data about the mean of the dependent variable. For example, the mean of the dependent variable "percent Whig" is 32 percent. The Whig rate in each sample unit, however, varies from 2 to 95 percent. This variance in the Whig vote is what the independent variables explain, or the extent to which variation in "Y" is explained by "X." The "RSQ Change" indicates the amount of variance that is explained by each variable and the "Simple R" is the correlation between each of the independent variables and the dependent variable. The multiple regression table also provides the coefficients for the straight line formula of $Y = a + b(X)$. The "constant" is the "a" and "Beta" is the standardized "b".

15.   *Freeport Journal,* 23 February 1854, 9 March 1854.

16.   *Rock Island Advertiser,* 5 April 1854.

17.   *Peoria Weekly Republican,* 16 September 1854.

18.   Elihu B. Washburne to Henry Robinson, 5 July 1854, James Franklin Aldrich Collection, CHS.

19.   *Rock Island Advertiser,* 13 September 1854.

20.   Ibid.

21.   See for example, Arthur M. Schlesinger, Jr., *The Age of Jackson* (Boston: Little, Brown and Company, 1945), pp. 480-83.

22.   *Alton Courier,* 7 November 1854.

23.   Ibid., 20 September 1855.

24. Ibid., 25 May 1854.

25. Ibid., 8 July 1854.

26. Mark M. Krug, *Lyman Trumbull: Conservative Radical* (New York: A.S. Barnes & Co., 1965), p. 102; *Alton Courier*, 12 August 1854, 30 August 1854, and 6 September 1854.

27. Don E. Fehrenbacher, *Chicago Giant: A Biography of "Long John" Wentworth* (Madison: The American Historical Research Center, 1957), pp. 130-36.

28. Stephen A. Douglas to Charles H. Lanphier, 13 February 1854, Charles H. Lanphier Papers, ISHL.

29. These percentages of non-voters are calculated from a bivariate analysis.

	a	b	SEE	r	r^2
Illinois	-4.65	.53	8.45	.25	.07
Other	7.95	.19	8.66	.27	.003
German	127.10	-1.13	9.99	.02	.0006

30. See Chapter 1, note 45.

31. Bivariate coefficients for the 1854 Democratic Treasurer's vote:

	a	b	SEE	r	r^2
Southerners	35.7	.51	20.0	.51	.26
Illinois	38.8	1.72	19.7	.53	.28
Germans	55.2	-.25	23.0	-.15	.02
Other	68.0	-.55	21.6	-.38	.14
Scandi-navian	53.0	-.13	23.3	-.01	.0003
French	54.8	-3.07	22.6	-.25	.06

32. See Chapter 1, note 49.

33. Bivariate coefficients for the 1854 Anti-Nebraska Whig Congressional vote:

	a	b	SEE	r	r^2
Southerners	3.90	.32	23.4	.33	.11
Illinois	19.7	-.04	24.1	-.01	.0002

34. William Pickering to Joseph Gillespie, 1 September 1857, Joseph Gillespie Collection, CHS.

35. John Wentworth to Mason Brayman, 20 June 1854, Mason Brayman Papers, ISHL.

36. Stephen A. Douglas to James W. Sheahan, 14 September 1854, Johannsen, *Letters*, p. 330.

37. For a good discussion of Wentworth's maneuverings, see Don E. Fehrenbacher, *Chicago Giant*, pp. 132-33.

38. By examining the Whig and Democratic newspapers in Madison, Peoria, Rock Island, and Stephenson counties in 1853, 1854 and 1856, it was possible to determine the names of the political leaders in each community. These men were traced in the county Histories and city directories, which provided information on each man's occupation, place of birth, year of settlement, age, religion, and party affiliation. A total of 569 of the political elite in these four counties were identified in this manner. Although there were no outstanding differences among these men as to age, occupation, religion and ethnicity, it was possible to identify their political movement.

39. *Aurora Guardian*, 18 October 1855.

40. *Free West*, 21 September 1854, Cole's Notes, IHS.

41. Lincoln to Ichabod Codding, 27 November 1854, *CWAL*, 2:288. Also see William H. Herndon, *Herndon's Lincoln*, ed. David Freeman Hawke (New York: Bobbs-Merrill Co., Inc., 1970), pp. 150-51.

42. *Illinois State Journal*, 4 August 1855.

43. David Davis to Rockwell, 15 July 1854, David Davis Papers, CHS.

44. *Illinois State Journal*, 27 July 1854.

45. Ibid., 24 November 1855.

46. *Chicago Daily Democrat*, quoted in *Belleville Advocate*, 15 August 1855.

47. *Rock River Democrat*, 12 September 1854, Cole's Notes, IHS.

48. *Weekly Chicago Democrat*, 23 June 1855.

49. Gustave Koerner, *Memoirs of Gustave Koerner*, ed. Thomas J. McCormack, 2 volumes (Cedar Rapids: The Torch Press, 1909), 1:617-8.

50. John M. Palmer, *Personal Recollections of John M. Palmer; The Story of An Earnest Life* (Cincinnati: Robert Clarke Co., 1901), p. 63.

51. On the Senatorial contest in 1854, see Mark M. Krug, *Lyman Trumbull*, pp. 112-14; Willard L. King, *Lincoln's Manager, David Davis* (Cambridge: Harvard University Press, 1960), pp. 102-8; and Don E. Fehrenbacher, *Prelude to Greatness; Lincoln in the 1850's* (Stanford: Stanford University Press, 1962), pp. 38-39.

52. Lincoln to Jacob Harding, 11 November 1854, *CWAL*, 2:286.

53. David Davis to Abraham Lincoln, 8 December 1854, David Davis Papers, CHS.

54. David Davis to Abraham Lincoln, 26 December 1854, Robert Todd Lincoln Collection, LC.

55. Lyman Trumbull to John M. Palmer, 23 November 1854, in George Thomas Palmer, ed., "A Collection of Letters from Lyman Trumbull to John M. Palmer, 1854-1858," *Journal of the Illinois State Historical Society*, 16 (April-July, 1923), p. 24.

56. Don E. Fehrenbacher, *Prelude to Greatness*, pp. 38-39.

57. *Joliet Signal*, 14 November 1854.

Chapter 4

1. See Michael F. Holt, *Forging a Majority: The Formation of the Republican Party in Pittsburgh, 1848-1860* (New Haven: Yale University Press, 1969); Ronald P. Formisano, *The Birth of Mass Political Parties: Michigan, 1827-1861* (Princeton: Princeton University Press, 1971); and Richard Jensen, "The Religious and Occupational Roots of Party Identification: Illinois and Indiana in the 1870's," *Civil War History* 16 (December, 1970), pp. 325-43.

2. For a good discussion of the effect of the Jacksonian revivals upon Calvinism, see T. Scott Miyakawa, *Protestants and Pioneers: Individualism and Conformity on the American Frontier* (Chicago: University of Chicago Press, 1964).

3. *Western Citizen*, 28 January 1851, Cole's Notes, IHS.

4. Ibid., 3 August 1852, Cole's Notes, IHS.

5. Ibid., 12 November 1850, Cole's Notes, IHS.

6. Ibid., 17 June 1851, Cole's Notes, IHS.

7. *Chicago Daily Democratic Press*, 10 March 1855.

8. *Urbana Union*, 15 February 1855, Cole's Notes, IHS.

9. The variables in the multiple regression table are significant at .01 or better.

10. Bivariate coefficients for the 1855 pro-temperance vote:

	a	b	SEE	r	r^2
Yankee	30.9	1.97	13.9	.69	.48
Southern	52.8	-.27	18.2	-.34	.11
Illinois	52.4	-1.07	17.6	-.41	.16
Other	24.1	.70	15.5	.59	.35
German	48.4	-.46	18.1	-.35	.12
English	39.1	1.07	18.6	.27	.07
Irish	44.4	-1.02	19.4	-.008	.00007
Scandinavian	44.4	-.10	19.4	-.01	.0002
Canadian	42.2	2.67	19.0	.20	.04
French	44.3	-.08	19.4	-.008	.00007

11. Bivariate coefficients for the 1855 anti-temperance vote:

	a	b	SEE	r	r²
Yankee	68.9	-1.97	14.0	-.69	.47
Southern	46.9	.27	18.3	.34	.11
Illinois	47.4	1.07	17.7	.41	.16
Other	75.8	-.70	15.6	-.59	.35
German	51.3	.47	18.2	.35	.12
English	60.7	-1.08	18.7	-.27	.07
Irish	55.7	.57	19.4	.009	.00009
Scandinavian	55.4	.11	19.4	.01	.0003
Canadian	57.6	-2.69	19.0	-.20	.04
French	55.5	.10	19.4	.009	.0001

12. Bivariate coefficients for non-voters in the 1855 temperance referendum:

	a	b	SEE	r	r²
Illinois	-18.0	.36	5.67	.03	.06
Southerners	-17.0	.25	6.32	.19	.20

13. Bivariate coefficients for non-voters in the 1855 temperance referendum:

	a	b	SEE	r	r²
Yankee	-3.31	.48	7.29	.48	.23
Canadians	-222.61	2.88	6.54	.05	.006

14. *Peru Daily Chronicle*, 1 February 1854, Cole's Notes, IHS.

15. See Holt, *Forging a Majority*; Formisano, *Birth of Mass Political Parties*; and Jensen, "The Religious and Occupational Roots of Party Identification."

16. *Ottawa Weekly Republican*, 6 December 1856, Cole's Notes, IHS.

17. Henry Winter Davis, "The Origin, Principles and Purposes of the American Party," David Davis Papers, CHS.

18. Ibid., p. 5.

19. Ibid., p. 6.

20. Ibid., p. 7.

21. Ibid., p. 11.

22. Ibid., p. 21.

23. Ibid., p. 15.

24. Ibid., p. 24.

25. Ibid.

26. Ibid.

27. Ibid.

28. See John P. Senning, "The Know-Nothing Movement in Illinois," *JISHS* 7 (April, 1914), pp. 7-34.

29. *Illinois State Register*, 16 August 1854.

30. See Gustave Koerner, *Memoirs of Gustave Koerner*, ed. Thomas J. McCormack (Cedar Rapids: The Torch Press, 1909), 1:617; Holt, *Forging a Majority*; Formisano, *Birth of Mass Political Parties*; and Jensen, "The Religious and Occupational Roots of Party Identification."

31. The variables in the multiple regression table are significant at .05 or better.

32. The categories of "none," "low," "medium," and "high" refer to the number and size of churches in each sampled community. See appendix.

33. *Free West*, 12 July 1855, Cole's Notes, IHS; *Ottawa Weekly Republican*, 12 July 1851, Cole's Notes, IHS.

34. Bivariate coefficients for the 1856 Presidential Know-Nothing vote:

	a	b	SEE	r	r^2
Yankee	20.8	-1.12	12.7	-.50	.25
Southerners	5.91	.37	13.2	.44	.19
Illinois	6.19	.62	13.2	.44	.19
Other	14.8	-.03	14.7	-.04	.001
German	14.9	-.10	14.7	-.11	.01
English	19.2	-1.16	13.7	-.36	.13
Irish	18.6	-.80	13.7	-.37	.14
Scandinavians	16.9	-2.02	13.6	-.38	.14
Canadian	17.4	-4.00	13.4	-.42	.18
French	13.9	-.14	14.8	-.03	.001

35. *Alton Daily Courier*, 8 November 1854.

36. Lyman Trumbull to Owen Lovejoy, 20 August 1855, Trumbull Family Papers, ISHL.

37. *Ottawa Weekly Republican*, 27 October 1855, Cole's Notes, IHS.

Chapter 5

1. Lyman Trumbull to Abraham Lincoln, 15 June 1856, Lyman Trumbull Family Papers, ISHL; *Belleville Advocate*, 15 August 1855.

2. William Jayne to Lyman Trumbull, 20 January 1856, Lyman Trumbull Family Papers, ISHL.

3. See the *Quincy Whig*, 28 February 1856. On the formation of the Republican party in Illinois, see Clarence W. Alvord, gen. ed., *The Centennial History of Illinois*, 4 volumes (Springfield: The Illinois Centennial Commission, 1919), volume 3: *The*

Era of the Civil War, by Arthur C. Cole; Green B. Raum, *History of Illinois Republicanism* (Chicago: Rollins Publishing Co., 1900); and Charles A. Church, *History of the Republican Party in Illinois, 1854-1912* (Rockford: Press of Wilson Brothers Co., 1912).

4. *Illinois State Journal,* 25 February 1856; *Belleville Advocate,* 5 March 1856; and *Rockford Republican,* 30 January 1856.

5. Ebenezer Peck to Lyman Trumbull, 24 Feburary 1856, Lyman Trumbull Family Papers, ISHL.

6. Elihu Washburne to Richard Yates, 2 April 1856, in Richard Yates and Catherine Yates Pickering, *Richard Yates, Civil War Governor,* ed. John H. Krenkel (Danville: The Interstate Printers & Publishers, Inc., 1966), p. 116.

7. William Herndon to Richard Yates, 1 May 1856, in Yates and Pickering, *Richard Yates,* p. 117.

8. Ebenezer Peck to Lyman Trumbull, 24 February 1856, Lyman Trumbull Family Papers, ISHL.

9. Ebenezer Peck to Lyman Trumbull, 17 January 1856, Lyman Trumbull Family Papers, ISHL.

10. Letter to John M. Palmer, 27 January 1856, John M. Palmer Papers, ISHL.

11. Lyman Trumbull to John M. Palmer, 24 January 1856, John M. Palmer Papers, ISHL. Also see Trumbull to Palmer, 2 January, 21 May 1856, John M. Palmer Papers, ISHL.

12. George T. Brown to Lyman Trumbull, 12 May 1856, Lyman Trumbull Papers, LC.

13. *Belleville Advocate,* 7 May 1856.

14. William Herndon to Richard Yates, 1 May 1856, in Yates and Pickering, *Richard Yates,* p. 117.

15. Raum, *History of Illinois Republicanism,* p. 28.

16. *Urbana Union,* 5 June 1856, Cole's Notes, IHS; and Lincoln to Trumbull, 7 June 1856, *CWAL,* 2:342-343.

17. See Chapter 3, note 37.

18. Of the 569 anti-Nebraska leaders surveyed in Peoria, Rock Island, Stephenson, and Madison counties, only 35.6 percent were politically active as Republicans or Democrats in 1856. The remainder of the surveyed group dropped out of public participation in politics. The survey indicated that of the local Republican leadership, only 30.8 percent were anti-Nebraska men and a full 69 percent had had no previous politically public experience.

19. Lyman Trumbull to Abraham Lincoln, 15 June 1856, Lyman Trumbull Family Papers, ISHL.

20. Gustave Koerner, *Memoirs of Gustave Koerner*, ed. Thomas J. McCormack, 2:24-25.

21. *Quincy Whig*, 7 June 1856.

22. The variables in the multiple regression table are significant at .001 or better.

23. Bivariate coefficients for the 1856 Republican Presidential vote:

	a	b	SEE	r	r^2
Yankee	24.6	3.15	18.6	.74	.55
Southern	71.5	-1.30	16.5	-.80	.64
Illinois	65.8	-1.74	21.1	-.65	.43
Other	76.9	-.25	13.5	-.24	.05
German	40.9	.32	27.5	.19	.03
English	29.9	3.11	23.9	.52	.27
Irish	33.8	-.08	25.1	-.43	.19
Scandinavian	38.0	4.19	25.4	.42	.17
Canadian	35.9	-1.35	23.8	-.52	.27
French	42.0	-1.64	27.3	-.21	.04

24. Koerner, *Memoirs*, 2:35.

25. The variables on the multiple regression table are significant at .05 or better.

26. Abraham Lincoln to Owen Lovejoy, 11 August 1855, *CWAL*, 2:316

27. Abraham Lincoln to Theodore Canisius, 17 May 1859, *CWAL*, 3:380.

28. Abraham Lincoln to James Berdan, 10 July 1856, *CWAL*, 2:347.

29. Abraham Lincoln to Lyman Trumbull, 11 August 1856, *CWAL*, 2:360. Also see form letter to Fillmore Men, 8 September 1856, *CWAL*, 2:374; Abraham Lincoln to John Bennette, 4 August 1856, *CWAL*, 2:358; and Abraham Lincoln to Hezekiah G. Wells, 4 August 1856, *CWAL*, 2:358.

30. Koerner, *Memoirs*, 2:21.

31. *Chicago Tribune*, 17 July 1860.

32. William Pickering to Joseph Gillespie, 20 July 1860, Joseph Gillespie Collection, CHS.

33. Quoted in *Joliet Signal*, 22 April 1856.

34. *Rock River Democrat*, 12 August 1856, Cole's Notes, IHS. The fact that W. W. Danenhower endorsed the Republican party in 1858 did not blunt the Republican argument that the Know-Nothings were tools of Douglas. Buckner S. Morris, John T. Stuart, and a number of other American party leaders joined the Democracy in the same year.

35. Trumbull to Palmer, 31 July, 3 August 1856, in George T. Palmer, ed., "A Collection of Letters from Lyman Trumbull to John M. Palmer, 1854-1858," *Journal of the Illinois State Historical Society* 16 (April-July, 1923), pp. 31-33.

36. Paul Selby to John M. Palmer, 8 August 1856, John M. Palmer Papers, ISHL.

37. Koerner to Lincoln, 4 April 1859, Robert Todd Lincoln Collection (hereinafter cited as RTL), LC.

38. Koerner, *Memoirs*, 2:22.

39. *Illinois State Journal,* 15 July 1857.

40. For the effect of Crittenden's endorsement of Douglas upon Lincoln and the Republicans, see Fehrenbacher, *Prelude to Greatness*, p. 118.

41. David Davis to Abraham Lincoln, 7 November 1858, RTL, LC.

42. Abraham Lincoln to Anson G. Henry, 19 November 1858, *CWAL*, 3:339-40; William Herndon to Lyman Trumbull, 30 November 1858, Lyman Trumbull Papers, LC.

43. John H. Bryant & Stephen G. Paddock to Abraham Lincoln, 4 June 1860, RTL, LC.

44. David Davis to Abraham Lincoln, 14 June 1858, RTL, LC.

45. Lincoln to Mark W. Delahay, 14 May 1859, *CWAL*, 2:378-79.

46. Lincoln to Trumbull, 30 November 1857, *CWAL*, 2:427.

47. Lyman Trumbull to W. B. Archer, 8 January 1858, Lyman Trumbull Collection, CHS.

48. Abraham Lincoln to Lyman Trumbull, 28 December 1857, *CWAL*, 2:430.

49. The "House Divided" speech as quoted in the *Illinois State Journal*, 18 June 1858. For a good discussion of the speech and the problem Douglas posed to the Republicans, see Don E. Fehrenbacher, *Prelude to Greatness*, pp. 70-95.

50. Abraham Smith to Abraham Lincoln, 20 July 1858, RTL, LC.

51. *Bureau County Republican*, 8 July 1858, Cole's Notes, IHS.

52. Speech delivered at Chicago by Lincoln, 10 July 1858, *CWAL*, 2:498.

53. Fourth Debate with Douglas at Charleston, Illinois, 18 September 1858, *CWAL*, 3:145.

54. Speech delivered at Springfield by Abraham Lincoln, 17 July 1858, quoted in *Illinois State Journal*, 20, 21 July 1858.

55. Lincoln to John L. Scripps, 23 June 1858, *CWAL*, 2:471.

56. For a complete analysis of the Republican ideology, see Eric Foner, *Free Soil, Free Labor, Free Men: The Ideology of the Republican Party Before the Civil War* (New York: Oxford University Press, 1970).

57. Fragment of Speech by Abraham Lincoln, 7 September 1858, *CWAL*, 3:462.

58. *Illinois State Journal*, 1 August 1860. Also see Proceedings of the Republican State Convention, Springfield, 16 June 1858, in Alton *Daily Morning Courier*, 18 June 1858, *Quincy Whig*, 3 June 1858, and for a complete discussion of Republican principles, see Eric Foner, *Free Soil, Free Labor, Free Men*.

59. The variables in the multiple regression table are significant at .01 or better.

60. Bivariate coefficients for the 1858 Republican election to previous elections:

	a	b	SEE	r	r^2
1856 Republican	66.6	.24	9.56	.53	.001
1856 Democrats	75.8	-.68	9.31	-.83	.69

61. Bivariate coefficients for the 1858 Republican State vote:

	a	b	SEE	r	r^2
Yankee	39.8	1.91	15.3	.58	.34
Southern	63.1	-.63	15.7	-.55	.31
Illinois	60.0	-.80	17.2	-.41	.17
Other	44.0	.19	18.6	.18	.03
German	48.8	.23	18.6	.18	.03
English	43.3	1.72	17.5	.38	.14
Irish	50.3	-1.14	18.9	-.07	.005
Scandinavian	49.8	.65	18.4	.24	.05
Canadian	51.8	-.19	18.9	-.09	.009
French	63.1	-.21	18.5	-.22	.05

62. Abraham Lincoln to Richard Yates, 30 September 1857, *CWAL*, 2:424; and Abraham Lincoln to Henry C. Whitney, 18 December 1857, *CWAL*, 2:429.

63. Gustave Koerner to Ozias M. Hatch, 20 April 1858, Ozias M. Hatch Papers, ISHL.

64. "'Letter to the Republicans of Illinois' from the Republican State Central Committee," 9 June 1859, CHS.

65. See, for example, letters from the Republican State Central Committee, 9 June 1858, 8 May 1860, 23 June 1860, Jesse W. Fell Papers, ISHL.

66. Abraham Lincoln to David Davis, 7 July 1856, David Davis Papers, CHS.

67. D. Clapp and others to Republican Central Committee of DeWitt County, 31 October 1856, David Davis Papers, CHS.

68. Ward H. Lamon to Abraham Lincoln, 9 June 1858, David Davis Papers, CHS.

69. Abraham Lincoln to Owen Lovejoy 8 March 1858, *CWAL*, 2:435-36; Abraham Lincoln to Ward H. Lamon, 11 June 1858, *CWAL*, 2:458-59.

70. For a complete discussion of the Wentworth-Judd feud, see Don E. Fehrenbacher, *Chicago Giant; A Biography of "Long John" Wentworth* (Madison: The American Historical Research Center, 1957); Willard L. King, *Lincoln's Manager, David Davis* (Cambridge: Harvard University Press, 1960); Mark M. Krug, *Lyman Trumbull: Conservative Radical* (New York: A. S. Barnes & Co., 1965). Also see Koerner, *Memoirs*, 2:83; David Davis to Abraham Lincoln, 1 January 1859 (misdated 1858), 21 February 1860, 23 April 1860, 4,5 October 1860, RTL, LC, 5 May 1860, 25 February 1860, David Davis Papers, CHS; Norman B. Judd to Lincoln, 1 December 1859, 11 December 1859, 21 February and May 25 1860, RTL, LC, 1 May 1860, David Davis Papers, CHS; John Wentworth to Abraham Lincoln, 21, 28 December 1859, 13 January 1860, 11, 22 February 1860, 21 April 1860, RTL, LC, 30 April (misdated May) 1860, David Davis Papers, CHS; Joseph Medill to Lincoln, 9 August 1860, 18 December 1860, RTL, LC; Leonard Swett to Lincoln, 25 May 1860, RTL, LC; Jesse W. Fell to Lincoln, 2 January 1861, Jesse W. Fell Papers, ISHL; Lyman Trumbull to Abraham Lincoln, 26 March 1860, David Davis Papers, CHS; George Dole, G.S. Hubbard, W.H. Brown to Abraham Lincoln, 12 December 1859, Lincoln Collection, CHS; Lincoln to Henry C. Whitney, 18 December 1857, *CWAL*, 2:429; Lincoln to Judd, 9 December 1859, *CWAL*, 3:505, 5 February 1860, *CWAL*, 3:516, 9 February 1860, David Davis Papers, CHS; and Lincoln to Dole, Hubbard & Brown, 14 December 1859, Lincoln Collection, CHS.

An interesting sidelight to the Wentworth-Judd feud was that Lincoln and Trumbull became involved in a direct confrontation. Lincoln had heard rumors that Trumbull was supporting someone else for the Republican Presidential nomination in 1860, and that the Senator hoped to ease him into political retirement. Lincoln wrote the following letter to Trumbull which put on end to the conflict, if in fact there ever had been one:

"A word now for your own special benefit. You better write no letters which can possibly be distorted into opposition, or quasi opposition to me. There are men on the constant watch for such things out of which to prejudice my friends against you. While I have no more suspicion of you than I have of my best friend living, I am kept in constant struggle against suggestions of this sort."

Lincoln to Trumbull, 29 April 1860, *CWAL*, 4:45-46.

71. For the 1856 election; a=95.6, b=.08 (SEE=1.92), and in the 1858 contest, a=21.2, b=.74 (SEE=2.09).

72. Bivariate coefficients for the 1860 Republican Presidential vote:

	a	b	SEE	r	r^2
Yankee	41.9	1.78	14.7	.58	.33
Southern	56.1	-.74	13.2	-.68	.46
Illinois	52.6	-1.01	15.6	-.50	.25
Other	44.6	.22	17.7	.21	.04
German	50.7	.18	17.9	.15	.02
English	46.2	1.25	16.9	.35	.12

	a	b	SEE	r	r²
Irish	51.7	-.63	18.1	-.07	.005
Scandinavian	51.2	.67	17.5	.26	.07
Canadian	52.1	.21	18.0	.11	.01
French	50.7	1.43	17.5	.25	.06

73. The variables in the multiple regression table are significant at .05 or better.

74. Fragment on Formation of the Republican Party by Lincoln, ca. 28 February 1857, *CWAL*, 2:391.

75. Address at the Cooper Institute, New York City, 27 February 1860, *CWAL*, 3:522-550.

76. Horace White to Lyman Trumbull, 30 December 1860, Lyman Trumbull Papers, LC.

Chapter 6

1. Stephen A. Douglas to Charles H. Lanphier, 18 December 1854, in Robert W. Johannsen, ed., *The Letters of Stephen A. Douglas* (Urbana: University of Illinois Press, 1961), p. 331.

2. Stephen A. Dougas to James W. Sheahan, 14 September 1854, in Johannsen, *Letters*, p. 330.

3. Stephen A. Douglas to Charles H. Lanphier, 18 December 1854, in Johannsen, *Letters*, p. 331.

4. *Illinois State Register*, 22 May 1856.

5. Ibid., 26 June 1855.

6. *Cairo Weekly Times & Delta*, 13 February 1856, Cole's Notes, IHS.

7. *Illinois State Register*, 25 June 1855.

8. *Joliet Signal*, 4 March 1855.

9. Quoted in the *Belleville Advocate*, 16 April 1856.

10. *Cairo Weekly Times & Delta*, 2 July 1856, Cole's Notes, IHS.

11. William A. Richardson to Stephen A. Douglas, 30 May 1856, quoted in Robert W. Johannsen, *Stephen A. Douglas* (New York: Oxford University Press, 1973), p. 653.

12. *Illinois State Register*, 1 April 1856.

13. Gustave Koerner, *Memoirs of Gustave Koerner*, ed. Thomas J. McCormack (Cedar Rapids: The Torch Press, 1909), 2:26-29.

14. *Our Constitution*, 24 July 1856, Cole's Notes, IHS.

15. *Chicago Citizen*, quoted in *Illinois State Register*, 19 January 1856.

16. *Illinois State Register*, 19 January 1856.

17. *Washington Union*, quoted in *Illinois State Register*, 17 February 1855.

18. Stephen A. Douglas to Twenty-five Chicago Clergymen, 6 April 1854, Johannsen, *Letters*, pp. 300-21.

19. Ibid.

20. Ibid.

21. Sermon from OS Presbyterian Minister, in *Illinois State Register*, 8 January 1855.

22. "'Olive Branch Speech' by John Reynolds at Springfield, Jan. 14, 1857," CHS.

23. All the variables in the multiple regression table are significant at .01 or better.

24. Bivariate coefficients for the 1856 Democratic Presidential vote:

	a	b	SEE	r	r^2
Yankee	54.5	-2.03	16.0	-.64	.41
Southern	22.5	.92	13.4	.76	.58
Illinois	28.0	1.12	17.2	.56	.31
Other	53.0	-.33	20.0	-.29	.08
German	44.1	-.22	20.6	-.17	.03
English	50.8	-1.94	18.8	-.43	.18
Irish	47.4	.95	19.8	.31	.10
Scandi-navian	45.0	-2.17	20.0	-.29	.08
Canadian	46.5	5.31	19.1	.39	.15
French	44.0	1.50	20.1	.26	.07

25. *Urbana Union*, 9 July 1857, Cole's Notes, IHS.

26. Stephen A. Douglas to John A. McClernand, 23 December 1856, John A. McClernand Papers, ISHL.

27. *Weekly Chicago Times*, 22 October 1857.

28. Stephen A. Douglas speech at Second Debate, Freeport, Illinois, 27 August 1858, *CWAL*, 3:49-70.

29. *St. Clair Tribune*, 6 October 1856, Cole's Notes, IHS.

30. *Cairo Weekly Times & Delta*, 25 March 1857, Cole's Notes, IHS.

31. *Rushville Times*, 22 August 1856, Cole's Notes, IHS.

32. *Joliet Signal*, 25 May 1858.

33. Speech by Don E. Morrison in *Belleville Advocate*, 16 April 1856.

34. Letter by E.B. Webb in *Illinois State Register*, 10 June 1856.

35. Curtis Goodsell to Stephen A. Douglas, 29 November 1858, Stephen A. Douglas Papers, UC.

36. *Winchester Chronicle*, in *Illinois State Register*, 5 September 1855.

37. Lyman Trumbull to John M. Palmer, 19 June 1858, in George T. Palmer, ed., "A Collection of Letters From Lyman Trumbull to John M. Palmer, 1854-1858," *JISHS* 16 (April-July, 1923), p. 38, Lincoln to John J. Crittenden, 7 July 1858, *CWAL*, 2:483, Crittenden to Lincoln, 29 July 1858, RTL, LC.

38. Thomas L. Harris to Stephen A. Douglas, 7 July 1858, Stephen A. Douglas Papers, UC.

39. In a regression of the 1858 Democratic State vote to the 1856 Fillmore vote, the Know-Nothing party had the following coefficients: $a = 22.7$, $b = 12.0$, SEE $= 12.0$. A regression of the Fillmore vote to the 1858 Republican vote could not be calculated by the computer.

40. All the variables in the multiple regression table are significant at .01 or better.

41. Bivariate coefficients for the 1858 Democratic State vote:

	a	b	SEE	r	r^2
Yankee	59.9	-2.02	15.3	-.61	.37
Southern	35.5	.65	15.9	.56	.31
Illinois	38.7	.83	17.5	.42	.18
Other	54.6	-.18	19.0	-.17	.03
German	50.4	-.25	19.0	-.20	.04
English	55.9	-1.77	17.8	-.38	.14
Irish	48.7	1.15	19.3	.07	.005
Scandi-navian	49.1	-.64	18.8	-.23	.05
Canadian	47.1	.21	19.2	.10	.01
French	49.8	.10	18.8	.24	.06

42. Lanphier to Douglas, 4 January 1859, and Douglas to Lanphier, 6 January 1859, Charles H. Lanphier Papers, ISHL.

43. Lincoln to Henry Ashbury, 19 November 1858, CWAL, 3:339.

44. Douglas to McClernand, 23 November 1857, John A. McClernand Papers, ISHL.

45. See Sheahan to Douglas, 8, 21, 31 March 1856, Stephen A. Douglas Papers, UC, Douglas to Sheahan, 28 March, 11, 19 April 1856, in Johannsen, *Letters*, pp. 353-54.

46. For a complete discussion of the Cook-Sheahan feud and of Cook's maneuverings as a Danite, see Robert W. Johannsen, *Stephen A. Douglas*, pp. 535, 553, 602, 621-26, 636, 648-50, 678, 703, 735.

47. D.G. Salisbury to Douglas, 15 November 1858, Stephen A. Douglas Papers, UC.

48. W. Coler to Douglas, 30 August 1858, ibid.

49. See I.N. Morris to Douglas, 22 August 1858, ibid.

50. See Alex Dunn to Douglas, 22 September 1858, ibid.

51. S.S. Marshall to Lanphier, 9 October 1858, Charles H. Lanphier Papers, ISHL.

52. Douglas to Sheahan, 23 February 1857, in Johannsen, *Letters,* p. 374.

53. All the variables in the multiple regression table are significant at .05 or better.

54. Murray McConnell to Douglas, 29 September 1859, and N.B. Thompson to Douglas, 9 September 1859, Stephen A. Douglas Papers, UC.

55. Douglas to McClernand, 21 February 1858, John A. McClernand Papers, ISHL.

56. Douglas to McClernand, 1 October 1859, Johannsen, *Letters,* p. 473.

57. J.B. Danforth to Douglas, 26 December 1859, and C.B. Dodson to Douglas, 15 July 1858, Stephen A. Douglas Papers, UC.

58. W.A. Monroe to Douglas, 12 June 1860, ibid.

59. Douglas to Samuel Treat, 28 February 1858, Johannsen, *Letters*, p. 418.

60. Douglas to J.W. Singleton, 31 March 1859, ibid., p. 439.

61. Douglas to William A. Richardson, 20 June 1860, ibid., p. 492.

62. Douglas to Henry K. McCoy, 27 September 1859, ibid., p. 468.

63. *Illinois State Register*, 29 January 1856.

64. *Ottawa Free Trader,* 18 October 1856, Cole's Notes, IHS.

65. *Ottawa Free Trader*, 6 August 1859, Cole's Notes, IHS.

66. For a good discussion of the 1860 Democratic Convention in Charleston and later in Baltimore, see Robert W. Johannsen, *Stephen A. Douglas*, pp. 749-59, 767-72.

67. Douglas to Lanphier, 5 July 1860, Johannsen, *Letters*, pp. 497-98.

68. R.E. Goodsell to Douglas, 3 September 1860, Stephen A. Douglas Papers, UC.

69. *Illinois State Journal,* 7 July 1860.

70. For a good discussion of Douglas' plans for 1864 and his cooperation with the Bell supporters, see Johannsen, *Stephen A. Douglas*, pp. 761, 787-92.

71. Bivariate coefficients for the 1860 Democratic Presidential vote:

	a	b	SEE	r	r^2
Yankee	56.6	-1.72	14.4	-.57	.33
Southern	33.3	.71	15.2	.67	.45
Illinois	36.7	.96	15.2	.49	.24
Other	54.1	-.21	17.2	-.21	.04
German	48.1	-.18	17.4	-.15	.02
English	52.3	-1.20	16.5	-.35	.12
Irish	46.9	1.11	17.6	.06	.003
Scandi-					
navian	47.5	-.63	17.0	-.26	.06
Canadian	46.7	-.18	17.5	-.09	.009
French	48.1	-1.40	17.0	-.25	.06

72. All the variables in the multiple regression table are significant at .05 or better.

73. See Frederick C. Luebke, ed., *Ethnic Voters and the Election of Lincoln* (Lincoln: University of Nebraska Press, 1971).

74. Douglas to August Belmont, 25 December 1860, Stephen A. Douglas Papers, UC.

75. Richardson to Douglas, 27 November 1860, ibid.

Chapter 7

1. Robert W. Johannsen, *Stephen A. Douglas* (New York: Oxford University Press, 1973), p. 857.

2. Douglas to Charles H. Lanphier, 25 December 1860, Robert W. Johannsen, ed., *The Letters of Stephen A. Douglas* (Urbana: University of Illinois Press, 1961), p. 504.

3. Douglas to Virgil Hickox, 10 May 1861, Stephen A. Douglas Papers, UC.

4. McClernand to Charles H. Lanphier, 4 February 1861, Charles H. Lanphier Papers, ISHL.

5. On Douglas in the secession crisis, see Robert W. Johannsen, *Stephen A. Douglas*, pp. 812-46, and Kenneth H. Stampp, *And The War Came: The North And The Secession Crisis, 1860-1861* (Baton Rouge: Louisiana State University Press, 1967), pp. 129-31, 210.

6. Virgil Hickox to Douglas, 8 January 1861, Stephen A. Douglas Papers, UC.

7. *Joliet Signal*, 15 January 1861; *Belleville Democrat*, quoted in the *Belleville Advocate*, 16 November 1860; *Cairo Gazette*, 6 December 1860, Cole's Notes, IHS.

8. *Illinois State Register*, 1 August 1861.

9. *Ottawa Free Trader*, 19 October 1861.

10. For a good discussion on the importance of the Union to the Republican ideology, see Eric Foner, *Free Soil, Free Labor, Free Men: The Ideology of the Republican Party Before the Civil War* (New York: Oxford University Press, 1970); David M. Potter, *The Impending Crisis, 1848-1861*, ed. Don E. Fehrenbacher (New York: Harper & Row, Publishers, 1976); and Kenneth M. Stampp, *And The War Came.*

11. Gustave Koerner, *Memoirs of Gustave Koerner*, ed. Thomas J. McCormack, two volumes (Cedar Rapids: The Torch Press, 1909), 2:96.

12. Quoted in Koerner, *Memoirs*, 2:98.

13. Theodore Glancy to Lyman Trumbull, 11 February 1861, Lyman Trumbull Papers, LC.

14. *Chicago Democrat*, 4 January 1861.

15. *Aurora Beacon*, 7 February 1861.

16. *Chicago Democrat*, 1 July 1861.

17. Clarence W. Alvord, gen. ed., *The Centennial History of Illinois*, four volumes (Springfield: Illinois Centennial Commission), 3: *The Era of the Civil War, 1848-1870*, Arthur C. Cole; Eugene F. Baldwin, "The Dream of the South–Story of Illinois During the Civil War", *Transactions of the Illinois State Historical Society* 16 (1911), 84-103; and William Jasper Cross, "Divided Loyalties in Southern Illinois During the Civil War" (Ph.D. dissertation, University of Illinois, Urbana, 1942).

18. John M. Palmer, *Personal Recollections of John M. Palmer; The Story of an Earnest Life* (Cincinnati: Robert Clarke Co., 1901), p. 91.

19. Anonymous to Richard Yates, 16 April 1861, in Richard Yates and Catherine Yates Pickering, *Richard Yates, Civil War Governor*, ed. John H. Krenkel (Danville: The Interstate Printers & Publishers, Inc., 1966), p. 86.

20. See Cole, *The Era of the Civil War*, p. 261, for a good account of Douglas' speech in Springfield.

21. Stanley L. Jones, "Agrarian Radicalism in Illinois' Constitutional Convention of 1862," *The Old Northwest: Studies in Regional History, 1787-1910*, ed., Harry N. Scheiber (Lincoln: University of Nebraska Press, 1969), pp. 312-22.

22. *Illinois State Journal*, 14 January 1862.

23. For the proceedings of the Constitutional convention, see Cole, *The Era of the Civil War*, pp. 267-72; Jones, "Agrarian Radicalism in Illinois' Constitutional Convention of 1862"; and Charles A. Church, *History of the Republican Party in Illinois, 1854-1912* (Rockford: Press of Wilson Brothers Co., 1912), pp. 86-88.

24. *Illinois State Register*, 2 April 1862.

25. S.S. Marshall to Lanphier, 31 May 1862, Charles H. Lanphier Papers, ISHL.

26. *Illinois State Register*, 10 April 1862.

27. Ibid., 12 June 1862.

28. *Peoria Union*, as quoted in the *Illinois State Register*, 17 April 1862.

29. *Illinois State Register*, 3 March 1862.

30. *Illinois State Journal*, 14 January 1862.

31. Ibid., 11 March 1862.

32. *Aurora Beacon*, 12 June 1862.

33. *Chicago Tribune*, 10 January 1862.

34. The variables are significant at .05 or better.

35. The simple correlations and explained variance for the vote for the Banking article and the Congressional Reapportionment section are:

	Bank Article		Congressional Reapportionment	
	r	r^2	r	r^2
Southern	.24	.49	.65	.05
Illinois	-.11	.002	.07	.06

36. *Rockford Register*, 25 September 1862, Cole's Notes, IHS.

37. *Rock River Democrat*, 16 September 1862, Cole's Notes, IHS.

38. *Illinois State Journal*, 20 August 1862.

39. *Aurora Beacon*, 10 July 1862.

40. *Chicago Tribune*, 31 March 1862.

41. "'Proceedings of the Democratic Congressional Convention for the First District,' speech by M.D. Gilman, Chicago, 14 October 1862", CHS.

42. *Joliet Signal*, 2 December 1862; *Illinois State Register*, 11 April 1862.

43. Bivariate coefficients for the 1862 Democratic State vote:

	a	b	SEE	r	r^2
Yankee	58.1	-1.86	16.1	-.60	.36
Southern	41.5	.65	16.5	.58	.34
Illinois	45.2	.91	18.1	.45	.20
Other	65.9	-.28	19.7	-.22	.05
German	57.0	-.15	20.2	-.08	.006
English	67.4	-2.50	17.2	-.53	.28
Irish	55.9	.64	20.3	.009	.00009

	a	b	SEE	r	r^2
Scandi-navian	57.6	-.75	19.1	-.32	.10
Canadian	60.7	-5.82	18.5	-.40	.16
French	58.1	-2.67	19.0	-.34	.11

Bivariate coefficients for the 1862 Republican State vote:

	a	b	SEE	r	r^2
Yankee	31.8	1.85	16.1	.60	.36
Southern	58.4	-.64	16.4	-.58	.34
Illinois	54.6	-.91	18.0	-.45	.20
Other	34.0	.28	19.7	.22	.05
German	42.8	.15	20.1	.08	.006
English	32.5	2.50	17.1	.53	.28
Irish	44.0	-.72	20.2	-.008	.00007
Scandi-navian	42.3	.75	19.1	.33	.10
Canadian	39.2	5.75	18.5	.40	.16
French	41.8	2.68	19.0	.34	.11

44. Of the 255,057 men from Illinois who served in the Union army during the course of the war, 135,440 had joined by 1862. The dramatic decline in voter turnout in 1862 must be understood in terms of the inability of these soldiers to vote in the field. Although Egypt provided its share of soldiers, the early enlistments were heaviest in the predominantly Republican counties of northern Illinois. John Moses, *Illinois Historical and Statistical*, two volumes (Chicago: Fergus Printing Co., 1892), 2:666.

45. *Belleville Advocate*, 28 August 1863.

46. *Ottawa Weekly Republican*, 20 June 1863.

47. For a good discussion of secession activities in Illinois, see Cross, "Divided Loyalties in Southern Illinois During the Civil War" (Ph.D. dissertation, University of Illinois, Urbana, 1942); Baldwin, "The Dream of the South," *Transactions of the Illinois State Historical Society*; and Theodore L. Agnew, "The Peace Movement in Illinois, 1864" (MA thesis, University of Illinois, Urbana, 1938).

48. Don E. Fehrenbacher, *Chicago Giant: A Biography of "Long John" Wentworth* (Madison: The American Historical Research Center, 1957), p. 72.

49. Davis blamed Trumbull for not getting an appointment from Lincoln and he accused the Senator of disloyalty to the administration. Willard L. King, *Lincoln's Manager, David Davis* (Cambridge: Harvard University Press, 1960), pp. 182-85.

50. For examples of typical letters of application for patronage in 1861, see J.H. Yager, 1 March; A.J. Swain, 13 March; John M. Palmer, 23 February; George T. Allen, 13 March, R.J. Oglesby, 28 February 1861; all to Lyman Trumbull, Lyman Trumbull Family Papers, ISHL.

51. *Belleville Democrat*, 27 February 1864.

52. *Illinois State Register*, 2 March, 30 May 1863; *Jonesboro Gazette*, 14 March 1863, Cole's Notes, IHS; *Belleville Democrat*, 26 September 1863.

53. *Chicago Times*, 24 September 1863; *Illinois State Register*, 1 September 1863.

54. *Champaign Union & Gazette*, 14 October 1864, Cole's Notes, IHS.

55. *Chicago Tribune*, 18 October 1864.

56. Robert Smith to Joseph Gillespie, 15 January 1864, Joseph Gillespie Collection, CHS.

57. John Middendord & others to Gillespie, 19 March 1864, Joseph Gillespie Collection, CHS.

58. Trumbull to H.G. Pike, 6 February 1864, Lyman Trumbull Papers, LC.

59. Richard Yates to Greeley, Godwin, Fulton, 6 September 1864, in Richard Yates and Catherine Yates Pickering, *Richard Yates, Civil War Governor*, p. 185.

60. Bivariate coefficients for the 1864 Republican Presidential vote:

	a	b	SEE	r	r^2
Yankee	45.2	1.39	16.5	.47	.22
Southern	59.7	-.27	18.2	-.24	.06
Illinois	62.9	-.79	17.2	-.40	.16
Other	54.2	-.008	18.8	-.006	.00004
German	52.7	.10	18.7	.09	.008
English	47.0	1.63	17.5	.36	.12
Irish	55.8	-.62	18.6	-.14	.02
Scandinavian	52.7	.55	18.2	.24	.05
Canadian	50.4	4.35	17.7	.33	.10
French	51.6	1.55	17.9	.29	.08

Bivariate coefficients for the 1864 Democratic Presidential Vote:

	a	b	SEE	r	r^2
Yankee	54.6	-1.39	16.5	-.47	.22
Southern	40.2	.27	18.2	.24	.06
Illinois	37.0	.79	17.1	.40	.16
Other	45.7	.007	18.8	.007	.00006
German	47.2	-.10	18.7	-.09	.009
English	52.9	-1.63	17.5	-.36	.13
Irish	44.1	.72	18.6	.14	.01
Scandinavian	47.2	-.55	18.2	-.24	.05
Canadian	49.5	-4.34	17.7	-.33	.10
French	48.2	-1.55	17.9	-.29	.08

61. Koerner to Trumbull, 4 January 1866, Lyman Trumbull Papers, LC.

62. *Chicago Tribune*, 8 April 1865.

63. *Aurora Beacon*, 8 June 1865.

64. *Belleville Advocate*, 14 July 1865.

65. *Joliet Signal*, 7 February 1865.

66. *Cairo Daily Democrat*, 17 September 1865, Cole's Notes, IHS.

67. For a discussion of the Johnson Reconstruction program, see Eric L. McKitrick, *Andrew Johnson and Reconstruction* (Chicago: University of Chicago Press, 1960); Kenneth M. Stampp, *The Era of Reconstruction* (New York: Vintage Books, 1965); LaWanda and John Cox, *Politics, Principle, and Prejudice, 1865-1866* (Chicago: The Free Press, 1963); David Donald, *The Politics of Reconstruction, 1863-1867* (Baton Rouge: Louisiana State University Press, 1965); and Michael Perman, *Reunion Without Compromise; The South and Reconstruction, 1865-1868* (New York: Cambridge University Press, 1973).

68. *Chicago Tribune*, 18 April 1865.

69. *Chicago Tribune*, 21 February 1866.

70. *Rockford Register*, 31 March 1866, Cole's Notes, IHS.

71. On the National Union Party, see McKitrick, *Andrew Johnson and Reconstruction*, pp. 394-421, and Stampp, *The Era of Reconstruction*, pp. 113-14.

72. *Cathage Republican*, 22 February 1866, Cole's Notes, IHS; *Jonesboro Gazette*, 6 October 1866, Cole's Notes, IHS; *Illinois State Register*, 29 August 1866; and Harris L. Dante, "Western Attitudes and Reconstruction Politics in Illinois, 1865-1872", *Journal of the Illinois State Historical Society* 49 (Spring, 1956), 149-62.

73. *Belleville Democrat*, 27 January 1866. Also see *Chicago Times*, 16 November 1865.

74. *Carthage Republican*, 30 August 1866, Cole's Notes, IHS.

75. For a good discussion of Johnson's personality and its effect upon politics, see McKitrick, *Andrew Johnson and Reconstruction*, pp. 85-92, and Stampp, *The Era of Reconstruction*, pp. 50-83.

76. See Arthur C. Cole, *The Era of the Civil War*, pp. 400-402; *Cairo Democrat*, 28, 30 September, 2, 21, 27 October 1866, Cole's Notes, IHS; *Illinois State Register*, 14 August and 27 September 1866; *Belleville Democrat*, 1 September and 6 October 1866; and the *Chester Picket Guard*, 5, 12 September 1866, Cole's Notes, IHS.

77. Speech of Richard Yates delivered at Jacksonville, Illinois, on 15 September 1866 in Yates and Pickering, *Richard Yates, Civil War Governor*, pp. 249-50.

78. Bivariate coefficients for the 1866 Democratic and Republican State vote:

Democratic

	a	b	SEE	r	r^2
Yankee	41.8	-.96	17.9	-.33	.11
Southern	22.5	1.26	11.9	.77	.60
Illinois	19.4	1.13	14.3	.65	.43
Other	35.7	-.04	19.0	-.03	.001
German	38.4	-.24	18.3	-.27	.07
English	43.8	-1.32	17.1	-.43	.19
Irish	39.6	.65	18.4	.25	.06
Scandi-navian	37.7	-1.54	18.2	-.28	.08
Canadian	37.9	-1.85	18.3	-.26	.07
French	35.2	-.35	18.9	-.13	.01

Republican

	a	b	SEE	r	r^2
Yankee	58.1	.96	17.8	.33	.11
Southern	77.3	-1.25	11.8	-.77	.60
Illinois	80.4	-1.13	14.2	-.66	.43
Other	64.2	.03	18.9	.03	.001
German	61.4	.24	18.2	.27	.07
English	56.1	1.30	17.0	.43	.19
Irish	60.2	-.66	18.3	-.26	.06
Scandi-navian	62.1	1.54	18.1	.29	.08
Canadian	62.0	1.85	18.2	.27	.07
French	64.6	.35	18.8	.13	.01

79. Variables are significant at .05 or better.

80. On Congressional Reconstruction, see Stampp, *The Era of Reconstruction,* pp. 119-55, and McKitrick, *Andrew Johnson and Reconstruction,* pp. 455-73.

81. *Chicago Tribune,* 13 March 1865.

82. *Illinois State Journal,* 4 April 1865.

83. See Koerner, *Memoirs,* 2:521.

84. *Rockford Register,* 5 September 1865, Cole's Notes, IHS.

85. *Chicago Tribune,* 9 November 1865.

86. Ibid.

87. *Jacksonville Journal,* 5 March 1868, Cole's Notes, IHS; *Chicago Tribune,* 3 March 1868.

88. *Champaign Union and Gazette,* 20 May 1868, Cole's Notes, IHS.

89. C.H. Ray to Trumbull, 15 January and 2 February 1866; Joseph Medill et al. to Trumbull, 27 February 1866; Medill to Trumbull, 1 July 1866; Horace White to Trumbull, 5 July 1866, Lyman Trumbull Papers, LC.

90. *Chicago Tribune*, 16 September 1867.

91. "Speech of John A. Logan in the House of Representatives, 16 July 1868," CHS.

92. *Cairo Daily Democrat*, 26 July 1867, Cole's Notes, IHS.

93. John Hoffman et al. to Kimberly, 12 March 1869, George S. Kimberly Collection, CHS.

94. *Carthage Republican*, 16 January 1868, Cole's Notes, IHS.

95. *Jacksonville Journal*, 28 January 1868, Cole's Notes, IHS.

96. *Chicago Tribune*, 3 November 1868.

97. "Speech of Senator Richard Yates at Springfield, Illinois, 22 August 1868," University of Illinois Library, Urbana.

98. John M. Palmer to John M. Palmer, [II], 10 November 1868, John M. Palmer Papers, ISHL.

99. Bivariate coefficients for the 1868 Democratic and Republican Presidential vote:

Democratic

	a	b	SEE	r	r^2
Yankee	47.1	-1.15	16.3	-.43	.18
Southern	27.2	1.31	9.6	.84	.71
Illinois	22.4	1.25	12.0	.74	.55
Other	42.4	-.12	.01	-.12	.01
German	42.1	-.23	17.3	-.27	.07
English	46.0	-1.00	17.0	-.34	.11
Irish	39.3	.70	18.0	.04	.002
Scandinavian	40.6	-.90	17.7	-.20	.04
Canadian	42.7	-2.17	17.0	-.33	.10
French	39.3	-.42	17.8	-.17	.02

Republican

	a	b	SEE	r	r^2
Yankee	52.8	1.16	16.3	.43	.18
Southern	72.7	-1.31	9.6	-.84	.71
Illinois	77.5	-1.25	12.0	-.74	.55
Other	57.5	.12	17.9	.12	.01
German	57.8	.23	17.3	.27	.07
English	53.9	1.00	17.0	.34	.11
Irish	60.6	-.70	18.0	-.04	.002

	a	b	SEE	r	r^2
Scandi-navian	59.3	.90	17.7	.20	.04
Canadian	57.2	2.17	17.0	.33	.10
French	60.6	.42	17.8	.17	.02

100. Variables are significant at .05 or better.

101. Shelby M. Cullom, *Fifty Years of Public Service* (Chicago: A.C. McClug & Co., 1911), pp. 78-79.

Chapter 8

1. *Rockford Gazette*, 22 July 1869, Cole's Notes, IHS.

2. The Pearson correlation between the 1868 and the 1870 elections was .93. There was some voter erosion in the Republican coalition, but none of major or sustaining proportions.

3. See for example, Earle Dudley Ross, *The Liberal Republican Movement*, introduction by John G. Sproat (Seattle: University of Washington Press, 1970) and Patrick W. Riddleberger, "The Break in the Radical Ranks: Liberals vs. Stalwarts in the Election of 1872," *Journal of Negro History* 44 (1959), 136-57.

4. See John G. Sproat, *"The Best Men"; Liberal Reformers in the Gilded Age* (Oxford: Oxford University Press, 1968): Kenneth M. Stampp, *The Era of Reconstruction* (New York: Vintage Books, 1965); Ross, *The Liberal Republican Movement*, and Riddleberger, "The Break in the Radical Ranks," *Journal of Negro History* (1959).

5. See David Montgomery, *Beyond Equality: Labor and the Radical Republicans, 1862-1872* (New York: Alfred A. Knopf, 1967); and Mario R. DiNunzio, "Lyman Trumbull, The State's Rights Issue, and the Liberal Republican Revolt," *Journal of the Illinois State Historical Society* 66 (Winter, 1973), 364-75.

6. David Davis to Rockwell, 24 February 1869, David Davis Papers, CHS.

7. Brown to Davis, 12 December 1871, ibid.

8. *Chicago Tribune*, 11 July 1870.

9. William Clun to John M. Palmer, 20 November 1871, John M. Palmer Papers, ISHL, John M. Palmer, *Personal Recollections of John M. Palmer: The Story of an Earnest Life* (Cincinnati: Robert Clarke Co., 1901), p. 495.

10. Palmer, *Recollections*, p. 283

11. Barton Able to O.M. Hatch, 10 February 1872, David Davis Papers, CHS.

12. See Mark M. Krug, *Lyman Trumbull: Conservative Radical* (New York: A. S. Barnes & Co., 1965).

13. Palmer, *Recollections*, pp. 283, 318, 495.

14. In 1864, the Chicago party was split between Congressman Isaac Arnold and postmaster John Locke Scripps. As the nominating convention approached, the party was on the verge of a complete rupture. A few days before the Republican convention, Wentworth, who had drifted into the Democratic party, made a powerful Union speech in response to an address delivered by the notorious copperhead Clement L. Vallandigham. Overnight, "Long John" became a hero again. The Chicago Republicans found Wentworth to be a solution to their problems and nominated him for Congress as a compromise between Arnold and Scripps. See Don E. Fehrenbacher, *Chicago Giant: A Biography of "Long John" Wentworth* (Madison: The American Historical Research Center, 1957), pp. 196-200.

15. Trumbull to William C. Bryant, 10 May 1872, Lyman Trumbull Family Papers, ISHL.

16. Gustave Koerner, *Memoirs of Gustave Koerner*, ed. Thomas J. McCormack, two volumes (Cedar Rapids: The Torch Press, 1909), 2:519.

17. *Chicago Tribune*, 25 August 1870.

18. William B. Lynn to John Palmer, 16 May 1872, John M. Palmer Papers, ISHL.

19. *Illinois State Register*, 6 January 1871.

20. Lyman Trumbull to John Palmer, 8 April 1872, David Davis Papers, CHS.

21. Quoted in James L. Sundquist, *Dynamics of the Party System* (Washington: The Brookings Institution, 1973), p. 93. Koerner expressed the same feelings in *Memoirs*, 2:538.

22. Koerner, *Memoirs*, 2:538.

23. Ibid., 2:540-41.

24. *Chicago Times*, 28 February 1872.

25. Lyman Trumbull to Gustave Koerner, 9 March 1872, David Davis Papers, CHS.

26. Horace White to Lyman Trumbull, 24 March 1872, ibid.

27. Ibid.

28. See Lyman Trumbull to Horace White, 27 January 1872, and Horace White to Lyman Trumbull, 9 March 1872, David Davis Papers, CHS. For an earlier discussion of the Logan-Grant dispute, see Lyman Trumbull to William Jayne, 18 November 1870 and 8 January 1871, William Jayne Papers, ISHL.

29. Jesse W. Fell to David Davis, 4 April 1872, David Davis Papers, CHS.

30. John Wentworth to David Davis, 17 March 1872, ibid.

31. Leonard Swett to Jesse W. Fell, 1 April 1872, Jesse W. Fell Papers, ISHL.

32. Koerner, *Memoirs*, 2:543-57.

33. See Koerner, *Memoirs*, 2:543-57 and Matthew T. Downey, "Horace Greeley and the Politicians: The Liberal Republican Convention in 1872," *Journal of American History* 53 (1967), 727-50.

34. John Wentworth to David Davis, 30 April 1872, David Davis Papers, CHS.

35. For reactions to the nomination of Greeley, see Ross, *The Liberal Republican Movement*, pp. 105-10; Fehrenbacher, *Chicago Giant*, p. 221; and Willard L. King, *Lincoln's Manager, David Davis* (Cambridge: Harvard University Press, 1960), pp. 282-83.

36. Koerner, *Memoirs*, 2:556.

37. Thomas A. Hendricks to David Davis, 4 May 1872, David Davis Papers, CHS.

38. Koerner, *Memoirs*, 2:558.

39. Ross, *The Liberal Republican Movement*, pp. 94-96.

40. Ibid., p. 105.

41. *Chicago Tribune*, 1 May 1872.

42. Horace White to Lyman Trumbull, 4 May 1872, David Davis Papers, CHS.

43. John A. McClernand to Lyman Trumbull, 3 May 1872, ibid.

44. Jesse K. Dubois to Lyman Trumbull, 2 June 1872, ibid.

45. Horace White to Lyman Trumbull, 4 May 1872, ibid.

46. David Davis to —, 4 June 1872, ibid.

47. *Chicago Times*, quoted in the *Illinois State Register*, 21 November 1871, *Illinois State Register*, 21 November 1871.

48. Ibid., 6 January 1872.

49. Ibid., 15 January 1872.

50. Ibid., 8 March 1872.

51. Ibid., 17 May 1872.

52. *Chicago Times*, 17 May 1872.

53. *Chicago News* quoted in the *Illinois State Register*, 8 May 1872.

54. *Carlinville Enquirer*, quoted in the *Illinois State Register*, 18 May 1872.

55. *Chicago Times*, 1 June 1872.

56. *Illinois State Register*, 15 May 1872; *Ottawa Republican*, 16 May 1872, Cole's Notes, IHS.

57. See Koerner, *Memoirs*, 2:560; *Ottawa Republican*, 4 July 1872, Cole's Notes, IHS; *Illinois State Register*, 27 June 1872.

58. "Speech of James W. Singleton delivered before the Illinois Straight-Out Convention," CHS.

59. Cyrus H. McCormick Circular, 20 September 1872, Cyrus H. McCormick Collection, IHS.

60. *Illinois State Register*, 3 May 1872.

61. Augustus Schell to Cyrus H. McCormick, 25 July 1872, Cyrus H. McCormick Collection, IHS.

62. See Cyrus McCormick to Cameron, 30, 31 July 1872; Horace White to Cyrus McCormick, 1 August 1872; Cyrus McCormick to Augustus Schell, 9 September 1872; Cyrus McCormick to Cameron, 11 September 1872, Cyrus H. McCormick Collection, IHS.

63. Circular from Cyrus H. McCormick, Chairman State Central & Liberal Executive Committees, 20 September 1872, Cyrus H. McCormick Collection, IHS.

64. *Illinois State Register*, 18 October 1872.

65. M.C. Kerr to Lyman Trumbull, 1 September 1872, Lyman Trumbull Family Papers, ISHL.

66. John G. Thompson to Lyman Trumbull, 3 August 1872, ibid.

67. S. M. Moore & B.C. Caulfield to Cyrus H. McCormick, 12 October 1872, Cyrus H. McCormick Collection, IHS.

68. U.S. Grant to Elihu Washburne, 26 May 1872, David Davis Papers, CHS.

69. *Illinois State Register*, 14 May 1872.

70. See *Chicago Tribune*, 24 July 1872.

71. Robert W. Topp to Lyman Trumbull, 1 September 1872, Lyman Trumbull Family Papers, ISHL.

72. Richard Yates to Uriah Reavis, 3 June 1872, Uriah Reavis Collection, CHS.

73. Ibid.

74. *Chicago Tribune*, 22, 23 May 1872; *Ottawa Republican* 30 May 1872, Cole's Notes, IHS.

75. *Illinois State Register*, 3 June 1872.

76. In *The Liberal Republican Movement*, Ross argues that the Liberal revolt was an "escape hatch" for the Democrats who had joined the Republican party in the 1850's. Riddleberger, in "The Break in the Radical Ranks," agrees, maintaining that the wartime coalition included only nominal Republicans who were Democrats at heart. The Liberal revolt allowed these men to return to their regular political home. The implication is that the Republicans in 1872 were no different from the original Whig coalition. The voter analysis disproves this suggestion. The Liberals had a negligible effect upon the voter coalitions.

77. The bivariate coefficients for the 1872 Presidential vote:

Liberal Republicans

	a	b	SEE	r	r^2
Yankee	48.6	-.97	14.6	-.38	.15
Southern	34.1	.74	12.7	.60	.36
Illinois	33.0	.68	13.8	.49	.24
Other	44.5	-.07	15.8	-.08	.006
German	47.3	-.31	14.5	-.39	.15
English	49.4	-1.17	14.4	-.41	.17
Irish	43.2	.61	15.8	.05	.003
Scandinavian	42.9	-.25	15.8	-.08	.007
Canadian	44.0	-1.05	15.6	-.17	.03
French	41.3	.28	15.5	.21	.04

Republicans

	a	b	SEE	r	r^2
Yankee	50.8	1.02	14.7	.39	.15
Southern	65.9	-.76	12.7	-.61	.37
Illinois	67.1	-.72	13.7	-.51	.26
Other	55.2	.07	16.0	.07	.006
German	52.2	.32	14.7	.40	.16
English	50.3	1.09	14.7	.40	.16
Irish	56.4	-.72	16.0	-.06	.003
Scandinavian	56.6	.27	16.0	.09	.009
Canadian	55.5	1.11	15.8	.18	.03
French	58.3	-.28	15.7	-.21	.04

78. D.W. Lusk, *Politics and Politicians: A Succinct History of the Politics of Illinois, From 1856 to 1884* (Springfield: H.W. Rokker Printer, 1884), p. 242.

79. David Davis to Thomas Drummond, 11 November 1872, David Davis Papers, CHS.

80. John Moses, *Illinois Historical and Statistical*, 2 volumes (Chicago: Fergus Printing Co., 1892), 2:819.

81. Fehrenbacher, *Chicago Giant*, pp. 223-25.

82. King, *Lincoln's Manager, David Davis*, pp. 304-5.

83. Horace White, *The Life of Lyman Trumbull* (New York: Houghton Mifflin Company, 1913), pp. 412-15.

Chapter 9

1.   *Cairo Evening Bulletin*, 6 February 1869, *Ottawa Free Trader*, 3 September 1870, Cole's Notes, IHS.

2.   *Chicago Tribune*, 10 June 1875.

3.   An examination of the lists of committeemen and candidates in Walter A. Townsend's *Illinois Democracy: A History of the Party and Its Representatives — Past and Present*, ed. Charles Boeschenstein (Springfield: Democratic Historical Association, Inc., 1935), reveals the change in the Democratic leadership. Quite suddenly, new names appeared among the Democratic leadership in 1870. The old party men who had served since the days of Douglas no longer held major positions.

4.   *Cairo Illinois Bulletin*, quoted in the *Illinois State Register*, 2 September 1874.

5.   *Missouri Republican*, 10 September 1880, Cole's Notes, IHS.

6.   Joel H. Silbey has argued in his study of Congressional voting behavior that discipline, regularity, and loyalty were the hallmarks of party behavior in the 1840s. While Silbey may be correct in his assessment of Congressional voting behavior, it is apparent that those values were not adhered to on the state level of politics in Illinois. Silbey, *The Shrine of Party: Congressional Voting Behavior, 1841-1852* (Pittsburgh: University of Pittsburgh Press, 1967).

7.   Richard Jensen, in *The Winning of the Midwest* (Chicago: The University of Chicago Press, 1971), p. 164, describes the typical election up through 1888 as the army style campaign. According to Jensen, the "election was conceived as a great battle pitting the strength of two opposing armies and the genius of their generals, with the spoils of victory being patronage positions and the seats of power."

8.   *Joliet Signal*, 21 September 1869.

9.   *Rockford Gazette*, 7 October 1869, Cole's Notes, IHS.

10. *Cairo Evening Bulletin*, 7 October 1869, Cole's Notes, IHS.

11. *Ottawa Republican*, 1 September 1870; *Illinois State Register*, 9 February 1869.

12. *Chicago Tribune*, 11 July 1870.

13. *Illinois State Journal*, 6 November 1869.

14. Lyman Trumbull to William Jayne, 5 August 1870, William Jayne Papers, ISHL.

15. *Chicago Tribune*, 5 October 1871; *Illinois State Register*, 18 October 1871.

16. For a good discussion of the fiscal situation, see Walter T. K. Nugent, *The Money Question During Reconstruction* (New York: W.W. Norton & Co., Inc., 1967), pp. 34-35, and Irwin Unger, *The Greenback Era: A Social and Political History of American Finance, 1865-1879* (Princeton: Princeton University Press, 1964), pp. 3-41.

17. The proposal to pay bonds in greenbacks was commonly referred to as the "Ohio idea" and was strongly endorsed by George H. Pendleton, Governor of Ohio. See Unger, *The Greenback Era*, pp. 81-82.

18. Part of the turmoil over the currency involved the balance between silver and gold. In the late 1860s, the great Comstock mines produced a silver bonanza. The fear that silver would replace gold as the monetary standard led to the demonetization of silver in the Coinage Act of 1873. The Coinage Act, however, did not become known as the "Crime of 73" until the Populist crusade began. In the 1870s, the demonetization of silver passed almost unnoticed. According to Nugent, the Coinage Act "was almost a detail amid the great problems of specie resumption, debt refunding, and currency stabilization." Nugent, *The Money Question*, p. 33.

19. *Illinois State Register*, 16, 20, 25 November 1872.

20. Ibid., 3 September 1873.

21. *Ottawa Republican*, 21 September 1873; also see 14 August and 3 September 1873.

22. *Chicago Tribune*, 6 February 1874, and *Freeport Bulletin* as quoted in the *Chicago Tribune*, 8 August 1874.

23. *Chicago Tribune*, 6 February 1874.

24. *Ottawa Republican*, 13 August 1874; *Illinois State Register*, 15 August 1874.

25. *Carlinville Enquirer*, quoted in the *Illinois State Register*, 15 August 1874.

26. *Freie Presse*, quoted in the *Illinois State Register*, 15 August 1874.

27. *Illinois State Register*, 2 January 1874.

28. *Chicago Tribune*, 29 May and 1 June 1874.

29. *Peoria Transcript*, quoted in *Chicago Tribune*, 20 May 1874.

30. *Ottawa Republican*, 4 June 1874.

31. *Chicago Tribune*, 28 May 1874.

32. Ibid., 11 June 1874.

33. Ibid., 27 August 1874. On currency and resumption, see the *Illinois State Register*, 1 August 1874.

34. *Illinois State Register*, 11 May 1874.

35. *Bloomington Pantagraph*, quoted in *Chicago Tribune*, 29 May 1874.

36. *Illinois State Register*, 10 May 1874.

37. Charles A. Church, *History of the Republican Party in Illinois, 1854-1912* (Rockford: Press of Wilson Brothers Co., 1912), p. 147.

38. *Illinois State Journal*, 11 July 1874.

39. *Chicago Tribune*, 27 April 1874.

40. Ibid., 19 June 1874.

41. Although the full details of the "Whiskey Ring" were not known until 1875, enough information had been gathered to indicate a conspiracy in Grant's Administration to defraud the government of liquor taxes. Many of Grant's friends were implicated, and before the affair could be forgotten another scandal was uncovered. In the War Department, Secretary Belknap was involved in granting fraudulent concessions in the Indian Territory.

42. The percentages in this table do not total 100 because of multicolinearity and the margin of error in the statistical routine of bivariate analysis.

43. The Republican bivariate coefficients for the 1874 State election:

	a	b	SEE	r	r^2
Yankee	35.4	1.20	15.4	.45	.20
Southern	50.8	-.67	14.6	-.53	.28
Illinois	53.0	-.65	14.2	-.57	.32
Other	33.5	.30	16.4	.32	.10
German	40.7	.16	17.0	.17	.02
English	37.3	.84	16.5	.29	.08
Irish	42.4	-.64	17.2	-.02	.0005
Scandi- navian	41.8	.35	17.1	.11	.01
Canadian	38.9	2.20	16.2	.33	.11
French	42.9	-.02	17.3	-.01	.0002

44. The Democratic bivariate coefficients for the 1874 State election:

	a	b	SEE	r	r^2
Yankee	52.3	-1.21	20.4	-.35	.12
Southern	38.4	.53	20.6	.33	.11
Illinois	38.3	.41	21.0	.28	.08
Other	48.3	-.11	21.8	-.10	.01
German	44.4	.01	21.9	.01	.0002
English	52.1	-1.13	20.8	-.31	.09
Irish	43.8	.69	21.9	.04	.001

	a	b	SEE	r	r^2
Scandi-navian	44.5	.07	21.9	.01	.0003
Canadian	47.1	-1.38	21.6	-.16	.02
French	45.9	-.38	21.4	-.21	.04

45. The Anti-Monopoly bivariate coefficients for the 1874 State election:

	a	b	SEE	r	r^2
Yankee	12.3	.008	18.7	.003	.00001
Southern	10.7	.13	18.6	.09	.009
Illinois	8.7	.23	18.4	.19	.03
Other	18.1	-.18	18.4	-.18	.03
German	14.6	-.18	18.5	-.16	.02
English	10.3	.31	18.6	.10	.01
Irish	13.5	-.13	18.7	-.06	.004
Scandi-navian	13.5	-.42	18.6	-.13	.01
Canadian	13.8	-.83	18.6	-.11	.01
French	11.07	.40	18.1	.26	.07

46. Breakdown of average ranked farm values, 1874:

Ranked Farm Values	Percent Democratic	Percent Republican	Percent Anti-Monopoly
None	68	31	0
Low	51	27	21
Medium	46	44	8
High	33	51	15

47. *Chicago Tribune*, 21 September 1876.

48. Ibid., 20 January 1876.

49. Ibid., 6 April 1876.

50. *Chicago Tribune*, 6 January 1875.

51. *Chicago Tribune*, 7 January 1875, describes some of the other ploys used by the Democrats to lure the independents into the party, such as creating bogus people's parties.

52. For a good description of the St. Louis convention, see Unger, *The Greenback Era*, p. 303.

53. *Chicago Tribune*, 28 July 1876.

54. For a good account of the Democratic platform, see John Moses, *Illinois Historical and Statistical*, two volumes (Chicago: Fergus Printing Co., 1892), 2:114.

55. *Illinois State Register*, 25 October 1876.

56. Ibid., 20 March 1876.

57. *Chicago Tribune*, 25 May 1876.

58. Ibid., 9 January 1875.

59. Ibid., 24 February 1876.

60. Ibid., 20 March 1876.

61. Ibid., 14 September 1876.

62. Ibid., 10 October 1876.

63. "'Conditions and Limits of Party Fealty,' Lecture Delivered by Matthew Hale April 26, 1880 at the New York Independent Republican Association," CHS.

64. Quoted in Jack Junior Northrup, "Richard Yates, Civil War Governor of Illinois" (Ph.D. dissertation, University of Illinois, 1960), p. 360.

65. The Democratic bivariate coefficients for the 1876 Presidential election:

	a	b	SEE	r	r^2
Yankee	50.7	-.99	15.1	-.37	.14
Southern	36.5	.73	13.1	.59	.35
Illinois	36.7	.56	14.4	.46	.22
Other	54.2	-.28	15.3	-.34	.12
German	45.6	-.01	16.3	-.02	.0006
English	50.4	-.82	15.5	-.30	.09
Irish	43.6	.19	16.2	.10	.01
Scandi-navian	45.9	-.27	16.2	-.09	.008
Canadian	47.4	-1.53	15.9	-.22	.04
French	46.0	-.22	16.1	-.16	.02

Republican bivariate coefficients for the 1876 Presidential election:

	a	b	SEE	r	r^2
Yankee	44.8	1.20	15.4	.43	.18
Southern	62.1	-.90	12.1	-.70	.49
Illinois	61.7	-.68	14.4	-.54	.29
Other	44.3	.22	16.5	.26	.06
German	49.8	.10	17.0	.12	.01
English	44.5	1.10	15.7	.39	.15
Irish	51.9	-.06	17.1	-.03	.001
Scandi-navian	50.4	.40	17.0	.12	.01
Canadian	48.7	1.93	16.5	.26	.07
French	50.5	.27	16.8	.19	.03

66. Greenback bivariate coefficients for the 1876 Presidential election:

	a	b	SEE	r	r^2
Yankee	4.4	-.21	5.7	-.22	.05
Southern	1.1	.17	5.4	.39	.15
Illinois	1.4	.12	5.6	.27	.07
Other	1.4	.05	5.7	.19	.03
German	4.4	-.08	5.6	-.29	.08
English	5.0	-.28	5.6	-.28	.08
Irish	4.3	-.13	5.7	-.20	.04
Scandi-navian	3.5	-.12	5.8	-.11	.01
Canadian	3.8	-.41	5.8	-.16	.02
French	3.4	-.05	5.8	-.10	.01

Conclusion

1. Allan Nevins, "A Major Result of the Civil War," *Essays on the Civil War and Reconstruction,* ed. Irwin Unger (New York: Holt, Reinhart and Winston, Inc. 1970), p. 329.

2. Brand Whitlock, *Forty Years of It,* quoted in James L. Sundquist, *Dynamics of the Party System* (Washington: The Brookings Institution, 1973), p. 91.

3. This table was calculated by determining the number of eligible voters in the census years and then by projecting the population growth in a linear progression.

4. This table is adopted from Ray Miles Shortridge, "Voting Patterns in the American Midwest, 1840-1872" (Ph.D. dissertation, University of Michigan, 1974), pp. 48-49.

5. Fragment of speech dated 1873 in Richard Yates and Catherine Yates Pickering, *Richard Yates, Civil War Governor,* ed. John H. Krenkel (Danville: The Interstate Printers & Publishers, Inc., 1966).

6. "'Conditions and Limits of Party Fealty,' Lecture Delivered by Matthew Hale April 26, 1880 at the New York Independent Republican Association," CHS.

7. See Chapter 7, p. xxx.

8. Shelby M. Cullom, *Fifty Years of Public Service* (Chicago: A.C. McClurg & Co., 1911), p. 160.

Appendix

1. The Illinois Constitution of 1870 authorized the division of all the counties in the State into townships. Consequently, the 1870 sample was composed entirely of townships.

2. This table does not represent the entire population of Illinois. Not only was there a scattering of people born in areas which could not be classified, but also there were

a number of residents in Illinois whose nativity could not be determined because of missing information.

3. Charles M. Dollar and Richard J. Jensen, *Historian's Guide to Statistics: Quantitative Analysis and Historical Research* (New York: Holt, Rinehart and Winston, Inc., 1971), p. 14.

4. See, for example, Lee Benson, *The Concept of Jacksonian Democracy: New York as a Test Case* (Princeton: Princeton University Press, 1961); Richard Jensen, *The Winning of the Midwest* (Chicago: University of Chicago Press, 1971); and Paul Kleppner, *Cross of Culture: A Social Analysis of Midwestern Politics, 1850-1900* (New York, The Free Press, 1970).

5. Frank S. Mead, *Handbook of Denominations in the United States* (New York: Abingdon-Cokesbury Press, 1949), and T. Scott Miyakawa, *Protestants and Pioneers: Individualism and Conformity on the American Frontier* (Chicago: University of Chicago Press, 1964). Richard Jensen, in *The Winning of the Midwest*, correctly saw the differences in the Baptist sects and was able to classify them into appropriate pietist and liturgical camps, but Jensen failed to recognize the diversity even among the Regular Baptists.

6. See for example, Ronald P. Formisano, *The Birth of Mass Political Parties: Michigan, 1827-1861* (Princeton: Princeton University Press, 1971) and Michael F. Holt, *Forging A Majority: The Formation of the Republican Party in Pittsburgh, 1848-1860* (New Haven: Yale University Press, 1969).

7. J. Morgan Kouser, "The 'New Political History': A Methodological Critique," *Reviews in American History* 4 (March, 1976), p. 2.

8. For a full discussion of multiple regression and the ecological fallacy, see F. Terrence Jones, "Ecological Interference and Electoral Analysis," *Journal of Interdisciplinary History* 2 (1972), pp. 249-62; J. Morgan Kouser, "Ecological Regression and the Analysis of Past Politics," *Journal of Interdisciplinary History* 4 (1973), pp. 237-62; Mattei Dogan and Stein Rokkaw, eds., *Quantitative Ecological Analysis in the Social Sciences* (Cambridge: The M.I.T. Press, 1969), and Eric A. Hanushek, et al., "Model Specification, Use of Aggregate Data, and the Ecological Correlation Fallacy," *Political Methodology* 1 (1974), pp. 89-107.

Bibliography

Primary Sources: Manuscripts

Chicago, Ill. Chicago Historical Society. James Franklin Aldrich Collection.
Chicago, Ill. Chicago Historical Society. Isaac N. Arnold Collection.
Springfield, Ill. Illinois State Historical Library. Mason Brayman Papers.
Chicago, Ill. Chicago Historical Society. Sidney Breese Collection.
Chicago, Ill. Chicago Historical Society. David Davis Collection.
Chicago, Ill. University of Chicago. Stephen A. Douglas Papers.
Chicago, Ill. Chicago Historical Society. Jesse K. Dubois Collection.
Springfield, Ill. Illinois State Historical Library. Jesse W. Fell Collection.
Chicago, Ill. Chicago Historical Society. Joseph Gillespie Collection.
Springfield, Ill. Illinois State Historical Library. Ozias M. Hatch Papers.
Springfield, Ill. Illinois State Historical Library. William Jayne Papers.
Chicago, Ill. Chicago Historical Society. Norman B. Judd Collection.
Chicago, Ill. Chicago Historical Society. George S. Kimberly Collection.
Springfield, Ill. Illinois State Historical Library. Charles H. Lanphier Papers.
Washington, D.C. Library of Congress. Robert Todd Lincoln Collection.
Springfield, Ill. Illinois State Historical Library. John A. McClernand Papers.
Urbana, Ill. Illinois Historical Survey. Cyrus H. McCormick Collection.
Springfield, Ill. Illinois State Historical Library. John M. Palmer Family Papers.
Springfield, Ill. Illinois State Historical Library. John M. Palmer [II] Family Papers.
Chicago, Ill. Chicago Historical Society. Uriah Reavis Collection.
Chicago, Ill. Chicago Historical Society. George Schneider Collection.
Springfield, Ill. Illinois State Historical Library. James W. Sheahan Collection.
Springfield, Ill. Illinois State Historical Library. Lyman Trumbull Family Papers.
Washington, D.C. Library of Congress. Lyman Trumbull Papers.

Primary Sources: Newspapers

Alton (Ill.) *Courier.*
Aurora (Ill.) *Beacon.*
Aurora (Ill.) *Guardian.*
Belleville (Ill.) *Advocate.*
Belleville (Ill.) *Democrat.*
Chicago Democrat.
Chicago Times.
Chicago Tribune.
Freeport (Ill.) *Bulletin.*
Freeport (Ill.) *Journal.*

Illinois State Journal.
Illinois State Register.
Joliet (Ill.) *Signal.*
Ottawa Free Trader.
Ottawa Weekly Republican.
Peoria Weekly Republican.
Quincy (Ill.) *Whig.*
Rockford (Ill.) *Republican.*
Rock Island Advertiser.
Rock Island and Western Illinois Times.

Primary Sources: Other

Chicago, Ill. Chicago Historical Society. "Address of Governor S.M. Cullom Before the Republican Convention of Sangamon County on April 13th, 1880."

Chicago, Ill. Chicago Historical Society. "'Conditions and Limits of Party Fealty' Lecture Delivered by Matthew Hale April 26, 1880 at the New York Independent Republican Association."

Chicago, Ill. Chicago Historical Society. "'Letter to the Republicans of Illinois' from the Republican State Central Committee June 9, 1859."

Chicago, Ill. Chicago Historical Society. "'Olive Branch Speech' by John Reynolds at Springfield, January 14, 1857."

Chicago, Ill. Chicago Historical Society. "'Proceedings of the Democratic Congressional Convention for the First District' speech by M.D. Gilman, Chicago, October 14, 1852."

Chicago, Ill. Chicago Historical Society. "Speech of James W. Singleton Delivered Before the Illinois Straight-Out Convention."

Chicago, Ill. Chicago Historical Society. "Speech of John A. Logan in the House of Representatives, July 16, 1868."

Urbana, Ill. Illinois Historical Survey. Arthur C. Cole Notes.

Urbana, Ill. University of Illinois. "Speech of Senator Richard Yates at Springfield, Illinois, August 22, 1868."

U.S. Census. Seventh Census of the United States, 1850: Illinois.

U.S. Census. Eighth Census of the United States, 1860: Illinois.

U.S. Census Ninth Census of the United States, 1870: Illinois.

Primary Sources: Published

Arnold, Isaac N. *The Life of Abraham Lincoln.* Chicago: Jansen, McClurg, & Company, 1885.

Basler, Roy P., et al., ed. *The Collected Works of Abraham Lincoln.* 9 vols. New Brunswick, N.J.: Rutgers University Press, 1953.

Church, Charles A. *History of The Republican Party in Illinois, 1854-1912.* Rockford, Ill.: Press of Wilson Brothers Co., 1912.

Cullom, Shelby M. *Fifty Years of Public Service.* Chicago: A.C. McClurg & Co., 1911.

Gillespie, Joseph. *Recollections of Early Illinois and Her Noted Men.* Chicago: Fergus Printing Co., 1880.

Greene, Evart B., ed. "Letters to Gustav Koerner, 1837-1863". *Transactions of the Illinois State Historical Society.* 12 (1907): 238-46.

Hawke, David Freeman, ed. *Herdon's Lincoln.* New York: Bobbs-Merrill Co., Inc., 1970.

Johannsen, Robert W., ed. *The Letters of Stephen A. Douglas.* Urbana, Ill.: University of Illinois Press, 1961.

Johnson, Charles B. *Illinois in the Fifties.* Champaign, Ill.: Flanigan-Pearson Co., 1918.

Koerner, Gustave. *Memoirs of Gustave Koerner.* 2 vols. Ed. Thomas J. McCormack. Cedar Rapids: The Torch Press, 1909.

Linder, Usher F. *Reminiscences of the Early Bench and Bar of Illinois.* Second edition. Chicago: Chicago Legal News Co., 1879.

Lusk, D.W. *Eighty Years of Illinois: Politics and Politicians, Anecdotes and Incidents, A Succinct History of the State, 1809-1859.* 2 vols. Springfield: H.W. Rokker, Printer, 1889.

————. *Politics and Politicians: A Succinct History of the Politics of Illinois.* Springfield: H.W. Rokker, Printer, 1884.

Moses, John. *Illinois Historical and Statistical.* 2 vols. Chicago: Fergus Printing Co., 1892.

Ormsby, R. McKinley. *A History of the Whig Party.* 2nd edition. Boston: Crosby, Nichols & Co., 1860.

Palmer, George Thomas, ed. "A Collection of Letters From Lyman Trumbull to John M. Palmer, 1854-1858." *Journal of the Illinois State Historical Society* 46 (April-July 1923): 20-41.

Palmer, John M., ed. *The Bench and Bar of Illinois, Historical and Reminiscent.* 2 vols. Chicago: The Lewis Publishing Co., 1899.

Palmer, John M. *Personal Recollections of John M. Palmer; The Story of an Earnest Life.* Cincinnati: Robert Clark Co., 1901.

Pease, Theodore Calvin and Randall, James G., eds. *The Diary of Orville Hickman Browning.* 2 vols. Springfield: The Illinois State Historical Library, 1925.

Raum, Green B. *History of Illinois Republicanism.* Chicago: Rollins Publishing Company, 1900.

Reynolds, John. *My Own Times, Embracing Also the History of My Life.* Belleville, Ill.: Printed by B.H. Perryman and H.L. Davison, 1855.

Rummel, Edward. *Illinois Hand-Book and Legislative Manual for 1871.* Springfield: Illinois State Register Printing Office, 1871.

Selby, Paul. "Genesis of the Republican Party in Illinois." *Transactions of the Illinois State Historical Society for the Year 1906.* Springfield: Illinois State Historical Library, 1906: 270-83.

Sheahan, James W. *The Life of Stephen A. Douglas.* New York: Harper & Brothers, 1860.

Townsend, Walter A. *Illinois Democracy: A History of the Party and Its Representative Members — Past and Present.* ed. Charles Boeschenstein. Springfield: Democratic Historical Assoc., Inc., 1935.

White, Horace. *The Life of Lyman Trumbull.* New York: Houghton Mifflin Company, 1913.

Yates, Richard and Pickering, Catherine Yates. *Richard Yates, Civil War Governor.* Ed. John H. Krenkel. Danville, Ill.: The Interstate Printers & Publishers, Inc., 1966.

Secondary Sources

Alvord, Clarence W., gen. ed. *The Centennial History of Illinois.* 4 vols. Springfield: Illinois Centennial Commission, 1919. Vol. 3: *The Era of the Civil War, 1848-1870,* by Arthur C. Cole.

Baldwin, Eugene F. "The Dream of the South — Story of Illinois During the Civil War." *Transactions of the Illinois State Historical Society* 16 (1911): 84-103.

Baringer, William E. "Campaign Technique in Illinois — 1860." *Transactions of the Illinois State Historical Society* 39 (1932): 203-77.

Baxter, Maurice Glen. "Orville H. Browning: Conservative in American Politics." Ph.D. dissertation, University of Illinois, 1948.

Bergquist, James M. "The Political Attitudes of the German Immigrant in Illinois, 1848-1860." Ph.D. dissertation, Northwestern University, 1966.

Blair, Cecil C. "The Chicago Democratic Press and the Civil War." Ph.D. dissertation, University of Chicago, 1947.

Cox, LaWanda and Cox, John. *Politics, Principles and Prejudice, 1865-1866.* Chicago: The Free Press, 1963.

Cross, Jasper William. "Divided Loyalties in Southern Illinois During the Civil War." Ph.D. dissertation, University of Illinois, 1942.

Dante, Harris L. "Western Attitudes and Reconstruction Politics in Illinois, 1865-1872." *Journal of the Illinois State Historical Society* 49 (Spring 1956): 149-62.

Davis, Granville D. "Factional Differences in the Democratic Party in Illinois, 1854-1858." Ph.D. dissertation, University of Illinois, 1936.

DiNunzio, Mario R. "Lyman Trumbull, The States' Rights Issue, and the Liberal Republican Revolt," *Journal of the Illinois State Historical Society* 66 (Winter 1973): 364-75.

_____. "Lyman Trumbull, U.S. Senator." Ph.D. dissertation, Clark University, 1964.

Doolen, Richard, "The Greenback Party in the Great Lakes Midwest." Ph.D. dissertation, University of Michigan, 1969.

Downey, Matthew T. "Horace Greeley and the Politicians: The Liberal Republican Convention in 1872," *Journal of American History* 53 (1967): 727-50.

Ellis, L.E. "The Chicago Times During the Civil War," *Transactions of the Illinois State Historical Society* 39 (1932): 135-81.

Fehrenbacher, Don E. *Chicago Giant: A Biography of "Long John" Wentworth.* Madison: The American Historical Research Center, 1957.

_____. *Prelude to Greatness: Lincoln in the 1850's.* Stanford: Stanford University Press, 1962.

Foner, Eric. *Free Soil, Free Labor, Free Men: The Ideology of the Republican Party Before the Civil War.* London: Oxford University Press, 1970.

Formisano, Ronald P. *The Birth of Mass Political Parties: Michigan, 1827-1861.* Princeton: Princeton University Press, 1971.

Herriott, F.I. "The Conference in the Deutsches Haus Chicago, May 14-15, 1860." *Transactions of the Illinois State Historical Society* 35 (1928): 101-91.

_____. "Senator Stephen A. Douglas and the Germans in 1854," *Transactions of the Illinois State Historical Society* 17 (1912): 142-58.

Hicken, Victor. "From Vandalia to Vicksburg: The Political and Military Career of John A. McClernand." Ph.D. dissertation, University of Illinois, 1955.

Holt, Michael F. *Forging A Majority: The Formation of the Republican Party in Pittsburgh, 1848-1860.* New Haven: Yale University Press, 1969.

James, Harold Preston. "Lincoln's Own State in the Election of 1860." Ph.D. dissertation, University of Illinois, 1943.

Jensen, Richard. "The Religious and Occupational Roots of Party Identification: Illinois and Indiana in the 1870's" *Civil War History* 16 (December 1970): 325-43.

_____. *The Winning of the Midwest.* Chicago: University of Chicago Press, 1971.

Johannsen, Robert W. *Stephen A. Douglas.* New York: Oxford University Press, 1973.

Johnson, Allen. *Stephen A. Douglas: A Study in American Politics.* New York: The MacMillan Company, 1908.

Jones, Stanley L. "Agrarian Radicalism in Illinois' Constitutional Convention of 1862," *The Old Northwest: Studies in Regional History, 1787-1910.* Ed. Harry N. Scheiber. Lincoln, Neb.: University of Nebraska Press, 1969: 312-22.

Kamphoefner, Walter D. "St. Louis Germans and the Republican Party, 1848-1860," *Mid-America* 57 (April 1975): 69-88.

King, Ameda Ruth. "The Last Years of the Whig Party in Illinois – 1847 to 1856," *Transactions of the Illinois State Historical Society* 32 (1925): 108-54.

King, Willard L. *Lincoln's Manager, David Davis.* Cambridge: Harvard University Press, 1960.

Kleppner, Paul. *Cross of Culture: A Social Analysis of Midwestern Politics, 1850-1900.* New York: The Free Press, 1970.

Krug, Mark M. *Lyman Trumbull: Conservative Radical.* New York: A.S. Barnes & Co., 1965.

Latner, Richard B. and Levine, Peter. "Perspectives on Antebellum Pietistic Politics," *Reviews in American History* 4 (March 1976): 15-24.

Luebke, Frederick C., ed. *Ethnic Voters and the Election of Lincoln.* Lincoln: University of Nebraska Press, 1971.

McCormick, Richard L. "Ethno-Cultural Interpretations of Nineteenth-Century American Voting Behavior," *Political Science Quarterly.* (June 1974): 351-377.

McCormick, Richard P. *The Second American Party System: Party Formation in the Jacksonian Era* New York: W.W. Norton & Co., Inc., 1966.

McKitrick, Eric L. *Andrew Johnson and Reconstruction.* Chicago: University of Chicago Press, 1960.

McPherson, James M. "Grant or Greeley? The Abolitionist Dilemma in the Election of 1872." *American Historical Review* 71 (1965): 43-61.

Mead, Frank S. *Handbook of Denominatons in the United States* New York: Abingdon-Cokesbury Press, 1949.

Miyakawa, T. Scott *Protestants and Pioneers: Individualism and Conformity on the American Frontier.* Chicago: University of Chicago Press, 1964.

Montgomery, David. *Beyond Equality: Labor and the Radical Republicans, 1862-1872.* New York: Alfred A. Knopf, 1967.

Nevins, Allan. "A Major Result of the Civil War," *Civil War History* 5 (September 1959): 237-50.

Nichols, Roy F. "The Kansas-Nebraska Act: A Century of Historiography," *The Mississippi Valley Historical Review* 43 (September 1956): 187-212.

Norton, Wesley L. "The Religious Press and the Compromise of 1850: A Study of the Relationship of the Methodists, Baptist and Presbyterian Press to the Slavery Controversy, 1846-1851." Ph.D. dissertation, University of Illinois, 1959.

Northrup, Jack Jr. "Richard Yates: Civil War Governor of Illinois." Ph.D. dissertation, University of Illinois, 1960.

Nugent, Walter T.K. *The Money Question During Reconstruction.* New York: W.W. Norton & Co., Inc., 1967.

Pease, Theodore Calvin. *The Story of Illinois.* Chicago: A.C. McClurg & Co., 1925.

Potter, David M. *The Impending Crisis, 1848-1861.* ed. Don E. Fehrenbacher. New York: Harper & Row, Publishers, 1976.

Prickett, Josephine G. "Joseph Gillespie," *Transactions of the Illinois State Historical Society* 17 (1912): 93-114.

Riddleberger, Patrick W. "The Break in the Radical Ranks: Liberals vs. Stalwarts in the Elections of 1872," *Journal of Negro History* 44 (1959): 136-57.

Robinson, Michael C. "Illinois Politics in the Post-Civil War Era: The Liberal Republican Movement, A Test Case." Ph.D. dissertation, University of Wyoming, 1973.

Ross, Earle Dudley. *The Liberal Republican Movement.* Introduction by John G. Sproat. Seattle: University of Washington Press, 1970.

Rozett, John M. "Racism and Republican Emergence in Illinois, 1848-1860: A Re-Evaluation of Republican Negrophobia," *Civil War History* 71 (Fall 1976): 101-15.

Sellers, James Lee. "The Make-Up of the Early Republican Party," *Transactions of the Illinois State Historical Society* 37 (1930): 39-51.

Senning, John P. "The Know-Nothing Movement in Illinois," *Transactions of the Illinois State Historical Society* 7 (April 1914): 7-34.

Shortridge, Ray Miles. "Voting Patterns in the American Midwest, 1840-1872." Ph.D. dissertation, University of Michigan, 1974.

Sproat, John G. *"The Best Men": Liberal Reformers in the Gilded Age.* Oxford: Oxford University Press, 1968.

Stampp, Kenneth M. *And The War Came: The North and the Secession Crisis, 1860-1861.* Second Edition. Baton Rouge: Louisiana State University Press, 1967.

_____. *The Era of Reconstruction.* New York: Vintage Books, 1965.

Stoller, Mildred C. "The Democratic Element in the New Republican Party in Illinois, 1856-1860," *Papers in Illinois History.* Springfield: The Illinois State Historical Society, 1944: 32-71.

Sundquist, James L. *Dynamics of the Party System.* Washington: The Brookings Institution, 1973.

Thomas, Benjamin P. *Abraham Lincoln.* New York: Alfred A. Knopf, 1952.

Tucker, Marlin Timothy. "Political Leadership in the Illinois-Missouri German Community, 1836-1872." Ph.D. dissertation, University of Illinois, 1968.

Unger, Irwin. *The Greenback Era: A Social and Political History of American Finance, 1865-1879.* Princeton: Princeton University Press, 1964.

Wilson, Bluford. "Southern Illinois in the Civil War," *Transactions of the Illinois State Historical Society* 16 (1911): 93-103.

Index